READING, WRITING, & LEARNING IN ESL

READING, WRITING, & LEARNING IN ESL

••••

A RESOURCE BOOK FOR K-8 TEACHERS

SUZANNE F. PEREGOY
San Francisco State University

OWEN F. BOYLE
San Jose State University

Longman

Reading, Writing, and Learning in ESL: A Resource Book for K–8 Teachers

Longman, 10 Bank Street, White Plains, N.Y. 10606

Associated companies:
Longman Group Ltd., London
Longman Cheshire Pty., Melbourne
Longman Paul Pty., Auckland
Copp Clark Pitman, Toronto

Senior acquisitions editor: Laura McKenna
Sponsoring editor: Naomi Silverman
Development editor: Susan Alkana
Production editor: Ann P. Kearns
Cover design: Joseph DePinho
Photo credits: pp. 14, 36, 62, 150, 194, 200, Linda J. Russell; pp. 12, 22, 39, 77, 85, 110,
    115, 127, 179, Suzanne Peregoy
Text art: ExecuStaff
Production supervisor: Anne P. Armeny

Library of Congress Cataloging-in-Publication Data

Peregoy, Suzanne.
    Reading, writing, and learning in ESL : a resource book for K–8
teachers / by Suzanne Peregoy and Owen F. Boyle.
        p.   cm.
    Includes bibliographical references and index.
    ISBN 0-8013-0844-5
    1. English language—Study and teaching—Foreign speakers.
I. Boyle, Owen.   II. Title.
PE1128.A2P39   1992
428'.007—dc20   92–32444
                                                                        CIP

6 7 8 9 10-CRS-99 98 97 96 95

To our parents
and to Uncle Ernesto

and

to the memory of
Walter Loban

Contents

CHAPTER 4   READING AND LITERATURE INSTRUCTION FOR SECOND LANGUAGE LEARNERS   111

Preface

The purpose of our book is to open a window on classrooms where second language children are actively involved in learning about themselves, their classmates, and the world around them. In these classrooms, students pursue topics of their own choosing, using oral and written English to discuss and confer with their classmates, read, write, report, and share in the ongoing process of learning. In so doing, they advance their knowledge of English, gradually expanding their discourse repertoires and refining their control of grammar and spelling.

FEATURES OF THE BOOK

Viewing learning as a social process, we will introduce you to the classroom cultures of some of the best teachers we know—classrooms where second language students of diverse language and cultural backgrounds demonstrate success in learning. In particular, we will describe various social contexts that maximize language and literacy development for second language learners, such as collaborative groups and teacher–student conferencing. At the same time, we will focus on specific instructional strategies that effective teachers use to promote literacy development for all their students. We trust that the product of our efforts will be a practical resource to help teachers organize literacy instruction for their second language students in a manner consistent with current understandings of language and literacy acquisition.

The idea for writing this book comes from our experiences working with teachers and children in the United States, Europe, and Central America. More and more often, we are asked how to accommodate second language learners into the "regular classroom" and how to organize literacy instruction for children who speak very little English. In our own university classes preparing reading/ language arts teachers for bilingual, English as a Second Language (ESL), and "regular" classrooms, we have found a need for a single, straightforward, theoretically sound yet practical book on second language reading and writing. This book is intended to provide such a resource.

As coordinators of bilingual programs, as assistant director of the Bay Area Writing Project, and as researchers in first and second language reading and writing, we have been trying to give teachers assistance and resources for working with second language students.

ORGANIZATION OF THE TEXT

In organizing our book, we have chosen chapter topics that correspond to those typically covered in standard reading/language arts textbooks. We begin with two chapters that provide background information on second language learning: chapter 1 describes characteristics of second language learners, while chapter 2 explains second language acquisition processes and oral language development. The next three chapters provide classroom strategies for second language literacy instruction: chapter 3, process writing; chapter 4, literature-based instruction; and chapter 5, content-area reading. In these chapters, we briefly explain current theory and research on second language reading and writing and provide techniques for adapting instruction to assist learners with limited English proficiency. By using topics parallel to those found in standard reading/language arts texts, we build on the current knowledge base in the field, utilize categories that are already familiar to most readers, and facilitate the use of our book as a supplementary text. Finally, in chapter 6, we provide a summary of the ideas presented in the book.

ORGANIZATION OF THE CHAPTERS

In presenting each chapter, we wish to engage our readers in a friendly conversation that will open their eyes to worlds of possibility in second language classrooms. Each chapter begins with focusing questions for readers to consider while reading the chapter. Material presented in the chapter then offers information with which to address these questions. Each chapter describes various social contexts of instruction and provides strategies appropriate for beginning and intermediate second language learners. In addition, we provide a list of learning acitivities for readers to carry out in order to extend their understanding of the chapter material.

In short, we expect the book to be both enjoyable to read and easy to use. Those who read it should look forward to the joys and challenges awaiting them in second language classrooms. Given the theoretically coherent and practical ideas in this book, readers should feel confident and prepared for opportunities to work with second language students.

ACKNOWLEDGMENTS

Because this book culls from our experiences and preparation past and present, we wish to acknowledge first of all Walter Loban, Lily Wong Fillmore, and Marilyn Buckley, for their influence on our ideas and passion for the importance of language and literacy development in the lives of children. We also wish to acknowledge our university students for their role in the development of our manuscript. Their questions, critiques, ideas, and enthusiasm have helped us to shape and refine the material in this book. In addition, we wish to acknowledge all the teachers who have welcomed us into their classrooms, in particular those who have shared materials with us: Linda Chittenden, Audrey Fong, Jennifer Jones, Jay Kuhlman, Anne Phillips, Reina Salgado, and Juana Zamora.

We also want to thank the principal and teachers of Coleman School, San Rafael, CA: Don Mar, Angela Campbell, Juana Feisel-Engle, Peggy Koorhan, Gloria López-Gutiérrez, Rosemarie Michaels, Elda Parise, Debi Quan, and Pam Thomas.

We would like to thank the following reviewers, whose helpful suggestions and insight have contributed greatly to the development of this book:

Richard P. Duran, University of California, Santa Barbara

Diane Bennett Durkin, University of California, Los Angeles

Sandra Fradd, University of Miami

Mary McGroarty, Northern Arizona University

Teresa Pica, University of Pennsylvania

Finally, we thank Naomi Silverman and other editors at Longman for their assistance throughout the stages in the publication of this book.

CHAPTER 1

Second Language Learners in School

In this chapter, we address the concerns of teachers when they first encounter non-English-speaking children in their classrooms, discussing such questions as the following:

1. Who are second language learners?
2. How can I get to know my second language students when their language and culture are new to me?
3. How do cultural differences affect how my students respond to me and to my efforts to teach them?
4. How can I ease newcomers into the routines of my class when they understand very little English?
5. What kinds of programs exist to meet the needs of second language learners?

First, come with us into Buzz Bertolucci's classroom. It is the first day of school in Mr. Bertolucci's first grade. All the children are seated on the rug and have just finished the opening routines with the calendar. After introducing the children to each other through a song, Buzz places a Big Book of *The Gingerbread Man* in front of the class. With its enlarged print and colorful illustrations, the 30-inch-tall Big Book not only captures the children's attention but also helps them understand the story's events. Mr. Bertolucci reads the book to the entire class, points to the pictures, puts on a gingerbread man mask, and acts out words such as "Run, run as fast as you can. You can't catch me. I'm the Gingerbread Man!" The entire book is "read" and acted out by members of the class on this, their first day of school. When the story is finished, one of the school cooks enters the class and hands a note to Mr. Bertolucci. He reads it to the class: "I jumped out of your book and ran to the cafeteria. Come and meet me! The Gingerbread Man." Teacher and children leave for the cafeteria but cannot find the Gingerbread Man there. They ask the cooks if they've seen the Gingerbread Man, but they haven't. Finally, one cook suggests that they look in the oven, and there they find another note from the Gingerbread Man: "I've gone to the janitor's storeroom by the bathrooms. See you there!" The class finds the janitor and asks if he's seen the Gingerbread Man, but he replies that the Gingerbread Man has gone to the nurse's office. When they meet the nurse, the children learn that the Gingerbread Man has gone to the counselor's office and then to the principal's office. Finally, the principal reports that the Gingerbread Man has returned to their classroom. When the children return to the classroom, each one finds a Gingerbread Man cookie sitting at his or her desk (Loban, 1968).

As the children eat their cookies, Mr. Bertolucci reads *The Gingerbread Man* again. He has introduced his children to literature in an involving way. In addition, he has introduced the new children to their school and to the many people and places in the school they will need to know. He has also presented the literature and its simple theme in a concrete and interesting manner. His children will look forward to the next book he reads in class, and they will look forward to reading and writing themselves.

It may surprise you to learn that more than half the children in Mr. Bertolucci's class are new to the English language, coming from homes in which languages such as Spanish, Cantonese, and Japanese are spoken. Such linguistic variety was not always the case, but changes in the neighborhood over the past ten years have been dramatic. Mr. Bertolucci has responded to these changes by keeping many of his favorite teaching routines such as the Gingerbread Man but modifying them to meet the needs of his limited English proficient (LEP) students. You may be facing similar changes in your school, given today's immigration patterns. In this book, we will show you how to develop and modify reading and writing instruction to meet the needs of your students who are new to English. But first, we want to introduce you to the great diversity among children called "second language learners" to help you better understand and integrate them into your classroom and school.

WHO ARE SECOND LANGUAGE LEARNERS?

Students who speak English as their second language live in all areas of the United States. A large number are sons and daughters of immigrants who have left their home countries to seek a better life. Many recent immigrants have left countries brutally torn by war or political strife in regions such as Southeast Asia, Central America, and Eastern Europe. Others have immigrated for economic reasons, as is often the case among Mexican immigrants, for example. Other second language students were born in the United States, and some of them, such as Native American students, have roots in American soil that go back for countless generations.

Whether immigrant or native born, each group brings its own history and culture to the enterprise of schooling (Heath, 1986). Furthermore, each group contributes to the rich tapestry of languages and cultures that form the basic fabric of the United States. Our first task as teachers, then, is to become aware of our students' personal histories and cultures, so as to understand their feelings, frustrations, hopes, and aspirations. By developing such understanding and knowledge, we create the essential foundation for meaningful instruction, including reading and writing instruction. As understanding grows, teacher and students alike can come to an awareness of universals in human experience, an important insight, as shared in this poem by a high school student who emigrated with her parents from Cambodia (Mullen & Olsen, 1990).

YOU AND I ARE THE SAME

You and I are the same
but we don't let our hearts see.

Black, White and Asian
Africa, China, United States and all other
countries around the world

Peel off their skin
Like you peel an orange

See their flesh
like you see in my heart

Peel off their meat
And peel my wickedness with it too

Until there's nothing left
but bones.

Then you will see that you and I
are the same.

by Kien Po (Kien Po, *You and I Are the
Same,* California Tomorrow, 1990.
Reprinted with permission of the author.)

HOW CAN I GET TO KNOW MY SECOND LANGUAGE STUDENTS?

Given the variety and mobility among second language groups, it is likely that most teachers, including specialists in bilingual education or English as a Second Language (ESL), will at some time encounter students whose language and culture they know little about. Perhaps you are already accustomed to working with students of diverse cultures, but, if you are not, how can you develop an understanding of students from unfamiliar linguistic and cultural backgrounds? Far from a simple task, the process requires not only fact-finding but also continual observation and interpretation of children's behavior, combined with trial and error in communication. Thus, the process is one that must take place gradually.

Getting Basic Information
When a New Student Arrives

When a new student arrives, we suggest three initial steps. First of all, begin to find out basic facts about the child: What country is the child from? How long has he or she lived in the United States? Where and with whom is the child living? What language or languages are spoken in the home? If the child is an immigrant, what were the circumstances of immigration? Some children have experienced traumatic events before and during immigration, and the process of adjustment to a new country may represent yet another link in a chain of stressful life events (Ovando & Collier, 1985).

Second, obtain as much information about the student's prior school experiences as possible. Since you are not likely to receive a cumulative folder forwarded from another country, you will need to piece the information together yourself. However, school records may be available if the child has already been enrolled in a U.S. school. Keep in mind that some children may have had no previous schooling, despite their age, or perhaps their schooling has been interrupted. Other students will have attended school in their home countries. Students with prior educational experience bring various kinds of knowledge to school subjects and may be quite advanced. Be prepared to validate your students for their special knowledge. We saw how important this was for fourth-grader Li Fen, a recent immigrant from mainland China who found herself in a regular English language classroom, knowing not a word of English. Li Fen was a bright child, though very quiet and seemingly shy during her first month in the class. She made a real turnaround, however, the day the class was studying long division. Li Fen accurately solved three problems at the chalkboard in no time at all, though her procedure differed slightly from the one in the math book. Her classmates were duly impressed with her mathematical competence, and none could hide their admiration. Her teacher, of course, gave her a smile with words of congratulations. From that day forward, Li Fen became more outgoing, having earned a place in the class.

When you are gathering information on your students' prior schooling, it's important to find out whether they are literate in their home language. If they are, you might encourage them to keep a journal using their native language, and, if possible, you should acquire native language books, magazines, or newspapers to have on hand for the new student. In this way, you validate the student's language, culture, and academic competence, while providing a natural bridge to English reading. Make these choices with sensitivity, though, building on positive responses from your students. Bear in mind, for example, that some newcomers may not wish to be identified as different from their classmates. I make this caveat because of my memory of a boy, recently arrived from Mexico, who attended an affluent, all-white school. He refused to speak Spanish to me, pretending that he did not know the language. When I visited his home and spoke Spanish with his parents, he was not pleased. At that point in his life, he wanted nothing more than to blend into the dominant social environment, in this case an affluent, white neighborhood saturated with English.

The discomfort felt by my student is an important reminder of the internal conflict experienced by many youngsters as they come to terms with life in a new culture. As they learn English and begin to fit into school routines, they embark on a personal journey toward a new cultural identity. If they come to reject their home language and culture, opting for maximum assimilation into the dominant culture, they must necessarily experience alienation from their parents and family. Even if immigrant students strive to adopt the ways of the new culture without replacing those of the home, they will nonetheless have departed significantly from many traditions their parents hold dear. Thus, for second language students, the "generation gap" necessarily widens to the extent that the values, beliefs, roles, responsibilities, and general expectations differ between the home culture and the dominant one. Keeping this in mind may help you empathize with students' personal conflicts of identity and personal life choices.

The third suggestion, then, is to become aware of basic features of the home culture, such as religious beliefs and customs, food preferences and restrictions, and roles and responsibilities of children and adults (Ovando & Collier, 1985; Saville-Troike, 1978). These basic bits of information, though sketchy, will guide your initial interactions with your new students and may help you avoid asking them to say or do things that may be prohibited or frowned upon in the home culture, including such common activities as celebrating birthdays, pledging allegiance to the flag, and eating hot dogs. Finding out basic information also provides a starting point from which to interpret your newcomer's responses to you, to your other students, and to the ways you organize classroom activities. Just as you make adjustments, your students will also begin to make adjustments, as they grow in the awareness and acceptance that ways of acting, dressing, eating, talking, and behaving in school are different to a greater or lesser degree from what they may have experienced before.

Classroom Activities That Let You Get to Know Your Students

Several fine learning activities may also provide some of the personal information you need to help you know your students better. One way is to have all your students write an illustrated book "All About Me" or "The Story of My Life." Each book may be bound individually, or all the life stories may be bound together and published in a class book, complete with illustrations or photographs. Alternatively, student stories may be posted on the bulletin board for all to read. This assignment lets you in on the lives of all your students and permits them to get to know, appreciate, and understand each other as well. Of particular importance, this activity does not single out your newcomers, since all your students will be involved.

Personal writing assignments like the one above lend themselves to many grade levels because personal topics remain pertinent across age groups even into adulthood. Students who speak little or no English may begin by illustrating a series of important events in their lives, perhaps to be captioned with your assistance or that of another student. In addition, there are many ways to accommodate students' varying English writing abilities. For example, if students write more easily in their native tongue than in English, allow them to do so. Then have a bilingual student or paraprofessional translate the meaning for you. Be sure to publish the student's story as written in the native language, because you will thereby both validate the home language and expose the rest of the class to a different language and its writing system. If a student knows some English but is not yet able to write, allow her or him to dictate the story to you or to another student in the class.

Another way to begin to know your students is to start a dialogue journal with them. Provide each student with a blank journal, and allow the student to draw or to write in the language of the student's choice. You may then respond to the students' journal entries on a periodic basis. Interactive dialogue journals, described in detail in Chapter 3, have proven useful for second language students of all ages (Kreeft, 1984). Dialogue journals make an excellent introduction to literacy and facilitate the development of an ongoing personal relationship between the student and you, the teacher. As with personal writing, this activity is appropriate for all students, and, if you institute it with the entire class, you provide a way for newcomers to participate in a "regular" class activity. Being able to do what others do can be a source of great pride and self-satisfaction to students who are new to the language and culture of the school.

Finally, many teachers start the school year with a unit on themes such as "Where We Were Born" or "Family Origins." Again, this activity is relevant to all students, whether immigrant or native-born, and it gives teacher and students alike a chance to know more about themselves and each other. A typical activity with this theme is the creation of a world map with a string connecting each child's name and birthplace to your city and school. Don't forget to put *your* name on the list along with *your* birthplace! From there, you and your students may go on to study more about the various regions and countries of origin. Clearly, this type of theme leads in many directions, including the discovery of people in the community who may be able to share their home countries with your class. Your guests may begin by sharing food, holiday customs, art, or music with students. Through such contact, you may become aware of some of the more subtle aspects of the culture, such as how the culture communicates politeness and respect, or how the culture views the role of children, adults, and the school. If you are lucky enough to find such community resources, you will not only enliven your teaching, but broaden your cross-cultural understanding as well.

Not all necessary background information will emerge from these classroom activities. You will no doubt want to look into cultural, historical, and geographical resources available at your school or community library. In addition, you may find resource personnel at your school, including paraprofessionals and resource teachers, who can help with specific questions or concerns. In the final analysis, though, your primary source of information is the students themselves as you interrelate on a day-to-day basis. For further information on multicultural teaching, the following list presents a few important books you may want to peruse.

Banks, J. A. (1991). *Teaching Strategies for Ethnic Studies* (5th ed.). Boston: Allyn & Bacon.

Ovando, C. J., & Collier, V. P. (1985). *Bilingual and ESL Classrooms.* New York: McGraw-Hill.

Saville-Troike, M. (1978). *A Guide to Culture in the Classroom.* Rosslyn, VA: National Clearinghouse for Bilingual Education.

Takaki, R. (Ed.). (1987). *From Different Shores: Perspectives on Race and Ethnicity in America.* New York: Oxford University Press.

Tiedt, P. L., & Tiedt, I. M. (1990). *Multicultural Teaching: A Handbook of Activities, Information and Resources* (3rd ed.). Boston: Allyn & Bacon.

HOW DO CULTURAL DIFFERENCES AFFECT TEACHING AND LEARNING?

In order to learn about your students through personal interactions, you may need to hone your skills in observing and interpreting their behavior. Such skills are especially important when you first meet your students, whether at the beginning of the school year or when they first enroll in your class. One procedure to help focus your observations is to keep a journal in which you jot notes at the end of each day concerning how your new student is doing. Does she understand basic school rules such as handraising? Is he starting to form friendships? What activities does your new student seem to be happiest doing: small-group activities, individual seatwork, listening to stories, drawing pictures? In which activities is the student reluctant? By noticing activities that are most comfortable for students, you can make sure that your newcomer has frequent opportunities to participate in them. In this way, you build a positive attitude toward what may as yet be an alien environment: school. From there, you may gradually draw the student into other school routines.

Culture in the Classroom Context

When you make observations in your classroom, you are actually using some of the tools used by anthropologists when they study another culture through ethnography (i.e., introspection, interviewing, observation, and participant-obser- vation). As the teacher, you are automatically both participant and observer in the classroom culture. However, you will need to step back at times to reflect introspectively on how your classroom operates. In addition, you may want to take time to observe your students during independent and small-group activity. In this way, you will have the opportunity to give full attention to how your students are functioning socially in your classroom.

In order to make the most of your introspective reflections and observations, you may need some concepts to guide interpretations. In other words, it's one thing to notice that Nazrene "tunes out" during whole-class lessons but quite another to figure out why, so that you can alter your instruction to reach her. To provide you with some interpretive touchstones, we suggest you consider for a moment some of the aspects that comprise culture, because these represent potential sources of overt conflict or silent suffering if your classroom rules and structures conflict with those already culturally engrained in your students.

Definitions of Culture and Its Content

Culture may be defined as the shared beliefs, values, and rule-governed patterns of behavior that define a group and are required for group membership (Goodenough, 1981; Saville-Troike, 1978). Thus defined, culture comprises three essential aspects: what people know and believe, what people do, and what people make and use. Every child is born into the culture of a particular group of people, and, through the culture's child-rearing practices, every child is socialized, to a greater or lesser extent, toward becoming first a "good boy" or "good girl," and ultimately a "good man" or "good woman" in the eyes of the culture. Thus, culture may be thought of as the acquired knowledge people use to both interpret experience and generate behavior (Spradley, 1980).

For the purposes of understanding your students, we summarize cultural content with questions outlined by Saville-Troike (1978). The content of culture may be categorized into various components, including: (1) family structure; (2) definitions of stages, periods, or transitions during a person's life; (3) roles of children and adults and corresponding behavior in terms of power and politeness; (4) discipline; (5) time and space; (6) religion; (7) food; (8) health and hygiene; (9) history, traditions, holidays, and celebrations. Table 1.1 provides a number of questions that you might ask yourself about these aspects of culture. As you read the questions, try to answer them for your own culture as well as for a different cultural group in order to get a sense of similarities and differences across cultures.

When students in our university classes discuss the questions in Table 1.1 according to their family traditions, interesting patterns emerge. While many students identify with mainstream, middle-class American cultural values, such as punctuality, some also add special traditions passed down from immigrant grandparents or great-grandparents, including special foods and holiday traditions. Other students come from families who have been in this country for centuries, yet maintain particular regional traditions such as herbal healing practices. In addition, some students have maintained strong religious traditions, including Judaic, Buddhist, Greek Orthodox Christian, Protestant, and Catholic beliefs. From these discussions, we find that each individual actually embodies a variety of cultures and subcultures.

One student found the cultural questions an interesting way to look at her own family. Her parents had met and married in Germany: her father an Egyptian and a Coptic Christian, her mother a German Catholic. From there they moved with their three young children to the United States. Najia reflected, with some amusement, on how different her German relatives were from her Egyptian relatives. For example, her German relatives visited once or twice a year, making

TABLE 1.1   Cultural Content and Questions

Cultural Content	Questions
Family structures	What constitutes a family? Who among these or others live in one house? What are the rights and responsibilities of each family member? What is the hierarchy of authority? What is the relative importance of the individual family member in contrast to the family as a whole?
The life cycles	What are the criteria for defining stages, periods, or transitions in life? What rites of passage are there? What behaviors are considered appropriate for children of different ages? How might these conflict with behaviors taught or encouraged in school? How is the age of the children computed? What commemoration is made of the child's birth, if any, and when?
Roles and interpersonal relationships	What roles are available to whom, and how are they acquired? Is education relevant to learning these roles? How do the roles of girls and women differ from those of boys and men? How do people greet each other? What forms of address are used between people of differing roles? Do girls work and interact with boys? Is it proper? How is deference shown and to whom and by whom?
Discipline	What is discipline? What counts as discipline and what doesn't? Which behaviors are considered socially acceptable for boys vs. girls at different ages? Who or what is considered responsible if a child misbehaves? The child? Parents? Older siblings? The environment? Or is blame ascribed? Who has authority over whom? To what extent can one person impose his/her will on another? How is behavior traditionally controlled? To what extent and in what domains?
Time and space	How important is punctuality? Speed in completing a task? Are there restrictions associated with certain seasons? What is the spatial organization of the home? How much space are people accustomed to? What significance is associated with different locations or directions, including North, South, East, West?
Religion	What restrictions are there concerning topics that should not be discussed in school? Are dietary restrictions to be observed, including fasting on particular occasions? When are these occasions? What restrictions are associated with death and the dead?
Food	What is eaten? In what order? How often? Which foods are restricted? Which foods are "typical"? What social obligations are there with regard to food giving, reciprocity, and honoring people? What restrictions or prescriptions are associated with handling, offering, or discarding food?
Health and hygiene	How are illnesses treated and by whom? What is considered to be the cause? If a student were involved in an accident at school, would any of the common first aid practices be considered unacceptable?
History, traditions, holidays	Which events and people are a source of pride for the group? To what extent does the group in the United States identify with the history and traditions of the country of origin? What holidays and celebrations are considered appropriate for observing in school? Which ones are appropriate only for private observance?

SOURCE: From *A Guide to Culture in the Classroom* by Muriel Saville-Troike, 1978, Rosslyn, VA: National Clearinghouse for Bilingual Education.

plans well in advance, and staying a short, predetermined amount of time. Her Egyptian relatives, in contrast, "couldn't seem to get enough of each other." They loved long visits, with as many of the family together as possible. Najia's German mother emphasized orderliness and punctuality in the home, with carefully scheduled and planned meals. The family ate at the specified hour, and all were expected to be there on time. With such differences concerning time and space, Najia wonders that her parents were able to make a highly successful marriage. She attributes their success in part to their individual personalities: her mother, an artist, is by nature easy-going and flexible; her father, an electronic engineer, is an organized thinker and planner. As individuals, they seemed compatible with many of each other's cultural ways. Najia's reflections are a reminder that people's behavior combines both cultural and individual differences.

Sociolinguistic Interactions in the Classroom

One particularly important aspect of culture that can affect teaching and learning has to do with the ways you use language during instruction. Because teaching and learning depend upon clear communication between teacher and students, the communicative success of teacher–student interactions is crucial. Early on, difficulties may arise from lack of a common language. However, communication difficulties may persist even after students have acquired the basics of English if the student and teacher are following different sociocultural rules about how to use language (Cazden, 1986). For example, if the home culture values strict authority of adults over children and if children are only supposed to speak when spoken to, then these same children may be reluctant to volunteer an answer in class. You might quite logically interpret this reluctance as disinterest or lack of knowledge, when in fact the student may simply be waiting for you to invite him or her to respond. On the other hand, some students may not want to answer your questions because displaying knowledge in class amounts to "showing off," causing them to stand out like a sore thumb (Philips, 1983). Some children consider enthusiastic knowledge display impolite because it could make their friends appear ignorant. These examples illustrate how cultural values affecting language use may impede teacher–student communication in either English or the home language.

Language use differences can be especially confusing in the realm of teacher questioning. Research has shown that teachers often do not allow much "wait time" after asking a question in class (Rowe, 1974). It turns out that what is considered enough wait time in normal conversations varies across cultures, as do rules concerning how and when to interrupt, and the number of people who may speak at once (Bauman & Scherzer, 1974; Ochs & Schieffelin, 1984; Schieffelin & Eisenberg, 1984; Shultz, Erickson, & Florio, 1982). In addition, children must learn what the teacher's rules are regarding who can speak with whom and when (Mehan, 1979). These rules may vary with the activity structure (e.g., teacher-led lesson vs. small-group projects). Another aspect of teacher questioning that may be problematic is the fact that teachers typically ask questions with a particular answer in mind, in order to assess what students know or have learned. For some students, these "known-answer" questions might be considered odd or of dubious purpose (Heath, 1983; Mehan, 1979), resulting in student reluctance to participate in such interrogations. You might want to reflect on your own questioning practices, in terms of wait time, question types, and the actual phrasing you use. If your questions are greeted with blank stares, try altering your questioning style. Another possibility is to introduce question–answer sessions with a brief explanation of what you are trying to accomplish and why. That way, if students are unaccustomed to your question types, you will at least help them understand your purpose for asking them.

Culturally Related Responses to Classroom Organization

There are other cultural differences that may interfere with student participation in learning activities in the classroom. One of these is the social organization of lessons (Mehan, 1979). Within the constraints of time and adult assistance, teachers typically utilize whole-class, small-group, and individualized formats for instruction. It is important to recognize that these formats represent distinctly different types of social structures within which students may experience various degrees of comfort or discomfort, based on both cultural and individual differences (Au & Jordan, 1981). For example, the use of small groups for cooperative learning has become a major thrust toward increasing learning for all students but especially for ethnic minority students (Kagan, 1986). The rationale is that many ethnic minority cultures instill strong values of group cooperation, and, therefore, such instruction will build upon home experience. In addition, cooperative groups provide students with practice in getting along with children different from themselves to the extent that groups consist of students with different backgrounds. We are convinced that cooperative group learning is a valuable tool for teachers, for the reasons described. However, it is important to keep in mind that some children may feel that the teacher, as the academic authority, is the only proper person to learn from in the classroom. If so, such students need to hear your reasons for using cooperative groups as reassurance that group learning is valid academically. In fact, parents may need to hear your reasons as well. We knew one child who was functioning beautifully in cooperative groups. Yet, during parent conferencing, his father politely asked when we were going to start teaching!

In summary, we know that different students may be more comfortable with some instructional formats than with others, and that their feelings stem from both cultural and individual preferences. We suggest the use of a variety of formats to meet the multiple needs of your diverse students. Your best route is to be aware of how you create the social formats of learning in order to observe and interpret student responses with thoughtful sensitivity, making modifications as needed.

Literacy Traditions from Home and Community

As you approach the teaching of reading and writing to second language students, you will want to be aware of the literacy knowledge your students bring with them. Literacy knowledge will stem not only from prior schooling but also from experiences with the ways reading and writing are used in the home and community (Au & Jordan, 1981; Boggs, 1972; Heath, 1983). Thus, it is helpful to become aware of how reading and writing are traditionally used in the community because these traditional literacy uses will influence your students' ideas, beliefs, and assumptions about reading and writing. You will want to build on these ideas, and make sure to expand them to include the functions of literacy required by U.S. schools and society. Let us make this more clear through some examples.

Gustavo, age seven, entered the first grade of an urban elementary school in February, halfway through the academic year. He had come from rural Mexico, and this was his first time in school. He didn't even know how to hold a pencil. At first, he was so intimidated that he would refuse to come into the classroom at the beginning of the school day. With persistent coaxing from the teacher and her assistant, he reluctantly complied. Once in, Gustavo was anxious to fit into the normal class routines. He loved to wave his hand in the air when the teacher asked a question, although at first he didn't know what to do when called upon. That part of the routine took a little time to master.

One day, as I was chatting with Gustavo, he began to tell me all about his little town in Michoacan, about the travails of the trip *pa' 'l norte* and then about an incident when his two-year-old sister became critically ill. His mother, he told me, knew what medicine the baby needed, but it was only available in Mexico. So they had to "find someone who could write" to send to Mexico for the medicine. They did, and Gustavo's baby sister recovered.

What does this story tell us about the concept of literacy that Gustavo offers for the teacher to build upon? First, we can surmise that Gustavo has not had

Children who know how to read and write in their first language can transfer much of this knowledge to literacy development in their second language.

extensive opportunities to explore reading and writing at home. He probably has not been read to much, nor provided with paper and pencils for dabbling in drawing and writing—the very activities so highly recommended today as the foundation of literacy development. On the other hand, he is well aware of how important it is to be able to write—it was a matter of life and death for his sister! Furthermore, he is aware of the inconveniences, not to say dangers, of illiteracy. Thus, Gustavo, at the tender age of seven, brings a deeper understanding of the importance of literacy than many children whose rich early literacy experiences allow them to take such things for granted. Gustavo's motivation and understanding provide the foundation for the teacher to build upon. Gustavo needs daily exposure to the pleasures and practical functions of print through stories, poems, rhymes, labels, letters, notes, recipes, board games, instructions, and more. With practice and hard work, his proudest moment will come when he himself writes the next letter to Mexico.

In contrast to Gustavo, students who immigrate at an older age often bring substantial experience and skill in reading and writing in their home language. These experiences and skills provide a good foundation for learning to read and write in English. Students who read in their home language already know that print bears a systematic relationship to spoken language, that print carries meaning, and that reading and writing can be used for many purposes. Moreover, literate students know that they are capable of making sense of written language. Such experience and knowledge will transfer directly to learning to read and write. in English, given English language development and appropriate literacy instruction (Cummins, 1981; Hudelson, 1987; Odlin, 1989; Thonis, 1981). Thus when students arrive with home language literacy skills, teachers do not have to start all over again to teach reading and writing (Goodman, Goodman, & Flores, 1979; Peregoy, 1989; Peregoy & Boyle, 1991). Rather, they can build on a rather sophisticated base of literacy knowledge, adding the specifics for English as needed, a topic developed fully in subsequent chapters.

HOW CAN I EASE NEWCOMERS INTO THE ROUTINES OF MY CLASSROOM WHEN THEY KNOW LITTLE OR NO ENGLISH?

As you begin to know more about your students, you will be better able to offer them social/emotional support. Only when new students become comfortably integrated into your classroom's social and academic routines will optimal second language acquisition and academic learning occur. Thus, you'll need to give special effort and attention to those who are newcomers to the country. Adapting from Maslow's hierarchy of human needs (Maslow, 1968), we discuss basic strategies for integrating new children into your classroom. Three basic needs you will want to consider are: (1) safety and security, (2) a sense of belonging, and (3) self-esteem.

First Things First: Safety and Security

When second language learners first arrive in school, a "first things first" approach is helpful, following Maslow's views. Thus, the first concern must be with creating a feeling of safety and security. To address this need, there are several things you can do. First of all, it is helpful to assign a "personal buddy" to each newcomer, if possible one who speaks the newcomer's home language. The buddy must be a child who already knows the school and is comfortable there. The buddy's job is to accompany the new child throughout the day's routines to make sure he or she knows where to find such essentials as the bathroom, the cafeteria, and the bus stop. The newcomer needs to learn not only where things are but also the various rules for using them. For example, each school has its own rules about how to line up and collect lunch at the cafeteria, where to sit, how to behave, and when to leave. Furthermore, there are culturally specific rules about how to eat particular kinds of food, rules that we take for granted but that may be totally foreign to a new arrival. Perhaps you yourself recall feeling tentative and intimidated the first time you ate in the school cafeteria. If so, you will have some idea of the anxiety that can accompany the first days of school for a youngster who is new not only to the school but also to the entire culture it represents. The personal buddy helps the new child through these initial days, helping alleviate anxieties and embarrassments that are bound to occur.

Another way to address the safety and security needs of newcomers is to follow predictable routines in your daily classroom schedule. Most teachers follow a fairly stable schedule within which instructional content varies. Predictability in routine creates a sense of security for all students, but it is especially important for students who are new to the language and culture of the school. In fact, your predictable routines may be the first stable feature some students have experienced in a long time, especially if they have recently immigrated under adverse circumstances.

Creating a Sense of Belonging

An additional way to promote security and create a sense of belonging is to assign your student to a "home group" that remains unchanged for a long period of time. In classrooms where student seating is arranged at tables, the home group may be defined by table. The purpose of the home group is to develop mini-communities of mutual interdependence, support, and identity. If such groups are an ongoing aspect of classroom social organization, with rules of caring, respect, and concern already in place, then the home group provides an ideal social unit to receive a newcomer.

Regardless of how you organize your classroom, it is always important to seat new students toward the middle or front of the classroom, rather than at the back or other far reaches of the room. In our experience, it seems that students who speak little or no English tend to be placed at the periphery of the classroom. There, they happily blend into the woodwork and are easy to forget about. In our own research, we have often noted teachers who rarely have eye contact with new, limited English speaking children. Even if you feel a child can't understand a word you are saying, you can integrate the child into the class by simply making eye contact occasionally while speaking. We encourage conscious integration of newcomers into the social fabric of the classroom so as to avoid unconscious marginalization.

By paying close attention to the social and emotional needs of your new students, you will be laying the foundation for the early stages of language acquisition. For example, the one-on-one attention of the personal buddy offers numerous opportunities for your newcomer to learn many basic English words and phrases at the "survival" level. In addition, repetition of classroom routines provides non-English speakers with ideal language learning opportunities because the words and phrases that accompany such routines are constantly repeated within a meaningful, concrete context. If you count up the number of times a child hears such functional phrases as "It's lunch time now," or "The quiet row may line up first," you will get an idea of how valuable such context-embedded language can be for rapid learning of basic English expressions. Finally, integrating newcomers into cooperative groups provides further social and academic language learning opportunities, as discussed in detail in chapter 2. Thus, by attending to the security and belonging needs of your limited English proficient students, you also lay a firm foundation for English language acquisition.

As second language acquisition progresses and as students begin to become a part of the social fabric of your class, they are well positioned to grow in self-esteem through successful participation in both the social and academic aspects of classroom life. Thus, Maslow's theory provides a useful way to look at the initial needs of newcomers. As the social-emotional foundation is laid, all the other aspects of personal growth may begin to interweave and support each other, with social and academic competence creating self-esteem and reinforcing feelings of security and belonging.

WHAT KINDS OF PROGRAMS EXIST TO MEET THE NEEDS OF SECOND LANGUAGE LEARNERS?

If you are fairly new to the enterprise of educating second language learners, you might be interested in what kinds of programs are in place throughout the country to serve them. We offer such information below so that you will have an idea of what some school districts are doing. If your school has just begun to experience growth in second language populations, these descriptions may provide a starting point for considering a more formalized language development program.

Bilingual Education Programs

Second language learners find themselves in a wide variety of school programs, from those carefully tailored to meet their specific linguistic and cultural needs to programs in which very little is done differently to accommodate them. Perhaps the simplest distinction among programs is whether two languages or one is used for instruction. In 1968, federal legislation was passed creating bilingual education programs, defined as educational programs in which two languages, one of which must be English, are used for teaching purposes. Bilingual education programs have taken many forms, but two goals are common to all: (1) to teach English and (2) to provide access to content area curriculum through the home language while students are gaining English language proficiency (Lessow-Hurley, 1990).

Several kinds of bilingual education programs have been established, including the following.

Transitional Bilingual Education. Primary language instruction, intended as a temporary bridge to English language instruction, is provided for one to three years, after which students are "transitioned" into all English instruction. No further language and literacy instruction in the home language is offered. The goal is to develop English language proficiency for limited English proficient students as soon as possible.

Maintenance Bilingual Education. Primary language instruction is offered as more than a bridge to English language instruction; instruction may extend beyond three years, with program goals including full bilingualism and biliteracy for limited English speaking students.

Immersion Education. A second language development program first developed in Canada to promote French language acquisition by English-speaking students. In the United States, immersion programs have been instituted in languages such as Spanish and Cantonese. Instruction takes place in the target language in the early grades, with the gradual introduction of English language arts as students move up the grades. The goal is full bilingualism and biliteracy for native English-speaking students.

Two-Way Immersion Programs. A variation on traditional immersion programs, two-way immersion programs group approximately equal numbers of English-speaking students and non-English-speaking students together for instruction. In the early grades the non-English language (e.g., Spanish or Cantonese) is used for instruction in an immersion approach. Instruction in English is gradually increased as students move up the grades. The goal is full bilingualism and biliteracy for all students. For example, the English speakers acquire Spanish or Cantonese and the Spanish or Cantonese speakers acquire English.

Newcomer Programs. These programs are designed to support the initial adjustment of students to the language, culture, and schooling of their new country. They emphasize the integration of academic and personal-social support to help students adjust (Chang, 1990). Newcomer programs may make use of students' home languages for instruction, but they also emphasize systematic English language instruction. All students in newcomer programs are recent arrivals from other countries. Newcomer programs are short-term, often only one year, and are intended to prepare students to succeed in regular schooling situations, where they may continue to receive bilingual instruction or ESL assistance and sheltered English instruction.

Bilingual education programs that aim to develop children's bilingual and biliterate abilities fully create the foundation for "additive bilingualism," or the addition of second language abilities concurrent with continued development of primary language abilities, including reading and writing (Lambert, 1987). In such programs, bilingualism is a major priority because it is viewed as a social, cultural, and economic asset to the individual and the community. Maintenance and development of a language that is not used widely in the larger community requires individual motivation and effort as well as community support. Bilingual education programs concerned with additive bilingualism are a major source of such support.

In contrast to additive bilingualism, subtractive bilingualism occurs when an individual develops a second language fully, while shifting away from identity with primary language and natal culture. This situation is quite common among immigrants to a new country. In fact, over the course of a few generations, loss of the ethnic language tends to be the rule rather than the exception (Fishman, 1981). School programs that do not aim for full bilingualism are most concerned with the need for students to develop English language proficiency. In such situations, it falls to the immigrant family and community to help children maintain and develop the home language. Not all families consider home language maintenance beneficial, deteriorating chances for primary language survival.

While the above definitions of bilingual programs appear crisp and clear-cut, real programs designated as "bilingual" vary a great deal and often do not adhere precisely to one model or another (Ovando & Collier, 1985). In any case, the practicality of bilingual instruction depends upon the existence of a sufficiently large linguistic community (e.g., Spanish, Vietnamese, French) to warrant instruction in the home language along with English. Many such communities do exist, and they have stimulated the growth of bilingual education in the United States to serve many American Indian/Alaskan Native languages as well as Spanish, Portuguese, French, Korean, Vietnamese, Cambodian, Cantonese, Arabic, Tagalog, and numerous others (Kloss, 1977).

ESL Programs

Bilingual education programs serve only a small percentage of eligible students. Much more common are instructional programs that make use of only one language, English, for teaching. In many urban and suburban areas today, classrooms include students from several language groups, making bilingual instruction impractical, if not impossible, for many students. Among program types that use only English for instruction are the following.

Sheltered English. In these programs, students are taught subject matter entirely in English. Subject matter instruction is organized to promote second language acquisition, while teaching cognitively demanding, grade-level-appropriate material. Special teaching techniques are used to help students understand English instruction even though they are still limited in English language proficiency.

ESL Pullout.   In these programs, second language students receive the majority of their instruction in regular classrooms alongside their monolingual English-speaking peers. However, they are "pulled out" of the regular classroom on a regular basis to receive additional help from an ESL teacher or aide. The help they receive consists of English language development activities as well as reinforcement of subject matter being taught in the regular classroom. The goal is to help students get by while becoming proficient in oral and written English.

English Language Development.   In these programs, students learn all subject matter including ESL in a class taught by a teacher with special knowledge of second language development. The majority of students in such classes are ESL or nonstandard English dialect speakers. The goal is full English language and literacy development.

Second Language Learners in the "Regular" Classroom

While various bilingual and monolingual English programs have been designed specifically for second language learners, many students find themselves in classrooms where little, if any, special assistance is provided. These students face a "sink-or-swim" situation. Increasingly, however, sound practices in second language teaching are reaching the "regular" classroom teacher. In this book, we offer information and ideas for developing literacy skills in English as a second language. We believe that these ideas can be applied by teachers, regardless of the type of program, bilingual, ESL, or English only. Just as our students bring diverse backgrounds, so also will programs exhibit diversity as we all join forces to move our students toward educational success and integration into the larger society.

SUMMARY

In this chapter, we have highlighted the rich diversity among students who are learning English as a second language in school. In our descriptions, we focus on children's different experiential backgrounds and strengths, while pointing out particular challenges they face in school. Because we believe strongly in building on each student's prior knowledge and experience, we suggest a variety of ways you can get to know your second language students, even though you may not yet share a common language. These activities include personal writing topics, interactive journal writing, and allowing students to write in their home language. Knowing that cultural differences can create an initial source of miscommunication, we have pointed out various components of culture defined by anthropologists, while suggesting ways to recognize and honor cultural differences among students in the classroom. We have also discussed how classroom organization and language use may be more or less comfortable for students due to both cultural and individual differences. We suggest cooperative group learning as one strategy for integrating students into the classroom fabric and promoting English language acquisition. Because we are convinced that social and emotional security form an essential base for learning, we have also provided a variety of ways to promote newcomers' sense of belonging from day one, using Maslow's hierarchy to give attention to their social-emotional needs. Finally, we offered an overview of the kinds of classrooms and programs in which second language learners find themselves. In the next chapter, we will present the details of second language acquisition, maintaining our emphasis on students' experiences and reactions to the processes and motivating factors that lead to learning their new language, English.

SUGGESTIONS FOR FURTHER READING

Ferguson, C., & Heath, S. B. (Eds.). (1981). *Language in the U.S.A.* New York: Cambridge University Press.

If you are interested in learning more about the rich language diversity in the United States, including Native American languages, immigrant languages, American English dialects, and language use in education, law, and medicine, this book is a must. Each chapter is written by a specialist on the topic. The book is readable and fascinating.

Lessow-Hurley, J. (1990). *The Foundations of dual language instruction.* White Plains, NY: Longman.

This well-written introductory text explains a broad range of complex issues that form the foundations of bilingual and ESL instruction. It includes discussion of topics such as language development in a first and second language, aspects of culture, national and international dual language programs, and the political and legal foundations of bilingual education.

Ovando, C. J., & Collier, V. P. (1985). *Bilingual and ESL classrooms: Teaching in multicultural contexts.* New York: McGraw-Hill.

A detailed introduction to issues in bilingual and ESL classrooms, including discussion of students, language, culture, academic achievement, program models and types, and curriculum options.

Roche Rico, B., & Mano, S. (1991). *American mosaic: Multicultural readings in context.* Boston: Houghton-Mifflin.

This book, an anthology of writings by members of various American ethnic groups, celebrates diversity and offers readers direct contact with diverse ethnic experiences through literature. It includes such diverse writers as Cesar Chavez, Cynthia Ozick, Alice Walker, Louise Erdrich, Martin Luther King, and Maxine Hong Kingston. Historical contexts are provided.

ACTIVITIES

1. As you look at Table 1.1, try to answer as many of the questions as you can regarding your own family traditions. Next, compare your answers with those of another adult. What are the similarities and differences?

2. Take the opportunity to visit a school near you that enrolls children newly arrived from other countries. Obtain permission from the principal to visit one of the classrooms. As you observe, try to find out where the children are from and what kinds of special help they are receiving.

3. Meet with a teacher who specializes in teaching English as a second language. Ask his or her views on the effects of children's cultural and prior educational backgrounds on their school performance. What accommodations does the teacher make to help children adjust?

4. Talk with a child who is learning English as a second language. Ask what it is like to learn English in school; what is the hardest part; what about it is fun, if anything; and how long it has taken so far.

5. Begin an informal study of an ethnic group that you would like to know more about. Look for literature by members of that group to read in order to get a feel of the culture from an inside view. If you don't know which group to pick, take a look at *American Mosaic,* listed above, to get an overview.

CHAPTER 2

Second Language Acquisition

In this chapter, we describe how students learn English as a second language, discussing such questions as the following:

1. What do we know when we know a language? What are some ways experts have defined language proficiency and communicative competence?
2. What kinds of processes and factors are involved in acquiring a second language?
3. What are some differences between being able to use a second language socially versus being able to use it for school learning?
4. How can teachers organize instruction to help students become more proficient in English while also teaching content?
5. For what purposes are students assessed in second language proficiency, and how is assessment accomplished?

We know a young Nicaraguan girl, Judith, who came to California at the age of seven. Her parents struggled to make a living for their seven children, and Judith was very protective of them, always looking to lighten their load. Once we asked about her younger brothers and sisters, but Judith admonished us never to mention the topic to her mother, who was still grieving the loss of an infant. Judith was virtually non-English-speaking in the third grade; her English grew very slowly in her fourth and fifth grades, though her native language remained fluent—she could make up extensive and complex Spanish stories on the spot, given a patient audience. For a long while, we didn't see Judith, but then we happened to visit her school one day. We entered the main office to check in, and there answering the telephone in fluent English was Judith, now a sixth-grader who had earned the prestigious job of student assistant. What a transformation! We greeted her at once, and complimented her on her efficient office management skills. And then, we just had to comment: "Your English is so good! How did you do it?" With hardly a moment's reflection, she replied: "I waited." And wait she had, a good four years, though much more went into it than her answer implied.

Judith's story gives a glimpse of second language acquisition from the inside view. In this chapter, we look at how researchers and theorists have described the process. As you read on, you will find that Judith's brief answer carried the weight of truth. There is, of course, more to be said in order to understand what it is like to learn the language of the school and the larger society as a second language. In the next few sections, we first discuss what you know when you know a language, in order to highlight the complex territory second language learners must cover to become proficient. Then, we discuss various factors that impinge upon the process, including the nature of the language learning situation, the effects of age, and the importanee of social interaction and "comprehensible input."

WHAT DO YOU KNOW WHEN YOU KNOW A LANGUAGE? DEFINING LANGUAGE PROFICIENCY AS COMMUNICATIVE COMPETENCE

In general, language proficiency can be defined as the ability to use a language effectively and appropriately throughout the range of social and personal situations normally required for daily living. In literate societies, language proficiency subsumes both oral and written language. You may have noticed that this definition emphasizes not only the grammatical rules governing sounds, word forms, and word orders to convey meaning (phonology, morphology, syntax, and semantics) but also knowledge of social conventions of language use (e.g., how to start and end a conversation smoothly; how and when to use informal expressions such as slang as opposed to more formal ways of speaking; how, whether, and when to establish a first-name basis in a formal relationship). Thus, as you can see, judgments concerning language proficiency are deeply rooted in social and cultural norms. For this reason, the term "communicative competence" is often used instead of "language proficiency" to emphasize the idea that proficient language use extends beyond grammar into the social conventions of language use (Canale & Swain, 1980; Wallat, 1984).

Demands on language proficiency vary, and people must often practice certain kinds of language use depending on the jobs they choose. Think for a moment of the different ways people listen, speak, read, and write in the following jobs: psychotherapist, teacher, grocery store clerk, construction worker, accountant, lawyer. While "active listening" may be one psychotherapeutic technique used to help people understand their problems, such intense listening would not be required for grocery store clerking. Teachers and lawyers must learn to speak clearly in a public forum, though in different ways: arguing versus professing or teaching. Lawyers probably do more writing than teachers as they prepare their briefs, but both must do quite a lot of reading. In addition to the different demands on people's language abilities, individuals often vary in their ability to use language from one situation to another. For example, a person might be verbally competent in managing an office, yet find it difficult to write a persuasive essay. You can probably imagine many other similarities and differences.

In summary, language proficiency represents a large and complex array of knowledge. As we have seen, appropriate language use involves both social and grammatical knowledge. People adjust their linguistic style from formal to informal, oral to written, according to their needs and purposes. Full language proficiency thus includes the development of a repertoire of oral and written language skills from which to choose for a range of social situations.

Students learning English as a second language face a complex task that must take place gradually over time. Simultaneously, many will also develop and maintain proficiency in their home language, including literacy skills, thereby becoming bilingual and biliterate. For children living in bilingual communities, maintenance of the home language represents a vitally important aspect of communicative competence: *bilingual* communicative competence (Grosjean, 1982). Consider, for example, the fact that the home language may be a child's only means of communicating with parents or grandparents. As a result, the home language becomes the primary vehicle for the transmission of cultural values, family history, and ethnic identity—the very underpinnings of self-esteem (Wong Fillmore, 1990). In addition to the important social and emotional advantages of home language maintenance, research suggests that primary language development supports second language development (Cummins, 1980, 1981) and that bilingualism itself may lead to cognitive flexibility (Hakuta, 1986). Although we focus on second language literacy in this book, we want to underscore the importance of the first language as an integral part of our students' lives: socially, emotionally, cognitively, and educationally.

LEARNING A SECOND LANGUAGE: PROCESSES AND FACTORS

Children learning English as a second language in school must gradually learn the words of the new language, along with how to pronounce and sequence them so as to convey meaning to serve a variety of functional communication goals. Considering that the average English-speaking five-year-old child understands an estimated 6,000 words and already knows enough English grammar to express ideas in the past, the present, and the future (Norton, 1989), you can see that young second language learners have a large amount of territory to cover! In addition to the basics of grammar and pronunciation, second language students must also learn how to use their new language in socially appropriate ways that are effective for school learning (Heath, 1986). How does second language learning take place? What are some of the processes and factors involved? We begin discussion of this question by contrasting formal study of a second language with the experience of living in a country where the language is spoken.

Second Language Acquisition Contexts: Formal Study versus Immersion in a Country Where the Language Is Spoken

One factor that affects second language acquisition is the social context in which the second language was learned. Have you ever studied another language, or do you know someone who has? How did you learn it? And how *well* did you learn it? When we ask our students this question, we hear a wonderful variety of second language learning stories. Most of our students have had the experience of studying a foreign language in high school or college. They often recall specific foreign language teaching techniques for learning the grammar, pronunciation, and vocabulary, usually of a European language such as French, German, or Spanish. They often remember activities such as choral repetition of sentence patterns, memorization of vocabulary items, and perhaps in-class opportunities to put these together in writing or simulated conversations.

Under these learning conditions, basic knowledge of the language may have developed. However, few people report reaching a substantial level of communicative competence unless they have spent time in a country where the language was spoken. The opportunity for foreign travel or residence often bears fruit for second language development based on the seed of classroom instruction. In contrast, students who have come to the United States as immigrants have a very different language learning story to tell. Many hold vivid memories of entering elementary or high school knowing not a word of English and feeling frightened and baffled at the world around them. They struggle for months, perhaps years, to become acclimated to the new language and culture. All too often, immigrant students are overcome by these demands and drop out of school. Yet others learn English well enough to be successful in university classes, though perhaps retaining a "foreign accent." Talking with people about how they learned a second language can provide insights into the process of second language acquisition as experienced by immigrants learning English and native-born students studying a foreign language in school. What can we learn from different language learning experiences?

Perhaps the first thing we can see is a distinction between studying a foreign language for one period a day in school versus language learning through immersion in a social environment, including the school, where the target language is used regularly for day-to-day communication. Differences between these two language acquisition contexts directly impact the language learning process. Students immersed in an environment where the new language is spoken have the advantage of being surrounded with opportunities to hear and use it. The larger social environment features the new language, not only in the classroom but also everywhere else—in shopping malls, at the theater, on television, in newspapers, and more. As a result, classroom learning can be solidified and expanded to the extent that learners interact within the larger community (Dulay, Burt, & Krashen, 1982). In addition, students learning the language of their new country are likely to be motivated, because success in acquiring strong English skills is important for day-to-day functioning and full participation in society.

In an immersion situation, second language acquisition is facilitated by the rich language exposure available and by the inherent need to communicate. At the same time, students are challenged to the highest levels of oral and written acquisition because they will need native-like skills in order to qualify for future education and employment opportunities. In contrast, foreign language study tends to be limited in opportunities and in the need to use the language for functional communication. Similarly, the expectations for accomplishment are correspondingly lower. When students enter your class knowing very little English, they have the benefit of the new language used both in school and in the larger environment. At the same time, they are apt to feel pressured by their need to learn the new language as quickly as possible.

Age and the Interplay of Social, Cultural, and Cognitive Factors

Another factor that affects the second language acquisition process is the age of the learner when second language acquisition begins (Collier, 1987, 1987/1988; Harley, 1986). For native-born children who speak another language at home such as Spanish, Navajo, Crow, or Cantonese, second language acquisition of English may begin during early childhood or upon entry to elementary school. For immigrants, the process may begin at any age, depending on how old they are when they come to this country. "Age on arrival" bears heavily upon second language acquisition processes and eventual levels of attainment. Why is this so?

The influence of age on second language acquisition stems from the complex interplay of social, cultural, and cognitive factors. Consider for a moment the language story told by Montha, a university student who came to the United States from Cambodia at age twelve, the eldest of six children. Montha remembers, first of all, how difficult it was to fit in at school where she knew neither the language nor the customs of her schoolmates. She felt frightened and isolated, as there were no other Cambodians in her neighborhood or school. To exacerbate the situation further, at age twelve, she was self-conscious and concerned about being different. Nonetheless, she gradually found her way into school social groups and began to acquire English. Reflecting on her language learning, Montha feels that her younger sisters and brothers seemed to have had an easier time. For one thing, as the eldest daughter, she was expected to help her mother daily with household chores, whereas her sisters were permitted to play with other children in the neighborhood. In addition, as an adolescent, she was not permitted to date or to go out with friends in cars, an accepted pastime of American teenagers. For these activities, she had to wait until she had graduated from high school and no longer lived with her parents.

From this brief example, we can see how age interacted with social and cultural factors to constrain Montha's language learning opportunities. First of all, she entered the American social scene at an age when cultural expectations of teenagers differed considerably between her home culture and that of the larger society. Remaining at home to help her mother, she was restricted from certain aspects of social participation that could have helped her learn English. In contrast, her siblings were young enough to be permitted to play with English-speaking neighborhood children, and this type of play was acceptable to Montha's parents. In other words, Montha's siblings, by virtue of their age, were permitted a broader range of age-appropriate social activity acceptable to both Cambodian and American parents, and this, very likely, facilitated language acquisition.

Montha did become proficient in English, however, and went on to earn a baccalaureate degree. Nonetheless, she retained some pronunciation features that set her apart from native English speakers. She also maintained fluency in Khmer and a strong ethnic identity. As a postscript, Montha tells us that her mother never did learn English. Being an adult, her mother was not required to attend school daily as her children were. Nor did she seek work outside the home as her husband did. Thus, she did not find herself in social contexts that could have provided the exposure needed for English language acquisition.

Differences in School Expectations of Younger and Older Learners

Another factor affecting second language acquisition is the level of cognitive-academic functioning normally expected at different ages, especially in school. A general task for all second language learners is to gain enough English proficiency to carry out school tasks about as well as their monolingual peers. For kindergarten and first-grade children, the linguistic performance gap between second language learners and their English-speaking agemates is relatively small. After all, monolingual children are still developing both language and concepts during the primary grades. Furthermore, learning for all young children is best derived from direct experience, manipulation of concrete objects, and social interaction with adults and peers. As kindergarten teachers know, younger children learn more by talking while doing than by listening to a long verbal explanation from the teacher. The same holds true for young second language learners. Thus, learning contexts that are age-appropriate for younger monolingual children tend to be optimal for young second language learners as well.

For older immigrant students, the classroom situation presents greater demands on second language proficiency than for younger newcomers (Ovando & Collier, 1985). They have further to go and less time to catch up than their younger brothers and sisters. From middle school on, and sometimes earlier, we expect students to be able to learn from lecture-style verbal instruction at least some of the time. Furthermore, subject matter grows increasingly more complex and abstract. Thus, students who are older upon arrival have a larger language gap to fill before they will be able to function academically in English at a level commensurate with their monolingual peers. On the other hand, precisely because they are older, they bring a well-developed cognitive and conceptual system. Moreover, they may have had sufficient schooling in their home country to be facile in literacy and numeracy skills. If so, they stand a good chance of academic success, provided that their new school offers systematic support for both second language development and continued content area learning. Other students may have had little schooling, or their educational opportunities may have been interrupted by war, political turmoil, or the struggles involved in leaving their home country. In such cases, students will have much work ahead of them in both language and content area learning.

FACILITATING FULL SECOND LANGUAGE DEVELOPMENT IN THE CLASSROOM

Neither we as teachers nor our students have any control over their "age on arrival." Yet, when students enter school with little or no knowledge of English, they are faced with the dual challenge of learning a new language while trying to fit into school routines both socially and academically: no small task! What do we know about second language acquisition processes that can facilitate these adjustments? First of all, we have seen that the process of acquiring a second language is facilitated when learners and speakers of the target language have the opportunity and desire to communicate with each other. Thus, students need opportunities to interact with fellow students and negotiate meaning—sharing experiences through activities such as speaking, drama, reader's theater, art, and writing. Making use of natural cognitive and linguistic processes similar to those involved in acquiring their first language, second language learners take the language they hear spoken around them and use it gradually to acquire the new language—its vocabulary, sound system, grammatical structure, and social conventions of use.

In the earliest stages of second language acquisition, students grapple with understanding their teacher and peers and with somehow making themselves understood. As speech emerges, learners grow in the ability to use their new language with fluency and ease, though as yet imperfectly. Eventually, as opportunities for higher-level thinking and problem solving are provided, students acquire the formal language competence necessary for instruction in mathematics, science, social studies, literature, and other subjects. Thus, students must learn to engage in complex social and cognitive transactions through their second language, both orally and in reading and writing.

When we say that students must become capable of complex social and cognitive transactions through their second language, we are putting forward the goal of full English language and literacy development. That is, we are expecting them to attain the same level of English language proficiency as their native English-speaking counterparts. For second language learners, this means acquiring the essentials of English phonology, syntax, and semantics and being able to integrate them for use in a wide variety of social contexts. Ultimately, we want our students to be at ease in English with their peers, with potential employers, with insurance agents, bank representatives, university recruiters, and the full range of social contacts that occur in daily life. Moreover, we want them to be capable of using both oral and written language in formal ways for academic purposes. This latter goal is one of the main charges of schooling for all students and represents access to the employment and social mobility available in U.S.

society. If, in addition to English language skills, students have been able to develop their primary language, they will enjoy further options afforded by their bilingualism.

Language Used for Social Interaction versus Language Used for Academic Learning

Some experts make a distinction between language used for basic social interaction and language used for academic purposes (Cummins, 1980). Research shows that students may demonstrate basic social competence in a second language within six months to two years after arrival to a new country; in other words, they can speak English well enough to interact with their peers, to talk on the telephone, and to negotiate meanings with adults. However, the ability to demonstrate academic competence in the new language at a level commensurate with that of their native-speaking peers may take five years or more (Cummins, 1979). In other words, newcomers may need five or more years to develop English skills such as those needed to read school texts efficiently and to write effectively. This information is important for teachers for two reasons. First of all, it reminds us that, even though students may appear fairly proficient in English during basic social interactions, they are still likely to need special support to be able to learn complex academic material through their second language. Secondly, it gives us a direct index of the long-term nature of the language acquisition process. We usually have students in class for just one year, and it is helpful to know that we are unlikely to witness full-blown language development in our students during that short period of time.

Although we may not control the timetable of language development, there are numerous strategies we, as teachers, can utilize to promote it. Thus, throughout this book, we will point out ways to assist second language students to develop the kind of linguistic competence that will facilitate their academic success. For now, let us take a closer look at two factors that bear heavily on the language acquisition process: comprehensible input and social interaction.

Comprehensible Input and Social Interaction

Comprehensible input refers to language used in ways that make it understandable to the learner even though language proficiency is still limited (Krashen, 1982). Paraphrasing, repetition of key points, reference to concrete materials, and acting out meanings are some of the ways speakers can help convey meaning and thus make language more understandable. When we pair two communication channels, the verbal and the nonverbal, words and meanings become discernible to the learner, as for example, when a picture of the digestive system is displayed and pointed to during an explanation of the digestive process. In this way, language is not only understood but also forms the raw material from which learners may gradually construct the new language system for themselves. During the earliest stages of language learning, face-to-face social interactions between learners and speakers of the target language provide optimal language learning opportunities.

This is because participants are likely to be focused on communicating with each other, and they will naturally make use of all their resources to do so—facial expression, dramatization, repetition, and so forth. Furthermore, the non–English speaker can communicate at a rudimentary level through actions, nods, and facial expressions. As communication is worked out or negotiated, a great deal of understandable language is generated, thereby providing comprehensible input from which language may be acquired.

Take for example an interaction we observed between two boys, Marcelino, new to English, and Joshua, a native English speaker. They were coloring a drawing they had created of a helicopter. When finished, it was to be posted on the bulletin board with drawings of other transportation vehicles.

> JOSHUA: Here, Marcelino. Here's the green [*hands Marcelino the green crayon*].
>
> MARCELINO: [*Marcelino takes the green crayon and colors the helicopter.*]
>
> JOSHUA: Hey, wait a minute! You gotta put some red stars right here. Okay?
>
> MARCELINO: Huh?
>
> JOSHUA: Red stars. I'm gonna make some red stars . . . right here. [*Joshua draws four red stars, while Marcelino continues coloring with the green crayon.*]
>
> MARCELINO: Okay.

In this interaction, the hands-on activity conveyed much of the meaning. Marcelino understood the purpose of the task and was able to interact with Joshua with minimal English to negotiate division of labor. With much of the meaning conveyed by the situation and the concrete materials, Joshua's language provided comprehensible input. Thus, Marcelino is apt to retain for future use words such as *green* and *red,* and phrases such as "Wait a minute." Working one-on-one with a partner also permitted Marcelino to convey his need for Joshua to clarify his concern over the red stars. While focused on the task of coloring the helicopter, Marcelino participated in the conversation with his minimal but functional vocabulary. At the same time, he was afforded quality English input from Joshua through conversation pertaining to the hands-on activity. Interactions such as this provide important essentials for language acquisition—functional communication situation, comprehensible input, and social interaction around a purposeful task.

Sheltered Instruction

Normal and natural classroom activities can provide comprehensible input in both quantity and quality. For example, one good source of comprehensible input, especially for academic language development, is teacher-directed instruction (Wong Fillmore, 1985). When teachers pair their verbal instruction with nonverbal cues such as pictures, demonstrations, and flow charts, they are providing comprehensible input from which their students will be able to acquire language. At the same time, by making their lessons understandable, they help insure student success in content area learning. In other words, teacher-directed instruction that is carefully tailored to students' language abilities serves two important goals at once: language development and content learning. The systematic use of such techniques is known as "sheltered instruction" (Northcutt & Watson, 1986; Schifini, 1985).

The example below describes a sheltered science lesson on owls from Ms. Bloom's fourth grade, a mixed group of native and non-native English speakers. After reading the example, look carefully at the sheltered instruction checklist below, adapted from Schifini (1985) and Los Angeles County Office of Education (n.d.), to identify the techniques used by the teacher.

> Ms. Bloom greeted her fourth-graders, who stood lined up at the door after mid-morning recess. She put her finger to her lips and quietly announced that today was the special day they had been waiting for. Then she asked them to tiptoe to their seats at their cooperative group tables. They took their seats, but not too quietly, because their curiosity was piqued by what they found at the center of each table: a small oval object wrapped in aluminum foil, a slender, five-inch probing instrument, and a graphing sheet depicting what turned out to be different kinds of rodent bones. Ms. Bloom waited for all to be seated and quiet. Then she proceeded to give her instructions:
>
> "Yesterday we visited the Natural History Museum and we saw a diorama of the life cycle of owls. Who remembers what Table Three wanted to know more about after visiting the museum? (Students at Table Three answer: 'We wanted to know more about what owls eat.') Okay, so I promised you I would give you a chance to investigate, or find out for yourselves. At your table, you have something wrapped in foil. (Ms. Bloom holds up an example.) This is called an *owl pellet.* After an owl finishes eating, it regurgitates the pellet, or throws it up out of its mouth. (Teacher dramatizes with a hand gesture.) After everyone understands what to do, I want you to take the pellet apart, examine it carefully, and together decide what information you can figure out, about what owls eat. I want you to look, to talk together, and to write down your ideas. Then each group will share back with the whole class. Take a look at the instruction card at your table, and raise your hand when you are sure you know what to do."
>
> Students went ahead, and with some assistance from the teacher, they got started. Because the groups included more advanced and less advanced English speakers, they were able to help each other understand what to do. After sharing back what they found, each group graphed the kinds of bones they found, and then discussed the original question further in light of their findings.

Sheltered English Instruction Checklist
1. The teacher organizes instruction around content (e.g., literature, math, science, integrated themes, social studies, etc.):
   a. instruction provides "access to the core curriculum"
   b. content is academically demanding
   c. topics are appropriate to grade level

2. The teacher modifies language used during instruction:
   a. may use slightly slower speech rate
   b. speaks clearly
   c. defines words within meaningful context
   d. paraphrases in simple terms when using more sophisticated forms of expression
   e. limits use of idiomatic speech
3. The teacher supports verbal explanations with nonverbal cues:
   a. gestures, facial expressions, action to dramatize meaning
   b. props, concrete materials
   c. graphs, pictures, visuals, maps
   d. films, videotapes, overhead projector, bulletin board displays
4. The teacher designs appropriate lessons:
   a. explains purpose of activity
   b. prepares students for information (e.g., builds background knowledge, provides vocabulary development in advance)
   c. helps students develop learning strategies: reading, writing, thinking, problem-solving
   d. offers opportunities for group work and problem solving
   e. provides many opportunities for student-centered activities
   f. adjusts lesson as needed (e.g., pace, language proficiency of student)
5. The teacher is sensitive to whether students understand the lesson and, therefore, checks frequently for understanding:
   a. monitors comprehension, asks students if they need clarification
   b. repeats, if necessary; reviews main ideas and key vocabulary
   c. provides opportunities for students to rehearse information in a variety of ways: oral, written, pictures, actions
   d. assesses mastery of objectives in a variety of ways

Even in this short example, you probably noticed how Ms. Bloom made use of many of the sheltering techniques, including the following: (1) organization of instruction around cognitively demanding content, in this case, science; (2) building background by visiting a museum; (3) careful use of language, including definition of words like owl pellet in context, developing meaning through direct experience with the actual object; acting out or paraphrasing the meaning of words like *regurgitated*; (4) use of direct experience when examining the owl pellets; (5) explanation of the lesson's purpose, with attention to understanding what was to be done; and (6) opportunities for students to help each other through cooperative groupwork. Perhaps you have found that you already include many of these "sheltering techniques" in your teaching. If so, keep up the good work. Much of what we know about teaching limited English proficient (LEP) students amounts to sound teaching for all students. That is why you can shelter your lessons and still keep your native English speakers involved.

As second language acquisition progresses, comprehensible input may be oral or written, but in either case it must be accompanied by sufficient nonverbal cues to make it understandable despite learner limitations in language proficiency. In subsequent chapters, we provide strategies for using reading and writing in ways that make it comprehensible to students with limited English proficiency.

Providing Opportunities for Social Interaction

Another excellent oral source of comprehensible input emanates from the students themselves. When teachers provide opportunities for limited English proficient students to interact with their English-speaking peers, language learning opportunities occur easily and often (Wong Fillmore, 1982). Imagine, for example, a small group of students working together to create a mural or an art project. Language will be used naturally in order to accomplish the task at hand. In addition, the language that is used will be "context-embedded" (i.e., directly related to concrete objects in a "here-and-now" situation—the mural, the paints, the children themselves and their actions). As a result, the children's speech will be comprehensible and, therefore, usable as input for language acquisition. Moreover, if words are used that are not understood, collaborative groupwork permits learners to ask for repetition and/or clarification if needed. Thus, learners themselves have some control over "fine-tuning" the input made available in carrying out the collaborative project. Collaborative groupwork offers opportunities for both social and academic language development. For these reasons, collaborative projects involving native English speakers and ESL students create particularly rich language learning environments. Table 2.1 depicts several different kinds of collaborative groups you may want to try in your class. Writing and literature response groups are described in detail in chapters 3 and 4, while cooperative groups are discussed in the next section of this chapter.

Organizing Groupwork

There are a variety of ways to organize groupwork to suit the purpose at hand; some are informal and student-centered, while others are more structured and require students to learn the cooperative processes before academic work can actually begin. For the purposes of language acquisition, the specific structure of collaborative groups is less important than the quality of the opportunities they provide for interaction. To create opportunities for informal groupwork, for example, you might provide activity centers as a free choice in the afternoon, with three to six students permitted at each center. By offering games, manipulatives, and problem-solving activities at each center, you encourage informal collaboration among students. In addition, you might create specific tasks for small groups to work on together. For example, to introduce a unit on animals, you could divide the class into groups of three or four students and provide each group with a set of photographs of different animals. One task would be to categorize the photos and then explain and justify the criteria for their groupings. The task is rich in natural opportunities for the use of academic language related to higher-level thinking such as comparing, contrasting, categorizing, explaining, and justifying. Furthermore, because students carry out the task in small groups, everyone gets a chance to contribute in a low-risk, low-anxiety atmosphere. The

TABLE 2.1 A Few Types of Collaborative Groups

Type	Procedure	Purpose
Buddy system	Pair students; one more capable is paired with a student less proficient in English. The buddy helps the student in and out of the class until the second language learner becomes proficient and knowledgeable about class and school routines.	Helps new second language learner become a member of the classroom society. Helps student become comfortable in the school.
Writing response groups	Students share their writing with one another, concentrate on what is good in the paper, and help one another improve their writing. The teacher begins by modeling good response partners and giving students specific strategies for improving their papers.	Writing response groups have several purposes: making students independent; helping students improve their writing; giving students an audience for their writing and immediate response to their writing.
Literature response groups	Teacher first models response to literature, emphasizing the variety of acceptable responses. Students learn to value individual responses and support responses with what they have read. Students focus on individual feelings first and later on structure and form of literature.	To help students use their own background knowledge to respond to literature. To value students' individual responses and to help them become independent readers of literature.
Cooperative groups	Students are given specific roles and responsibilities for group work. Students become responsible for the success of one another, and they teach and learn from one another, creating success for all members of the group.	Build individual and group responsibility for learning. Build success for all members of the group. Develops creative, active learners.

relaxed atmosphere is considered conducive to language acquisition (Krashen, 1981; Dulay et al., 1982).

To the extent that the target language, English, is used during groupwork, students practice their new language and gain context-embedded input for further acquisition. In some situations, you may explicitly encourage the use of English for group activities. For example, if most students in the class speak the same native language as well as varying levels of English, students may tend to use the home language instead of English. If so, you may choose explicitly to encourage English as the designated language for activity centers. In multilingual classrooms, English becomes the one language common to all students, the *lingua franca,* and students consequently choose it as a matter of course. The ideal situation occurs when the class includes advanced English speakers with whom newcomers may interact and learn from during groupwork. However, research suggests that group interaction may promote second language acquisition even when all participants are non-native English speakers (Varonis & Gass, 1985).

Working in groups while using English promotes academic learning, social development, and second language acquisition.

Cooperative Learning Methods

In addition to informal group collaboration, a great deal of work has been carried out on more structured cooperative learning methods (Cohen, 1986; Dishon & O'Leary, 1984; Johnson, Johnson, & Holubec, 1986; Kagan, 1986). Cooperative learning can be defined as an instructional organization strategy in which students work collaboratively in small groups to achieve academic learning goals. In cooperative learning, grouping is heterogeneous. That is, members are either randomly assigned, or else you set up membership to ensure that each group includes a variety of students in terms of gender, ethnicity, language proficiency, and academic achievement. You may also balance groups in terms of personality characteristics: shy/outgoing, quiet/talkative, and so forth. In addition to heterogeneous grouping, procedural roles are assigned to students in each group such as recorder, observer, encourager, or reporter. These roles are rotated so that all group members have a chance to experience them. In this way, leadership and other roles are distributed among all students, rather than falling upon certain ones all the time.

In addition to heterogeneous grouping and role distribution, cooperative learning procedures are set up to build positive interdependence among group members. That is, students come to share and support each other's learning in socially appropriate ways. This occurs because members of a cooperative group succeed only if every member succeeds. Thus, in order to be successful, all students must care about the work of all the other group members. To build positive interdependence, assignments are established that require group members to cooperate smoothly. For example, you may assign a group project with each group member responsible for one part. In this way, the final goal cannot be achieved without each member contributing. Furthermore, the quality of the final project depends on the quality of each member's contribution. Thus, individuals are accountable for their own learning as well as that of the group.

Jigsaw

In one cooperative technique called jigsaw (Aaronson, 1978) one segment of a learning task is assigned to each group member, who then works to become an "expert" in that area. After researching their special areas, the experts from each group meet to compare notes and extend their learning. Finally, the original groups meet again, and the experts reports back to their original group. For example, Mary Ann Smith created "base groups" consisting of three students each to help her students learn about spiders. She then assigned each member in the base group different pages from a selection on "spiders." One student in each base group was responsible for pages 1–3, another for pages 4–6, and the third student was responsible for the final three pages. When students had read the assigned pages, Mary Ann met with the specialists on each section. These students became "experts" on the information they read, discussing and sharing their under-standing of the reading with their expert peers and planning how they would teach the information to members in their base groups. All experts returned to their base groups and shared their special expertise with their peers. In this way, all group members were availed of the whole spectrum of information on spiders. In jigsaw processes such as this, students may then apply their knowledge to a group task or to an individual task, assuring individual accountability for all information.

A final aspect of cooperative learning is the development of group autonomy. That is, groups become responsible for their own learning and smooth func-tioning. Thus, the teacher needs to step back at times to let students solve their own procedural and academic problems. In this way, students use their critical thinking abilities and social skills to accomplish the task at hand.

To summarize our discussion thus far, we have seen that second language learners, by virtue of their immersion in a new language and culture, have the benefit of natural exposure to the new language both in and out of school. In addition, they have real and immediate life needs that motivate them to learn. At the same time, they must reach high levels of proficiency in order to succeed. In order to learn their new language, they need comprehensible input and opportunities to use the new language in day-to-day social interactions. Teachers can provide high-quality comprehensible input for both social and academic language use in the classroom by using sheltering techniques and by creating opportunities for collaborative groupwork where English will be used with peers. Another excellent strategy to use with second language learners is thematic instruction within an integrated language teaching model. The next section explains why and how.

THEMATIC INSTRUCTION: OVERVIEW
AND RATIONALE FOR USE WITH
SECOND LANGUAGE LEARNERS

For many years, teachers have used themes or topics as focal points for organizing curriculum content (Enright & McCloskey, 1988; Pappas, Kiefer, & Levstik, 1990). One teacher we know, Reina Saucedo, uses "corn" as the central topic for a unit that integrates math, social studies, science, and language arts. She begins the unit with a feast of *quesadillas,* toasted corn tortillas filled with melted cheese. Next comes a discussion about corn as the basic ingredient for tortillas. From there, the class embarks on a study of corn, a native American plant originally cultivated by many tribes in North, Central, and South America. Reina's students read, illustrate, and dramatize corn legends; sprout corn seeds and record their growth; and create a world map, citing locations where corn is grown and eaten today. Some students choose to research how corn is prepared in different countries, creating an illustrated international corn cookbook. The class learns about the nutritive value of corn, finding out, for example, that it combines with beans to form a complete protein. They also learn how to dye corn kernels and string them into necklaces to wear themselves or to give as a gift. Finally, they create a menu based on corn and prepare a nutritionally balanced meal for the class as a culminating activity.

Though more prevalent in the primary grades, thematic instruction lends itself to virtually any content and any grade level. For example, an extensive cooperative theme project, "Building Toothpick Bridges" (Pollard, 1985) would be appropriate for upper elementary grades through high school. In this project, students work in groups of six, forming construction companies, to design and build a bridge out of toothpicks. The unit begins with readings on the brief history of bridge development, analysis of bridge designs, and information about how bridges work. Each company member assumes a role selecting from project director, architect, carpenter, transportation chief, and accountant. The goal is to design and build the strongest bridge possible, staying within the company's projected budget. In the planning stage, companies design their bridges, estimating the quantity and cost of necessary materials. On certain days, the "warehouse" is open for purchase of materials, paid for by check. At the end of the project, the strength of the bridges is tested to the breaking point, and the strongest bridge wins a prize. The bridge-breaking is an exciting media event, described by students in an article for the local newspaper. This collaborative project is thus a highly involving, fun project that integrates the use of oral and written language with a wide variety of math concepts.

We recommend the use of thematic instruction for second language learners for several reasons. First of all, thematic instruction creates a meaningful conceptual framework within which students are invited to use both oral and written language for learning content. The meaningful context established by the theme supports the comprehensibility of instruction, thereby increasing both content learning and second language acquisition. In addition, theme-based collaborative projects create student interest, motivation, involvement, and purpose. Moreover,

When students share information about their home countries, they grow in self-esteem while broadening the horizons of their peers.

as students work together on their projects, they naturally use both oral and written language to question, inform, problem-solve, negotiate, and interact with their peers. Through such engagement, both social and academic language development is challenged and promoted. Thus, when combined with opportunities for collaboration, thematic instruction creates optimal language and literacy learning opportunities for both first and second language learners.

Distinguishing Theme Units from Theme Cycles

In current discussions on thematic instruction, a distinction has been made between traditional thematic units and theme cycles (Altwerger & Flores, 1991; Harste, 1988). The crux of the difference between the two lies with the degree of student input and choice at every step in the learning process—topic choice, the selection of materials and resources, the organization of projects, grouping, and manner of presenting final products of learning, such as plays, reports, murals, etc. Traditionally, the teacher has been responsible for all these decisions. In the theme cycle, the teacher and children negotiate these choices together. When students have input and choice in the direction of their own learning, they become motivated to pursue ideas and information. They also become active questioners and learners. Furthermore, they begin to see themselves as capable of initiating and carrying out their own learning. Finally, they evaluate their own learning based on the extent to which they are satisfied with the answers they have found.

Even though clear distinctions can be drawn between theme units and theme cycles, we believe that, in practice, a continuum exists depending upon the degree to which students are free to choose and negotiate their own learning with the teacher. For that reason, we use the term "thematic instruction" to subsume both units and cycles. We define thematic instruction as a learning sequence organized around a theme or a topic offering students opportunities to use oral language, reading, writing, and critical thinking for learning and sharing ideas. The criteria for thematic instruction listed below reflect our own preference for student choice in the learning process. At the same time, we view the teacher as ultimately responsible for the quality of learning opportunities available in the classroom. Thus, the teacher does not abrogate this responsibility but uses careful judgment, reserving the right to the final say on how the learning sequence will be implemented.

Organizing Thematic Instruction

We offer six criteria for organizing thematic instruction to promote language development, critical thinking, independence, and interpersonal collaboration for both first and second language learners. Our criteria represent basic learning principles that we have adapted from Enright and McCloskey (1988), a book we describe in our suggested readings at the end of this chapter.

Meaning and Purpose.   The content of the thematic unit/theme cycle is interesting and relevant to the students. One way to ensure interest and relevance is to provide opportunities for the students themselves to guide the choice of the theme and the activities and projects undertaken during the course of study. As students make choices, they invest themselves in their own learning, thereby creating self-direction and purpose.

Build on Prior Experience.   The thematic unit/theme cycle builds on students' prior experiences, both in-class experiences, such as previous instruction, as well as prior knowledge and experience students bring from home. In this way, students' varied cultural experiences can be incorporated into their schoolwork, providing an understanding of themselves and others.

Integrated Opportunities to Use Oral and Written Language and Literacy for Learning Purposes.   The teacher is conscious of creating opportunities for oral language and literacy to be used for learning purposes established in concert with students. The teacher broadens the students' experiences with different forms and functions of print suited to student interests and goals.

Scaffolding for Support.   Thematic instruction is provided within a classroom atmosphere that supports students' efforts and values their accomplishments. One way to support students is to use sheltering techniques and various kinds of scaffolds, discussed fully below, to assist students in participating successfully, even if their language/literacy proficiency is as yet limited. Another way is to provide students opportunities to display their learning and share it with others.

Collaboration.   Students are provided many opportunities to work together on theme-related projects and activities. Collaboration in pairs and small groups provides students with opportunities to process complex information actively in a low-risk, low-anxiety situation. In this way, language and content learning is productive. At the same time, language and literacy are used purposefully, promoting acquisition.

Variety.   Variety permeates the learning process—in topics of study, in the ways that learning is shared with others, in the functions of oral and written language used, in roles and responsibilities, and in task difficulty. Variety and flexibility characterize learning groups—pairs, small groups, and the whole class. Thus, interest remains high.

The process of developing thematic instruction is a dynamic one, ideally involving input from the students themselves at all levels of decision-making. The first step is to choose the topic or theme that will serve as the focus of interest. There are many sources for themes and topics, including state and local curriculum guidelines, as well as personal interests and curiosities expressed by the students. Not least of all, your own special interests provide an excellent source of topics and themes, and you are likely to have or know of resources and materials to share with your students. Enthusiasm is contagious, and, when you bring your own curiosity and joy for learning into the classroom, you reveal your personal self, thereby deepening your relationship with your students and modeling life-long learning. Likewise, when you build on your students' interests and curiosities, you can catch their wave of enthusiasm and embark on exciting new learning adventures yourself.

Once a theme is chosen, the next step is to brainstorm ideas related to the theme. One way to conduct the brainstorming is to create a cluster or word web on the chalkboard as you and your students generate ideas around the theme. During brainstorming, it is important to accept and write down every idea contributed by your students. Based on the words generated during brainstorming, related ideas can be grouped together, resulting in a map of the major subtopics to be investigated. Under each subtopic, activities and projects are listed together as shown in the map in Figure 2.1. It is helpful to post the thematic map in the classroom to keep the organization and planning available at a glance.

Another way to generate and organize learning activities and projects around a theme is to write the chosen theme or topic on a large piece of butcher paper and invite students to list "what we know already" and "what we wonder about." Students may then form interest groups around the "wonder topic" of their preference and, together with the teacher, establish a plan to find out more. In this approach, groups conduct research with teacher guidance as needed, each group presenting its findings to the class in some form, either oral, written, pictorial/graphic, or dramatic. Students are encouraged to combine at least two or three of the presentational modes so as to "shelter" their presentations for

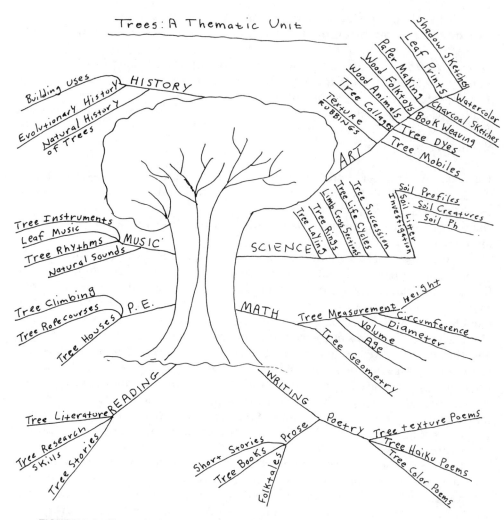

FIGURE 2.1 Trees: An Integrated Thematic Unit

SOURCE: From *Mapping the Writing Journey* (p. 28, Fig. 15) by Marilyn H. Buckley and Owen Boyle, 1981, Berkeley, CA: Bay Area Writing Project. Reprinted with permission of the publisher.

their classmates. For example, an oral presentation to the class might explain a mural. Finally, the butcher paper list is reviewed and revised with a new category: "What We Know Now." This "theme cycle" (Altwerger & Flores, 1991) may then be repeated by adding, "What We Wonder Now," as students pose new questions and choose new areas of investigation. The thematic units and cycles provide students with opportunities for functional and purposeful language use in the classroom, which we discuss in more detail below.

Functional Language and Literacy Uses in Thematic Instruction

From the standpoint of second language learning, one of the teacher's major responsibilities is to make sure a variety of functional language and literacy uses are incorporated into the projects and activities undertaken by the students (Heath & Mangiola, 1991). The following list describes different forms and functions of reading and writing to consider as you expand students' repertoires.

Forms of Print Used in Class	Sample Functions of Print Used in the Classroom
Lists	Organizing and remembering
Order forms	Purchasing items for class activities
Checks	Paying for book orders
Ledgers	Keeping account of class responsibilities
Labels and captions	To accompany pictures on bulletin board or other class displays
Personal journals	Generating ideas on a project, etc.
Buddy journals	Promoting a personal relationship
Record-keeping journal	Keeping track of a project or experiment
Interactive journal with teacher	Conversing in writing; promoting a personal relationship
Notes	Taking information down to remember it
Personal letters	Sharing news
Business letters	Applying for a job; complaining about a product; recommending a procedure
Narratives	Relating stories; telling and learning about people
Scripts (e.g., reader's theater)	Entertaining the class by acting out a story
Essay forms: Compare/contrast Problem/solution Cause/effect Enumeration Thesis/proof	To persuade or explain; to prove or explain; to solve problems or develop an argument

In addition to exposing students to a variety of literacy forms and functions, you will want to make sure that there are supports available to facilitate student participation, even if English language proficiency is limited. Therefore, as the final step in developing a theme cycle, you will want to examine the project and activity plans and consider the students involved in each, using the following questions to guide your students' involvement.

1. Which aspects of the project can be carried out by students with minimal English proficiency (e.g., painting, coloring, short answers, the use of the child's native language)?

2. Which aspects of the project involve literacy uses that may be supported by literacy scaffolds and/or by peer assistance [e.g., re-creating a pattern book such as *Brown Bear, Brown Bear What Do You See?* (Martin, 1967) or *Fortunately* (Charlip, 1964) writing a story based on the story parts *Someone/Wants/But/So*; writing a letter in cooperative pairs; paired reading]?

3. What special resources might be of help to a particular group (e.g., books, encyclopedias, films, community members, school personnel)?

4. How might this project lend itself to particular kinds of language and literacy uses (e.g., a letter to a company protesting its use of laboratory animals, the contribution of an article to the school newspaper, oral reading of the poems discovered in researching the theme, the use of a log to record plant growth)?

Creating Variety in Language and Literacy Uses

Your role in generating a variety of oral and written language uses is crucial for optimal language and literacy development through thematic instruction. To support students' successful involvement, you will want to consider the students' performance levels and find ways to stretch them. As you consider how to assist your students with their projects, two questions should be kept in mind: (1) How can I assure successful participation by each student? (2) How can I encourage each student to perform at his or her best?

We believe that both participation and motivation are promoted by encouraging students to make choices. For example, if your curriculum requires the study of your state's history, you might start with local history by posing the question: "Has our town always been here? What do you suppose it was like here 100 years ago?" Your discussion may lead students to other questions, such as: "What and who were here? How did people live, work, and learn? How did they dress? What did they use for transportation? What did they do for fun?" Students may form interest groups by choosing which question or questions they want to work on. Further choices may be made as to the books and materials they will use to answer their question. Perhaps some students will choose to interview long-time local residents. Finally, students may choose the format they wish to use for presenting their findings—publishing a factual book on local history, creating a mural to depict the town as it was 100 years ago, creating a diary that might have been written by a local child 100 years ago, or creating a series of letters that might have been written to a cousin in another state. Your job is to be on hand to listen to students and make suggestions as needed. By offering students choices, you broaden their horizons, while allowing them to invest more fully in their own learning, thus sparking interest and involvement as well.

Active participation is also enhanced when students work in groups to accomplish self-selected tasks. Groups provide support and motivation to get things done. Your limited English proficient students may prove more capable than anticipated when allowed to work in a small group.

In any case, you will want to meander from group to group to observe students' progress and interaction. If necessary, you may suggest ways to involve new second language learners. For example, if a student speaks virtually no English, you might pair him or her up with another student to illustrate the group's book or to copy captions for the illustrations. You need to be observant, intuitive, and imaginative when making such suggestions for newcomers and others with limited English proficiency. Therein lies the art of teaching—knowing when to encourage and when to stand back!

Finally, as students reflect on their new knowledge, they are in a position to evaluate their own learning. Through the process of posing their own questions, researching to find possible answers, and presenting their findings to their classmates, they can see for themselves how much they have learned. At the same time, they may wish to note those areas still open to question, thereby generating questions for their next theme cycle study. The theme cycle thus replicates the knowledge generation process used in formal research.

VYGOTSKY'S ZONE OF PROXIMAL DEVELOPMENT

Russian psychologist Lev Vygotsky (1896–1934) introduced a useful concept about learning and development when he pointed out that **what the child can do with assistance today, he or she can do alone tomorrow**. Teaching, he urged, must aim not at today's, but at tomorrow's, development or, as he called it, the "zone of proximal development" (Vygotsky, 1962). Thus, students need to be challenged, but with support and encouragement. With support and assistance, they can exercise their next level of development and, thus, progress in learning and development. The support and assistance that permits this performance has been referred to as "scaffolding."

One educational program that has applied Vygotsky's ideas is the Kamehameha Elementary Education Program (KEEP) in Honolulu, Hawaii. KEEP was established two decades ago as a research and development center to meet the educational needs of native Hawaiian children descended from the original Polynesian inhabitants of the island chain (Tharp & Gallimore, 1988). These children, ethnic minority group speakers of Hawaiian Creole English, were not achieving well in school, particularly in reading (Au & Jordan, 1981). Through the concerted efforts of a team of psychologists, anthropologists, linguists, and educators, an innovative educational program was established, which became a laboratory and demonstration school.

Two especially interesting innovations were made. First, a communication feature of the children's home culture was incorporated into reading lessons. That is, discussion of stories was carried out through conarration, or the joint narration of a story by two people. Conarration, the researchers had found, was a feature of the native Hawaiian storytelling tradition to which the children were accustomed. In their home culture, conarration of a story not only conveyed information; it also served to reaffirm the relationship between the conarrators. With this familiar communication style incorporated into reading lessons, children were more inclined to feel "at home" and participate in lessons. In time, reading achievement scores increased and remained at national-norm levels for over a decade (Tharp & Gallimore, 1988, p. 116).

The second KEEP innovation over the decades has been the implementation of a teaching model based on the Vygotskian notion of assisted performance in the child's "zone of proximal development." The teaching model emphasizes the teacher's ability to respond to the child's developmental level and to stretch the child's performance accordingly through modeling, feeding-back, instructing, questioning, and other processes (Tharp & Gallimore, 1988). In so doing, the teacher "scaffolds" the child's development to the next level.

Scaffolding: A KEEP Example

To illustrate the complex nature of scaffolding, as carried out in a KEEP kindergarten, Tharp and Gallimore (1988, pp. 138–146) provide a detailed description of a language-experience activity (LEA) in which the teacher leads a group of six children in making peanut butter and jelly sandwiches. This experience will later serve as the basis of a dictated story, following traditional LEA procedures (Allen, 1976; Stauffer, 1970). The "instructional conversation" between the teacher and children during the sandwich-making creates natural opportunities for the teacher to model, question, and instruct, thereby scaffolding children's linguistic and cognitive performance.

Gathering the children at a small table, the teacher begins with an improvised chant about making peanut butter and jelly sandwiches. Placing the peanut butter and jelly jars on the table with a loaf of sliced bread, she introduces the activity with a statement and a question (Tharp & Gallimore, 1988)[1]:

> TEACHER: We're gonna make our peanut butter sandwich. What is the first thing I'm going to need?
> [*Produces a jar of peanut butter, a jar of jelly, and a loaf of sliced bread in a bag.*]
>   J: Get the bread!
> [*Child points to bread; reaches across the table and pats the bag of bread.*]
> TEACHER: I need to get a piece of bread. What am I going to do with it?
> [*Reaches into the bag and retrieves a slice. J. nods approval.*]
>   J: Put this first . . . and put this second.
> [*Touches peanut butter jar; touches jelly jar.*]
> TEACHER: Put it . . .
> [*Hesitates*]

---

[1] From *Rousing Minds to Life: Teaching, Learning and Schooling in Social Context* (pp. 138–139) by Roland Tharp and Ronald Gallimore, 1988, New York: Cambridge University Press. Reprinted with permission of the publisher.

J: Oh, no. Put this first . . . and this second.
[*Touches jelly jar; touches peanut butter jar.*]

R: Get the knife first, no get the knife in and spread it.

JK: Put the jelly on the sandwich, then that on the sandwich.
[*Points to peanut butter.*]

TEACHER: I put the jelly on top of the sandwich?
[*Places jelly jar on top of sandwich.*]

CHILDREN: (chorus) No! No! No!
[*Two stand up; another points; they laugh and smile with surprise and amusement.*]

R: You open it.
[*Takes jelly jar from teacher and removes lid.*]

JK: Then you put it in.

TEACHER: Oh I need to twist the lid off the jar?

CHILDREN: Yes, yes and then you make like that.

R: First you have to do peanut butter . . .

J: No. That!
[*Gestures toward jelly, disagreeing about which ingredient is applied first.*]

R: [*Shakes head in disagreement.*]

TEACHER: I have to spread the peanut butter first? Are you sure?

R: Yeah, cause I tried it, that's that's [the truth] everybody's [looking at it].

TEACHER: How do I spread it? Do I take my finger, stick it in, and rub it all over the bread?

J: No this! You stick that in . . .
[*Picks up knife; makes spreading motion with knife over bread.*]

At this point, the children get the idea that they are going to have to tell their teacher methodically, sequentially, and step-by-step exactly how to make this sandwich. The instructional conversation continues, with questioning, modeling, and feedback from the teacher. By requiring the children to organize the procedure logically and to provide explicit directions through language, not gesture, she is inviting them to perform in their zone of proximal development both cognitively and linguistically. Making language clear enough to stand on its own without gestures or reference to objects in the environment is a cognitive-academic skill required for school literacy.

The teacher facilitates the children's performance by asking questions that require them to reflect on their prior peanut butter and jelly experiences and then analyze and organize the task into a logical sequence. She then provides feedback on the efficacy of their communication by following their directions literally. When she makes her sandwich-making response obviously wrong, the children rephrase their directions for her with greater specificity. If a child seems to lack the language necessary to make instructions clear, the teacher elaborates the child's meaning, thereby modeling vocabulary and structure in context. For example, R says, "First you have to do peanut butter," and the teacher replies, "I have to spread the peanut butter first?" Embedded in her request for clarification is the more specific verb *spread*. A single reply by the teacher thus serves several purposes. Throughout the lesson, these means of assistance are not set up in the form of a drill but rather emerge naturally in the course of the fun and engaging sandwich-making activity.

What we have described was the oral language interaction phase of a language experience activity. The precision in organization and language that the teacher pressed for during the instructional conversation paved the way for putting the procedure into writing. The means of teacher assistance during the instructional conversation were questioning, modeling, and feedback. This phase of the activity guided children's thinking and language toward forms acceptable for schoolwork and academic literacy, an important transition for students whose ways of using language differ from those of the school (Michaels, 1979; Heath, 1983).

Scaffolding in First Language Acquisition Research

Scaffolding techniques similar to those used in the KEEP kindergarten lesson were originally identified by researchers studying first language acquisition (Bruner, 1978; Ninio, 1980; Ninio & Bruner, 1978). Adults, it was observed, sometimes helped young children verbally elaborate upon a topic, thereby facilitating communication at a more sophisticated level. For example, a young child may exclaim, "Mommy, kitty!" to which the mother replies, "Yes, kitty wants to play with you, doesn't she?" In her response, the mother provides a scaffold, elaborating on the child's topic and unconsciously modeling linguistic and conversational patterns through natural social interactions with the child.

Language games and routines such as book-reading provide another, more complex type of scaffold. In book-reading, for example, children become accustomed to a question-answer sequence, "What's that?" That's a _____." (Ninio & Bruner, 1978). The first time the book is read, the adult may provide the answer, but, through repetition of the routine, the child acquires the ability to either fill in the blank or make the entire response. With further repetition, the child may ask the question and let the adult answer. All of these stages provide language practice at a level that stretches somewhat beyond the child's capability unassisted. Reading aloud to children at home was subsequently found to be of such great importance to later reading success (Wells, 1986) that the practice has been encouraged in first and second language communities where the practice was previously less prevalent or nonexistent (Ada, 1988; Edwards, 1989).

The importance of the repeated routine in the scaffolding process is paramount. As noted by Snow (1977) in her study of mothers' communication with their infants, "We think of routines as simple and unsophisticated . . . but their simplicity allows for the introduction, into slots created by the routine, of fillers considerably more complex in structure and/or content than could possibly be dealt with elsewhere" (quoted in Cazden, 1983, p. 9). The routines themselves scaffold performance at a higher level.

It is important to note that routines provide effective learning scaffolds to the extent that they are sufficiently familiar and appropriate to students' prior cultural experiences. For example, researchers in the KEEP found that the traditional round-robin oral reading routine went against the social norms of the children's home culture. Using ethnographic information, KEEP educators modified the reading instruction routine, incorporating "talk-story" conarration from the home culture, as described earlier. The new, culturally consistent reading instruction routine provided an effective scaffold, whereas the traditional routine did not.

Few classroom teachers have the luxury of a research team to inform them of the nuances of their students' home cultures. However, classroom teachers have something that research teams generally do not have—the benefit of a deep, on-going reciprocal relationship with students over time. Through the special teacher–child relationship, and, through thoughtful and sensitive trial and error, you will be in a position to judge which scaffolding routines work with your students and which do not. In fact, as you systematically observe your students, reflect on what you know about their families, and interpret their responses to you and your teaching, you will be expanding your role from teacher to teacher–researcher.

Scaffolding Applied to Second Language Acquisition

In our work with children learning a second language in school, we have found that teachers provide a variety of scaffolding routines for second language learning (Peregoy, 1989; Peregoy & Boyle, 1991). In one kindergarten, for example, we noticed that the teacher created two overarching scaffolds by offering (1) a stable physical space arrangement and (2) a daily schedule that remained the same throughout the school year. Within the stable physical and temporal routines, content and structure changed, becoming more complex as the year progressed. For example, in the library corner at the beginning of the year, children just looked at pictures in trade books. As the year progressed, however, they began to publish their own books, based on predictable pattern books their teacher had read to them. Soon, they were able to read these books aloud to each other at the library corner. The stability of the routines made the kindergarten predictable for children who were just learning a new language, freeing their attention for learning.

The predictable room arrangement and schedule helped students know what to expect each day. Rules of behavior also remained constant for different centers and different times of the day (e.g., storytime, free choice at learning centers, recess and lunch). Through the repetition of daily routines, the children came to understand classroom events and rules, even though their second language proficiency was limited. At the same time, as the routines were repeated, the language that accompanied them was also repeated and rapidly learned by the youngsters. In this way, their second language development was supported.

In observing the kindergarten, we noticed that, within routine instructional events, the teacher actually embedded a succession of other scaffolds to assist children in performing at a level just a bit beyond their budding language capabilities. During roll call and calendar activities with the whole class seated at the rug, for example, children were encouraged to make a gestural response to indicate whether they would be having hot lunch or cold lunch. If a child had cold lunch, he or she would walk over to the jacket rack and point to his or her lunch box. Gradually, they were able to answer verbally, "Hot lunch" or "Cold lunch," modeling after native speakers in the class and prompted by the teacher's simple question, "Hot lunch or cold lunch?" In addition, from the first day of school, the teacher would repeat the classroom rules. For each rule, she had a corresponding picture to convey the meaning. Thus, for "Speak softly," she had a picture of an index finger over a pair of lips, and for the raise-your-hand rule, she had a picture of a hand waving in the air. These pictures made the language associated with the routines comprehensible, creating daily language learning opportunities within a functional classroom event such as roll call.

Scaffolds for First and Second Language Reading and Writing

While most research has examined scaffolding in relation to oral language acquisition, we have applied it to literacy acquisition as well, creating criteria for what we call "literacy scaffolds" (Boyle & Peregoy, 1990; Peregoy & Boyle, 1990b). Criteria defining literacy scaffolds are as follows:

1. Literacy scaffolds are applied to reading and writing activities aimed at functional, meaningful communication found in whole texts such as stories, poems, reports, or recipes.
2. Literacy scaffolds make use of language and discourse patterns that repeat themselves and are, therefore, predictable.
3. Literacy scaffolds provide a model, offered by the teacher or by peers, for comprehending and producing particular written language patterns.
4. Literacy scaffolds support students in comprehending and producing written language at a level slightly beyond their competence in the absence of the scaffold.
5. Literacy scaffolds are temporary and may be dispensed with when the student is ready to work without them.

Perhaps the clearest example of a literacy scaffold is the interactive dialogue journal in which the student and teacher carry on a written conversation. Dialogue journals may be used with any age student, and they have proven useful for second language learners of all ages (Kreeft, 1984.) Typically, the student makes a written entry in his or her journal, perhaps accompanied by an illustration, and the teacher then responds in writing with a comment or question that furthers the conversation. The dialogue journal thus duplicates, in written form, the scaffolding opportunities we saw earlier in the informal instructional conversations between adults and young children at home and at school. Specifically, the student initiates the topic to which the teacher responds. The teacher responds to the meaning of the journal entry, thereby encouraging further elaboration of the topic. In their responses, teachers may model written language patterns by incorporating and expanding upon the students' entry, just as adults sometimes do in conversations with young children. Thus, the dialogue journal affords the teacher regular opportunities for scaffolding through questioning, modeling, and feedback. However, the scaffolding is always embedded within the natural flow of the written conversation between the student and teacher. Thus, the focus remains on interpersonal communication between teacher and child.

Dialogue journals meet the literacy scaffold criteria in the following ways:

1. They are part of a functional communication activity—a conversation with the teacher.
2. They make use of a discourse pattern that repeats itself and is therefore predictable (i.e., a written conversation in which participants alternate turns).
3. They provide modeling of written language patterns by the teacher.
4. The teacher's questions and encouragement help students comprehend and produce written language beyond what they might accomplish if unassisted.
5. Dialogue journals may be replaced with other forms of writing as students gain fluency.

Other examples of literacy scaffolds include shared reading, patterned writing, mapping, directed listening–thinking activities, reader's theater, and interactive journal writing, described in detail in chapter 4. We saw earlier how daily school routines may create a scaffold for language acquisition. Similarly, routines such as process writing and literature study circles create overarching scaffolds within which other scaffolding activities may be embedded to promote reading and writing development. These routines are presented in chapters 3 and 4.

In summary, scaffolding helps students perform at a level somewhat beyond their capability if unassisted. As teachers, we are constantly aiming to assist our students at their next developmental level in oral language and literacy, as well as in other areas of learning and development. In subsequent chapters, we develop the idea of scaffolds specific to literacy development and provide many sample activities to show you how to apply the concept to reading and writing development.

ORAL LANGUAGE DEVELOPMENT IN SECOND LANGUAGE ACQUISITION

Walter Loban, a favorite professor of ours and a pioneer in researching oral language development of students from kindergarten through twelfth grade (Loban, 1968), used to say: "We listen a book a day, talk a book a week, read a book a month, and write a book a year" (personal communication, October 20, 1980). With this quote, he highlighted the pervasiveness of oral language in our lives; so pervasive, in fact, that we take it easily for granted, until plagued with a case of laryngitis. Reading and writing also play vitally important roles in our lives, but oral language interactions account for the bulk of our day-to-day communications, remaining the primary mode of discourse throughout the world.

For students learning English as a second language in school, oral language development plays a key role as well. When children are working or playing together, their conversations are based on concrete, "here-and-now" topics of current interest. As a result, opportunity abounds for them to negotiate meaning through requests for clarification, reference to objects at hand, and other face-to-face communication strategies. As a result, the language used becomes comprehensible and usable as input for second language acquisition. To optimize classroom oral language learning opportunities, we need to offer daily opportunities for students to *talk* to each other while working in a variety of situations (e.g., paired reading, group research projects, group work at learning centers, brainstorming a writing topic, sharing news with the entire class, and just visiting quietly while carrying out tasks). Language development should be *heard,* not just seen, in classrooms where talk is valued as a learning tool.

Task-directed talk is thus useful in and of itself for second language acquisition, including teacher talk during instruction, provided that sheltering techniques are used, as discussed earlier. Talk is also important for helping students clarify concepts and arrive at their own understandings. As academic content increases in complexity, the use of small- and large-group discussion remains important as a means of assisting students in concept development. Consistent with the value we place on oral language facility, we incorporate opportunities throughout this book for students to develop their own thinking through talking and responding as they read, write, and learn in English, for it is the integrated use of oral and written language for functional and meaningful purposes that best promotes the full development of second language proficiency.

Assessing Second Language Oral Proficiency

Assessment of students' second language oral proficiency is an important matter because instructional and programmatic decisions are dependent upon the outcome. For example, a carefully administered program for second language students must first identify students who are in need of special services, and then monitor their progress in order to determine when they have achieved sufficient second language proficiency to exit the special service program and enter the mainstream educational program. A common procedure for identifying such students is to send a bilingual survey questionnaire to parents asking about the language or languages spoken in the home. Survey results identify students from homes where a language other than English is used. These students are then individually tested for English oral language proficiency, generally using a standardized oral proficiency test. Students whose oral English is limited may then be enrolled in a bilingual or English language development program to support their academic development while they develop English language proficiency.

Characteristics of Oral Language Proficiency Tests

Many bilingual and ESL programs use commercially available, standardized oral language proficiency tests to determine whether students need special assistance in second language development. Publishing companies offer training in the procedures for using their tests. Among the most commonly used tests are the

Language Assessment Scales (Duncan & De Avila, 1977), the Bilingual Syntax Measure (Burt, Dulay, & Hernandez-Chavez, 1975), and the Basic Inventory of Natural Language (Herbert, 1977). Tests such as these generally consist of three parts: (1) oral language data collection, that is, tape-recorded samples of children's speech, (2) data analysis, and (3) interpretation. Oral language sampling, carried out individually, may be accomplished by asking the child questions about pictures or by asking the child to tell a story about a picture. The child's responses then form the "language sample" to be analyzed. Analysis is usually carried out by school language specialists, or the samples may be sent back to the publishing company for analysis. In the analysis, specific aspects of comprehension, vocabulary, and grammatical development are noted and scored. Scores are then interpreted to yield a "level" or "phase" of second language proficiency development. Oral proficiency tests vary in the number of levels or phases that they discriminate, but three general categories emerge as meaningful for programmatic decisions: (1) Non–English Proficient (NEP), (2) Limited English Proficient (LEP), and Fully English Proficient (FEP). Programs that aim to serve second language learners must provide services for NEP and LEP students, with eventual reclassification to FEP as the ultimate goal.

The main problem with standardized oral language proficiency tests is that they are based on a single performance sample, usually elicited out of the context of routine classroom activity. Performance is thus easily affected by nonlinguistic variables such as lack of familiarity with the testing procedure, disinterest, and fatigue. Furthermore, to the extent that a child feels the pressure of a testing situation, performance may be affected by anxiety. Because of these limitations, schools need to use oral language test scores in combination with other sources of information about the child's performance, including teacher judgment, parental input, and direct observation of the child's performance in day-to-day classroom activities.

Teacher Observation of Oral Language Use

Teacher judgment is one of the most important and accurate measures of children's oral language development. One observational instrument that teachers can use to assess their students' oral proficiency is the Student Oral Language Matrix (SOLOM) shown in Figure 2.2. In this type of assessment, your observations of student oral language use stand in place of formally elicited language samples used by the commercial tests described above. As the teacher, you will be able to observe your students periodically over the year in a variety of naturally occurring classroom situations. As a result, your "sampling" of student oral language use will be much richer, more natural, and more educationally relevant than a standardized test (Goodman, Goodman, & Hood, 1989). In addition, your students will be focused on the classroom task, alleviating the anxiety factor typical of testing situations.

While you observe students during day-to-day classroom activities, the SOLOM observation matrix is organized to focus your attention on general traits such as fluency, vocabulary, and pronunciation. Thus, you are, in fact, evaluating

	1	2	3	4	5
A Comprehension	Cannot be said to understand even simple conversation.	Has great difficulty following what is said. Can comprehend only "social conversation" spoken slowly and with frequent repetitions.	Understands most of what is said at slower-than-normal speed with repetitions.	Understands nearly everything at normal speed, although occasional repetition may be necessary.	Understands everyday conversation and normal classroom discussions without difficulty.
B Fluency	Speech is so halting and fragmentary as to make conversation virtually impossible.	Usually hesitant; often forced into silence by language limitations.	Speech in everyday conversation and classroom discussion frequently disrupted by the student's search for the correct manner of expression.	Speech in everyday conversation and class-room discussions generally fluent, with occasional lapses while the student searches for the correct manner of expression.	Speech in everyday conversation and classroom discussions fluent and effortless, approximating that of a native speaker.
C Vocabulary	Vocabulary limitations so extreme as to make conversation virtually impossible.	Misuse of words and very limited vocabulary; comprehension quite difficult.	Student frequently uses the wrong words; conversation somewhat limited because of inadequate vocabulary.	Student occasionally uses inappropriate terms and/or must rephrase ideas because of lexical inadequacies.	Use of vocabulary and idioms approximates that of a native speaker.
D Pronunciation	Pronunciation problems so severe as to make speech virtually unintelligible.	Very hard to understand because of pronunciation problems. Must frequently repeat in order to make himself or herself understood.	Pronunciation problems necessitate concentration on the part of the listener and occasionally lead to misunderstanding.	Always intelligible though one is conscious of a definite accent and occasional inappropriate intonation patterns.	Pronunciation and intonation approximate that of a native speaker.
E Grammar	Errors in grammar and word order so severe as to make speech virtually unintelligible.	Grammar and word-order errors make comprehension difficult. Must often rephrase and/or restrict himself or herself to basic patterns.	Makes frequent errors of grammar and word order that occasionally obscure meaning.	Occasionally makes grammatical and/or word-order errors that do not obscure meaning.	Grammatical usage and word order approximate that of a native speaker.

FIGURE 2.2 SOLOM: Student Oral Language Observation Matrix

SOLOM PHASES: Phase I: Score 5–11 = non–English proficient; Phase II: Score 12–18 = limited English proficient; Phase III: Score 19–24 = limited English proficient; Phase IV: Score 25 = fully English proficient.

SOURCE: Courtesy of California State Department of Education.

Based on your observation of the student, indicate with an "X" across the block in each category that best describes the student's abilities. The SOLOM should only be administered by persons who themselves score at level "4" or above in all categories in the language being assessed. Students scoring at level "1" in all categories can be said to have no proficiency in the language.

student language in several dimensions. Your ratings are ultimately subjective and require substantial linguistic sensitivity to be accurate and meaningful. However, we believe that you can develop such sensitivity through guided experience in language observation and analysis. Research, in fact, supports teacher efficacy in rating students' second language oral proficiency, using procedures similar to the SOLOM (Jackson, 1980; Mace-Matluck, 1980, 1981).

In summary, observational matrices or checklists are useful because they are descriptive and easy to understand, thus offering meaningful information. Another strength stems from the fact that evaluation is based on holistic observations of students in the course of day-to-day classroom language use. For the purpose of documenting language growth over time and for gaining a sense of how well students are getting along with English for classroom purposes, we believe that observational instruments such as the SOLOM matrix are more useful to teachers than tests that rely on an artificial sampling procedure.

Reclassification of Students

Reclassification of students to the category of FEP is a critical task. This is because a student who is reclassified as FEP must be prepared to be educationally successful in a mainstream classroom. If a student is evaluated as FEP, then special language services are, by definition, no longer needed. Due to the potential cessation of special educational assistance, reclassification requires careful consideration of multiple measures of student competence including oral and written English proficiency measures, primary language development measures, and achievement test scores along with input from teachers, parents, and any other resource personnel who have worked with the student.

DESCRIBING BEGINNING AND INTERMEDIATE SECOND LANGUAGE ORAL PROFICIENCY

In this book, we have undertaken to provide instructional strategies for second language learners who are still limited in English language knowledge. We assume that FEP second language learners will be able to benefit from mainstream instructional programs, provided they are validated personally and culturally in the educational process. Many of the reading, writing, and learning ideas in this book are appropriate for all students, not just those limited in English language proficiency. Thus, you may use them with FEP students as well, according to your judgment.

In keeping with our concern for LEP students and in order to facilitate your use of this book, we have taken the larger category of "LEP" and divided it into two subcategories: (1) beginning and (2) intermediate ESL learners. We use these categories in this chapter to describe oral proficiency and, in subsequent chapters, to describe second language reading and writing proficiency. We include non–English speakers in our beginner category because the strategies we suggest work as well for them as for children who have already begun to speak the new language. As you read on, bear in mind that these are broad, general guidelines, not lock-step levels set in stone. We designate activities as appropriate for beginning and intermediate ESL students for your convenience. However, please keep in mind that no activity should be "withheld" from any particular student on the basis of perceived English language proficiency. It is all too easy to misjudge a child's ability because language performance varies across situations and from week to week due to the dynamic and context-specific nature of language proficiency. Moreover, motivation tends to stretch children's performance. Therefore, we recommend that you allow students the choice to take part in more difficult activities according to their interests and desires. You may be in for some pleasant surprises!

Second Language Oral Proficiency of Beginning ESL Learners

The beginner phase of second language development starts immediately upon exposure to the new language. Early on, the child may neither understand nor speak a word of English. Soon, however, language comprehension develops as a result of opportunities for social interaction with speakers of the new language. While it is important not to force children to speak, the fact is that very shortly, within perhaps a week to a few months, most children will naturally begin to speak on their own (Terrell, 1981). At this point, their speech is likely to be limited to simple phrases and day-to-day expressions that have highly functional communicative payoff, such as "Okay," "No," "Wanna play," "I wanna she go, too," and "I donno" (Wong Fillmore, 1983). As beginners develop, they are able to generate utterances according to simple grammatical rules, enabling them to carry out various tasks through conversations according to their needs and purposes. The following example cited by Lily Wong Fillmore (1980) shows a young beginner's attempt to get an eraser back from her friend Cathy.

> Kim-girl is at the table doing seatwork. Cathy, Sin Man, Suh Wah, and Chui-Wing are at the same table; they have been arguing over the possession of a pink eraser all morning.
>
> CATHY: Gimme 'raser! [*Takes Kim-girl's eraser.*]
>
> KIM-GIRL: [*Looks up crankily. Turns to LWF and complains:*]
> Can I eraser? Se took my 'raser. Se want 'raser.
> This Edlyn gip me.
> [*She grabs microphone which has been placed right in front of her, and says into it:*]
> Gip me 'raser, yah!
> Gip me pencil, yah!
> Gip me chopstick, no!
> Gip me crayon, yah!
> Can I hab color? No way!
> That's all! Bye-bye!
>
> (p. 323)

Kim-girl makes use of various formulaic expressions, such as "That's all," "Bye-bye," and "No way." In addition, in this conversation, she demonstrates her ability to use simple present-tense grammar for statements and questions when she says: "Can I eraser? Se took my 'raser. Se want 'raser. This Edlyn gip me." Her pronunciation shows some influence from her native language, Korean, in the use of *se* for *she* and *gip* for *give*. As a beginner in English, Kim-girl is resourceful in using her rudimentary English knowledge to try to get her eraser back. She also takes the opportunity for pattern practice with her litany of "Gip me _____" sentences.

The key to participation during the beginner phase is to provide social-emotional support by assigning new students to a home group and to a buddy, preferably one who speaks the child's home language. The buddy accompanies the newcomer everywhere throughout the school day, including to the bathroom, cafeteria, and bus stop. Meanwhile the home group assumes responsibility for the new child during routine classroom activities. Some teachers set up home groups of four to five students each at the beginning of the school year. These groups remain fairly stable throughout the year in order to create interpersonal support and cohesion. With such groups in place, much responsibility for caring for a new student may be transferred from the teacher to the home group. These assignments help meet the safety, security, and belonging needs of a new student and create the social interaction matrix from which language acquisition begins.

At the beginner level, support for participation in lessons comes from three sources—the teacher, the other students, and the newcomers themselves. Early on, the teacher may provide some tasks that do not require speech but rather invite a nonverbal participatory response. For example, if a group is working on a thematic project, the newcomer may be involved in drawing, painting, or coloring a mural with the assistance of the other group members. In this way, the child contributes actively to the group project. At the same time, through active involvement in a low-risk, small-group activity, a good deal of talk will go on, providing excellent input for language acquisition. Similarly, the teacher and the other students can make use of sheltering techniques to help make lessons and routine activities more understandable to the newcomer. Finally, the teacher can make sure that small-group activities take place frequently, in order to create numerous opportunities for social interaction. With this kind of support, beginners will gradually advance toward the intermediate phase described next.

Second Language Oral Proficiency of Intermediate ESL Learners

Intermediate second language learners are able to understand and speak English in face-to-face interactions, and they are able to speak with minimal hesitation and few misunderstandings. Nevertheless, because their grammatical abilities (syntax, semantics, phonology) are still developing, you may still notice features in their speech that are not typical of standard English. For example, they may at times confuse *he* and *she*. They may not conjugate verbs conventionally, saying things like: "My friend, she like to read a lotta books," using *like* instead of *likes*. Even though these speech differences may nag at you for correction, you should control the natural tendency to correct children's grammar. Instead, make a point of noticing how much the child can now do with language. Show interest by asking questions that focus on the activity at hand, encouraging the student to elaborate and tell you more. You may be surprised to find that your student is able to understand and discuss ideas at a fairly complex level with patient listening. For example, intermediate students may be able to recall the details of a story, identify main ideas, predict what will come next, and, perhaps, summarize a plot. However, at this phase of development, students are likely to struggle to formulate their ideas in their new language, both orally and in writing. To get an idea of an intermediate ESL learner's oral language, take a look at how Teresa described the movie *Poltergeist* to us. Teresa is a fifth-grader whose first language is Spanish, and she has been learning English since the third grade.

SUZANNE: Was it scary?

TERESA: No it wasn't escary. But, well . . . First it was scary but then the other one no. Because there was . . . First a little girl . . . There was a television and the father was sleeping in the . . . in a . . . *sillón*? in like a chair. And then the little girl passed the television and she said: "Right here!" Then . . . then a hand get out of the television and she said: "Ouch!" And then a little boy was sleeping and the little girl sleep here and the boy here and then he see all the time a tree and then. then. there was outside a tree. a tree. but it look ugly in the night. It look like a face . . . And then he was escary. Then he tell his father and his father said OK. Just count 1, 2, 3 to not escare. Then. then. the. he . . . the little girl and the little. the two brothers go in with the mother and her father because they're still escare.

As you can see, Teresa is quite expressive in English and is able to provide a rather detailed account of the movie. She employs her developing vocabulary with a variety of grammatical rules, utilizing both past and present tense forms. Furthermore, she is able to coordinate her linguistic knowledge without hesitation much of the time. The aspects of Teresa's speech that indicate her intermediate level of English language development consist primarily of (1) her nonconventional verb use (e.g., "hand get out," "little girl sleep," "it look ugly"), (2) nonidiomatic expressions (e.g., "he see *all the time a tree*," "the little girl passed the television"), and (3) occasional groping for appropriate vocabulary items (e.g., "*sillón*, in like a chair" and variations of the word *scare: scare, scared, scary*).

During the intermediate phase of second language development, you can support students' participation in learning activities by continuing with the sheltering techniques and small-group collaboration discussed earlier. In addition, now is the time to involve students in somewhat more linguistically demanding tasks. For one thing, intermediate ESL learners know sufficient English to be able to serve as the buddy of a newly arrived non–English speaker. In terms of classroom learning activities, the intermediate student will be able to hold a speaking part in a story dramatization or reader's theater, or any other more formal language activity that permits rehearsal. In addition, during this phase, students may enjoy participating in small-group discussions of stories, science experiments, and other activities.

As intermediate-level ESL learners progress, they may appear able to use English with nearly as much facility as their native English-speaking counterparts. Their speech may be fluent, and you might find them responding with enthusiasm during whole-class as well as small-group discussion. Their reading and writing may be relatively fluent as well. At this point, it is important to continue both sheltering techniques as well as group collaboration. More advanced intermediate students are capable of understanding steady streams of verbal instruction, but the words should continue to be accompanied by charts, graphic organizers, concrete objects, and pictures to convey meaning. In addition, intermediate students can benefit from hearing the teacher use technical vocabulary, provided that it is introduced with concrete experiences, visual support such as graphs and pictures, and verbal explanations of meaning.

SUMMARY

In this chapter, we discussed second language acquisition as children experience it in school. First, we defined language proficiency, pointing out grammatical and social aspects of both communicative competence and communicative performance. We then examined a variety of factors that researchers and theorists have noted as important in second language acquisition—the language learning environment (immersion versus foreign language); age; cognitive development; the cultures of the home and school; and ways in which all of these interact to motivate and give purpose to second language acquisition. We then focused on differences between social and academic language development, drawing implications for teachers. Given the challenge students face as they attempt to learn through their second language, we described and illustrated three important teaching strategies: sheltered instruction, collaborative groupwork, and thematic units and cycles. Finally, we discussed ways of assessing oral language proficiency, and sketched characteristics of beginning and intermediate phases of second language development.

SUGGESTIONS FOR FURTHER READING

Enright, D. S., & McCloskey, M. L. (1988). *Integrating English: Developing English language and literacy in the multilingual classroom.* Reading, MA: Addison-Wesley.
   Addressing school-age children who are learning English in addition to their native language, this book describes an integrated language teaching model and how to implement it in the classroom. The appendix includes several fully developed integrated thematic units and sample classroom schedules for carrying them out.
McLaughlin, B. (1985). *Second language acquisition in childhood* (Vol. 2). Hillsdale, NJ: Lawrence Erlbaum Associates.
   A thorough critical review of research on children learning English, and other languages, subsequent to entering elementary school. Issues related to bilingual instruction are discussed as well as program types and academic achievement of students schooled in a second language.

Richard-Amato, P. (1989). *Making it happen: Interaction in the second language classroom.* White Plains, NY: Longman.
This textbook introduces a variety of approaches and classroom strategies for teaching English as a second language to students of any age. Examples of classrooms in different types of programs are provided.

ACTIVITIES

1. If you have studied another language, share your language learning story with the group. As other group members share their language learning stories, use the stories for discussing the effect of differences such as age, culture, and language learning situation on second language acquisition among the people in your group.

2. Reflecting on your own experiences studying a foreign language, what do you recall as the hardest part? Why was it hard? What was easy? Why was it easy? How proficient did you become? What affected your degree of proficiency?

3. Think back to a memorable learning experience you had in elementary school. Jot down the experience as you remember it, making note of what you were learning about and what you were doing in the process of learning. Now analyze the lesson to see how many, if any, "sheltering" techniques were used. If none were used, to what do you attribute the strength of your memory? What implications can you draw for your own teaching?

4. Take a lesson plan from a published source or one you have written yourself. Critically review the plan to analyze its comprehensibility for LEP learners. What modifications or additions could you make to ensure comprehension and participation by LEP students?

5. Try a theme cycle with a small group of children. Begin by brainstorming the question, "What are some things we would like to know more about?" Next, as a group, choose one topic to focus on. Write the topic on a piece of butcher paper, and create two columns for listing "what we know" and "what we want to know." With the children, decide which question to investigate and how. With student input, create a list of books, people, and places to go to get the needed information. Students may choose to work alone or in pairs to present the final product of their learning to the rest of the group. When finished, make a new butcher paper list of "what we know now" and "new questions we have now."

CHAPTER **3**

Second Language Learners and the Writing Process

In this chapter, we look at how second language learners benefit from the process approach to writing instruction. We address the following questions:

1. What does research tell us about writing in English as a second language?
2. What is process writing, and how can it be used with second language writers?
3. Which contexts and strategies can best assist second language writers?
4. What does the writing of beginning and intermediate second language writers look like, and how can it be assessed?

We have a friend, Paul, who has taught immigrant kindergartners in an inner-city school for twenty years. Each year, on the first day of school, he invites the children to write. He shows a few examples of student writing from previous years, including drawings, scribble writing, and invented spelling, written in whichever language the child has chosen. Given the invitation to express themselves freely, his students begin to write. Some scribble, some draw pictures, some copy letters and words from the board, some write their names, and a few write messages. Whatever they write, however, Paul listens to their stories and praises their accomplishments, letting them know they're "on their way and getting better every day."

Paul views writing differently from some teachers we know. He doesn't expect each student to construct elaborate messages upon entering kindergarten, nor does he believe in teaching children each little skill before allowing them to begin writing. Rather, he assumes that the best way for them to learn is to express themselves with pencil and crayon from the start—to learn to write by writing. This view, original twenty years ago, has now grown into the highly researched fields of emergent literacy and process writing.

The process approach to teaching writing has gained prominence among educators from kindergarten to college over the last decade. In recent years, the process approach has also been successfully applied with second language writers. In this chapter, we describe theory and research supporting the rationale for using process writing with second language learners. We describe ways in which students may collaborate to practice and improve their writing. In addition, we provide general descriptions of beginning and intermediate second language writers and outline various teaching strategies to facilitate their progress. Samples of student writing are interspersed to give you a sense of what children are able to do in writing and to illustrate how their writing reflects both written language knowledge and general second language development. Finally, we conclude with procedures for assessing writing progress.

RESEARCH ON SECOND LANGUAGE WRITING

Current research documents the similarity of writing processes for both first and second language writers. For example, second language writers make use of their budding knowledge of English as they create texts for different audiences and different purposes, just as first language writers do (Ammon, 1985; Edelsky, 1981a; 1981b). As students develop control over the language, their writing gradually begins to approximate standard English (Hudelson, 1986). In addition, at the early stages, children writing in a second language support their efforts with drawings (Hudelson, 1986; Peregoy & Boyle, 1990a) just as their first language counterparts do (Dyson, 1982). It makes sense that the task of English writing should be similar for both first and second language learners. After all, the problems writers face are either specific to the conventions of written English, such as spelling, grammar, and rhetorical choice, or they relate to more general aspects of the writing process, such as choosing a topic, deciding what to say, and tailoring the message to the intended audience—elements that go into writing in any language.

While the processes of English writing are essentially similar for both first and second language writers, there are some important differences in what the two groups bring to the task. First of all, students new to English are apt to experience some limitations in expressive abilities in terms of vocabulary, syntax, and idiomatic expressions. In other words, second language proficiency plays a role in writing. In addition, LEP students may not have had much exposure to written English, exposure that comes from reading or being read to. As a result, they may not have a feel for the way that English conventionally translates into written form. The more they read or are read to in English, however, the easier it will be for them to write (Krashen, 1982).

Some students know how to write in their native language, and this knowledge facilitates the English writing task. For example, they are apt to display a sophisticated understanding of the nature and functions of print as well as confidence in their ability to produce and comprehend text in their new language (Hudelson, 1987). In addition, to the extent that their native language alphabet is similar to the English alphabet, first language letter formation and spelling strategies will transfer partially to English writing (Odlin, 1989). Finally, research demonstrates that students can profitably engage in reading and writing in their second language well before they have gained full control over the phonological, syntactic, and semantic systems of spoken English (Goodman, Goodman, & Flores, 1979; Hudelson, 1984; Peregoy & Boyle, 1991). In fact, providing students with opportunities to write not only improves their writing, but also promotes second language acquisition.

Given the similarity between first and second language writing processes, it is not surprising that effective teaching strategies for first language writers tend, with some modifications, to be effective for second language writers as well. One such strategy is the process approach to writing instruction. In fact, process writing has been enthusiastically embraced by bilingual and ESL teachers, and researchers have pointed out the importance of teaching students composing processes (Krapels, 1990; Silva, 1990).

WHAT IS PROCESS WRITING?

Process writing is an approach to teaching writing that has been researched in depth over the past several years with both first language learners (Calkins, 1986; Emig, 1981; Graves, 1983) and second language learners (Kroll, 1990). In process writing, students experience five interrelated phases: prewriting, drafting, revising, editing, and publishing. During the prewriting phase, students choose a topic and generate ideas, often through brainstorming and oral discussion. Once they have found and explained their topic, they begin drafting. As they compose their first draft, they are encouraged to let their ideas flow onto the paper without concern for perfection in form or mechanics. After completing the first draft, students reread their papers and, with feedback from the teacher or their peers, get ready to revise. Revisions are aimed at conveying the writer's ideas as effectively as possible. Finally, the paper is edited for correct punctuation, spelling, and grammar in order to be presented for publishing. Table 3.1 describes the purpose of each phase of the writing process and provides examples of strategies to use with each.

The writing process approach thus breaks the writing act into manageable parts and integrates oral language, reading, and writing at the service of the child's communication goals. As a result, process writing allows students to concentrate on one task at a time and to experience the value of peer feedback in developing their ideas for effective written expression (Boyle, 1982). Because their writing is published, children learn to tailor their message for a particular audience and purpose. Moreover, as students share their polished pieces, a great deal of

TABLE 3.1 Writing Process Phases and Strategies

Phase	Purpose	Strategies
Prewriting	To generate and gather ideas for writing; to prepare for writing; to identify purpose and audience for writing; to identify main ideas and supporting details.	Talking and oral activities; brainstorming, clustering, questioning, reading, keeping journals in all content areas.
Drafting	Getting ideas down on paper quickly; getting a first draft that can be evaluated according to purpose and audience for paper.	Fast writing; daily writing; journals of all types: buddy journals, dialogue journals, learning logs.
Revising	Reordering arguments or reviewing scenes in a narrative; reordering supporting information; reviewing or changing sentences.	Show and not tell; shortening sentences; combining sentences; peer response groups; teacher conferences.
Editing	Correcting spelling, grammar, punctuation, mechanics, etc.	Peer editing groups; proofreading; computer programs for spelling, etc.; programmed materials; mini-lessons.
Publishing	Sharing writing with one another, with students, with parents; showing that writing is valued; creating a classroom library; motivating writing.	Writing may be shared in many formats: papers placed on bulletin boards, papers published with computers, papers shared in school book fairs, etc.

excitement and enthusiasm is generated about writing. Not least important, students evolve into a community of writers who know how to listen to what others have to say and to critique each other's writing in a positive and sensitive manner.

Using the process writing approach, teachers encourage children to write daily and to select a few papers for occasional revising, editing, and publishing. They also respond positively to the message of the child's writing first and later to the form of the writing when it is deemed appropriate to do so. Moreover, they concentrate on what the child is doing right rather than on errors in the papers. When children are doing something right, we should encourage them to continue. Finally, teachers ask children to write to different audiences for different purposes, and they engage children in writing in many domains, including stories, letters, biographical pieces, and persuasive essays.

To give you a feel for the process approach to writing, we invite you to try the procedure described below, a writing activity based on a personal memory that works well with any age (Caldwell, 1984). After trying it, you may wish to use it with your own students. As you follow the procedure, notice how the five phases of process writing are included: prewriting, drafting, revising, editing, and publishing.

Experiencing Process Writing

TEACHER: I want you to think of five things that have happened to you. Write down each of the five things, beginning with the phrase: "I remember. . . ." When you have finished, share your ideas with a partner.

TEACHER: Now, write down one name associated with each of the five things you selected.

TEACHER: Can you name our five senses? [*Students generate the five senses: touch, sight, smell, hearing, and tasting.*]

Write down the most important sense that goes with each of your "I remember. . . ."

TEACHER: Now, select the "I remember" you would most like to write about. Share the memory with your group.

TEACHER: Next, write the part of the memory that makes it memorable or very important to you; share it with your group.

TEACHER: Now, writing as fast as you can for ten minutes, see how much of the memory you can get on paper. Don't worry about punctuation or spelling; you can think about that later, if you like what you've written.

TEACHER: [*Ten minutes later.*] Share your papers with your group and ask them to make suggestions that will make your paper clearer.

Questions for Discussion
1. In what ways did the exercise help your writing?
2. In what ways do you suppose the process approach might help second language children with their writing?

Children's Responses to "I Remember"

The "I remember . . ." activity ties well into literature study because published authors often make use of their own personal and family memories as the basis of their fiction. For example, in the foreword to *Mirandy and Brother Wind* (McKissack, 1988), author Patricia McKissack briefly relates the "I remember. . ." family story that inspired the book. Mildred Taylor offers a similar note to her readers in *Roll of Thunder, Hear My Cry* (Taylor, 1976). When students read literature, it is important to discuss the authors and make explicit the connection between professional and student authors. Authors are real people who face the same essential challenges when writing as do the students themselves. By discussing authorship in the context of their own reading and writing experiences, students come to see themselves in a new light and gain a deeper understanding of the relationship between reading and writing.

Using literature in this way, teacher Anne Phillips read her second graders the autobiographical piece *When I Was Young in the Mountains* (Rylant, 1989) to introduce the "I remember. . ." process writing activity. Figure 3.1 shows Peter Aguirre's first draft based on the "I remember. . ." procedure.

Writing such as this does not happen by chance. Peter has been taught to use descriptive words, he has heard and read numerous stories, and he has used the writing process as outlined in the "I rememberh. . ." activity above. After generating his first draft, he listened to advice from his group, which suggested that he needed an introduction to make clearer why he was cutting down a tree in his backyard. In addition, he added information at the end of the story to make the milk and sandwich scene fit. He then worked with his teacher to edit his story for publication. In the final draft, he corrected most of his original errors and,

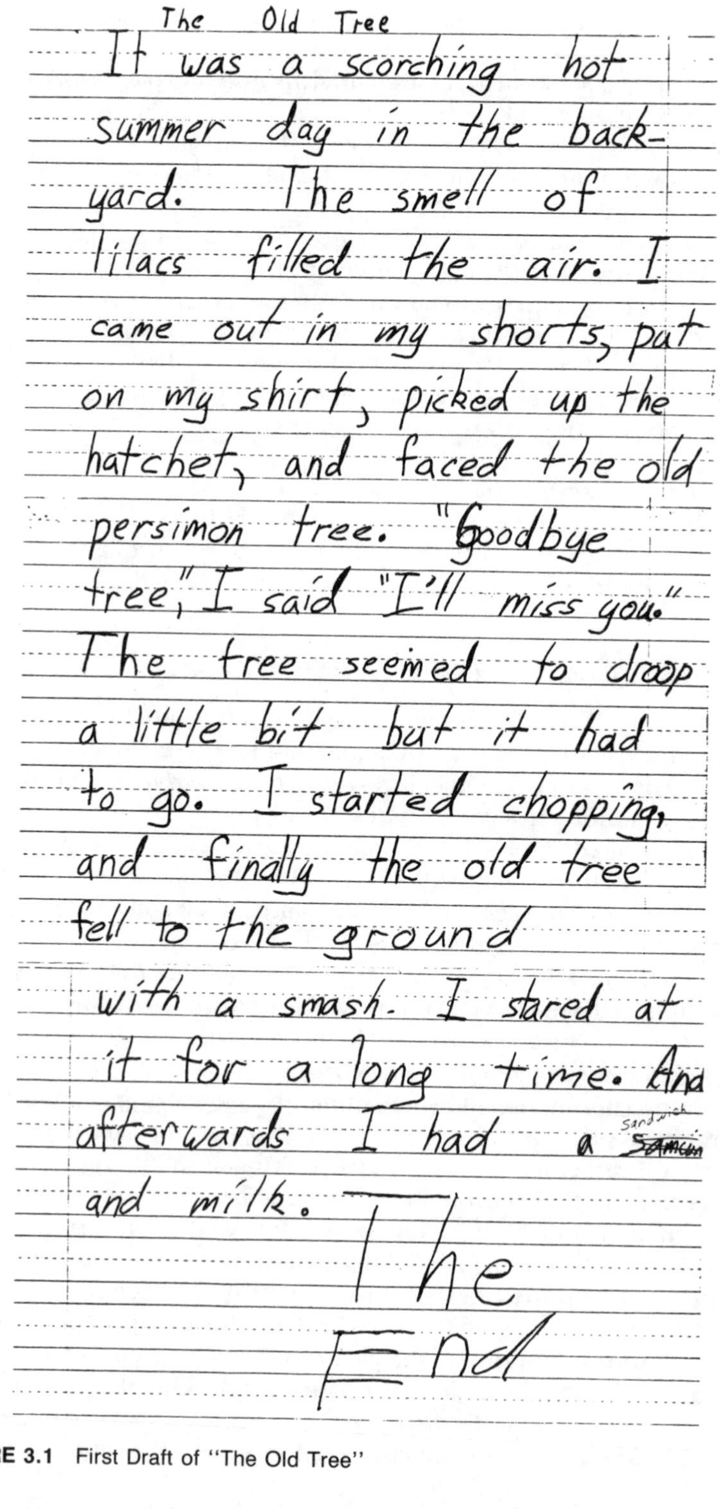

The Old Tree

It was a scorching hot summer day in the back-yard. The smell of lilacs filled the air. I came out in my shorts, put on my shirt, picked up the hatchet, and faced the old persimon tree. "Goodbye tree," I said "I'll miss you." The tree seemed to droop a little bit but it had to go. I started chopping, and finally the old tree fell to the ground with a smash. I stared at it for a long time. And afterwards I had a sandwich and milk.

The
End

FIGURE 3.1 First Draft of "The Old Tree"

incidentally, added a few new ones. Ms. Phillips then asked the students to create a cover for their story and write a dedication, just as their favorite published authors do. For his story, Peter drew a picture of "the old tree" and dedicated it to his pet parrot. Here is Peter's final draft:

The Old Tree

My favorite memory was when my Dad tought me how to chop down a tree and today was my first test. It was a scorching hot summer day in the backyard. The smell of lilacs filled the air. I came out in my shorts put on my shirt, picked up the hatchet and faced the old persimon tree. "Goodbye tree," I said "I'll miss you. The tree seemed to droop a little but it had to go. I started chopping, and finally the old tree fell to the ground with a smash. I stared at that tree for the longest time. Then it hit me. I went inside the house. Mom asked what I was sad about. "I miss the tree" I said. "Don't worry" she said I'll fix you some milk and a sandwich.

The End.

Abel, a classmate of Peter's who immigrated from Mexico, produced the following final piece during the "I remember. . . ." activity. He dedicated his story to "Mrs. Grazvawni because she help me with my story."

My Favorite Memory

I was in Mexico. It was cold. I was with my uncle. My horse was big and black. I rode slow in the street. I gave grass to him to eat. My uncle jumped in the river; it felt good and cold.

Abel, age 7

As children write about their memories, we find that they bring a wealth of experience to personal writing topics. One reason personal writing is so useful with second language students is that it provides a bridge between their previous experiences and those of the classroom. In this way, they are validated for what they know, and their teacher and classmates come to understand them better. Years ago, when Vietnamese children first began to arrive in U.S. classrooms, one well-meaning teacher shared her frustration over a new child in her classroom: "Truc has come along okay with her English, but she never seems to get anything down in writing. She never has anything to say." The resource teacher, however, was able to elicit several pages of writing from Truc during their weekly sessions together. Truc shared the horrors of war, her family's perilous escape by boat, the death of loved ones, and what it felt like to be in a new country with twelve people in a one-bedroom apartment. Why, we asked, was Truc so reluctant to write in her regular class? In further conversations with her teacher, we found out that writing topics were always assigned. Students almost never chose their own. Truc had difficulty generating ideas under these circumstances. In contrast, she was able to write much more fluently with the resource teacher because there she was free to choose her own topic. She may have felt more comfortable in the small-group situation afforded by the resource program. However, there can be no doubt that a great deal of power resides with the freedom to choose one's own topic: power in choice, power in knowing something about the topic, and power in having something to say. All children bring rich personal experiences into the classroom. If they are given the opportunities to voice these experiences orally and in writing, you will find that they will always have valid topics to write about and plenty to say.

HOW PROCESS WRITING HELPS SECOND LANGUAGE STUDENTS

The process approach to writing is especially valuable for LEP students because it allows them to write from their own experiences. As they share their writing during writing groups and publishing, their teacher and friends get to know and appreciate them. Thus, personal relationships are enhanced. In addition, second language writers benefit from cooperative assistance among students during both revising and editing. As a result, there are numerous opportunities for supporting both clear self-expression and correctness in the final product. Cooperative groups not only promote better writing, but also they provide numerous opportunities for oral discussion within which a great deal of "comprehensible input" is generated, promoting language development. Furthermore, the supportive interaction that takes place in effective response groups helps students appreciate and accept each other, another positive factor for second language learning. Finally, by setting aside "editing" as a separate phase, process writing frees second language students to elaborate their ideas first and make corrections last. Yet, through the editing process, they grow in their awareness of English grammar, punctuation, and spelling.

In summary, you can assist children with their writing by assisting them with strategies for generating, drafting, revising, and editing. By introducing children to the writing process, you can show them that they will need to concentrate on various aspects of writing at different times in the process. They must first generate ideas, then form them for different audiences and different purposes, and then revise and edit them to prepare them for publication and sharing. When good literature is combined with opportunities to write often, when strategies are offered to solve problems in writing, and when writing is shared and published, your students will grow both in writing and overall second language development.

COLLABORATIVE CONTEXTS FOR PROCESS WRITING

When you use the writing process approach, writing ceases to be a solitary activity and becomes a highly interactive group endeavor. Of course, individuals ultimately "own" their own work. However, throughout the phases of the writing process, they have worked with the whole class, in pairs, and in small groups: brainstorming ideas, focusing their topics, considering ways to express themselves, revising their papers, getting ready for publication, and, finally, sharing their final pieces with the entire class. Thus, the process approach calls for group collaboration and support at every phase: prewriting, writing (drafting), revising, editing, and publishing.

While cooperative groups are useful during any phase of process writing, groupwork is particularly crucial during revision and editing. Groups that help the writer during revision are called "peer response groups," while those concerned with editing are called "peer editing groups" (Beck, McKeown, Omanson, & Pople, 1984). For both kinds of groups, students need explicit guidelines on what kinds of things to say and how to say them so as to benefit their group members. Thus, students need to learn both the social rules of groupwork and specific elements of good writing and editing in order to be effective participants.

Response Groups

After students have chosen a topic and produced a first draft of their papers, they are ready to work in response groups. The purpose of response groups is to give writers a chance to try out their writing on a supportive "audience," the members of their response group. Response groups usually include three to five people, although other configurations are possible. Each student gets a chance to read his or her paper aloud to the group for feedback, which the writer considers when making revisions to improve the paper (Calkins, 1986; Graves & Hansen, 1983; Healy, 1980). At this point, comments should focus on expression of ideas, not on mechanics, as those will be addressed later during editing. Responding to another's writing is a very high-level task, both cognitively and socially, involving careful listening to the author's intent and critical thinking about possible questions and suggestions. Clearly, students need direct instruction in how to respond effectively and sensitively. How can this be taught? Table 3.2 outlines general procedures for preparing students to work in response groups; it is followed by a description of how teachers prepare students to be responsive peer group partners.

TABLE 3.2　Initiating Peer Response Groups

A	By responding to students' content rather than to the form of their writing, you model response to writing.
B	By teaching students specific strategies such as show and not tell, you give them the vocabulary and means to truly improve their writing in peer response groups.
C	By sharing sample papers with students on the overhead projector, you can model responding to writing and give the students an opportunity to practice response.
D	By sharing papers before and after revision, you can show students the effects of response groups' efforts.
E	By taping or videotaping successful response groups or having successful groups show how they work together, you can assist all children in learning how to be a successful response group member.
F	By continually sharing good literature with children, you can help them recognize good writing.

Before asking students to respond in groups, we suggest that you model the responding process by displaying an anonymous first draft paper on an overhead projector and commenting on it yourself. This may be done with the whole class or with a smaller group. First, find one or two things you like about the paper. The golden rule is "Find something positive to say first." Next, you need to model questions you would ask the writer if there are parts you don't understand. You might also look for flow of ideas, sequencing, organization, and other elements of good writing such as those illustrated in Table 3.3. Next, place another paper on the overhead and invite students to respond to it following the procedure you have just modeled. This procedure gives students a chance to practice responding before they work with one another and boosts their chances of success in collaboration.

Later on, as a variation, you might role-play a good response partner and a poor response partner. Contrasting constructive and sensitive responses with those that are unhelpful or unkind may help beginning responders become effective in their response groups. Children need to see what a good response partner is like and hear the kinds of questions that partners use to assist writers. Once students have practiced as a class with your modeling and guidance, they will be ready to act positively in their groups.

The acts of reading and discussing quality literature also provide students with ideas about how to respond to each other's writing. When your students read and share literature, ask them to select writing that is particularly vivid or interesting to them. You might ask them to point out good examples of "showing and not telling," of sentence combining, or sentence models to try themselves. (These strategies are described in detail subsequently.) Ask your students to underline or highlight their favorite parts of a story to share with one another. By sharing the good writing of students and professionals alike, you heighten your students' awareness of the author's craft.

TABLE 3.3 Elements of Good Writing

Element	Description of Element
Leads	The opening of a paper, whether the first line, the first paragraph, or the first several paragraphs, must capture the reader's interest and/or state purpose clearly.
Focus	The writers must choose and limit a single focus for their writing, omitting information that does not directly contribute to the point of the piece.
Voice	Voice in a paper is that element that lets you hear and feel the narrator as a real person, even if the narrator is fictitious. Voice should remain consistent throughout a piece.
Show not tell	Good writers learn to create pictures for their readers rather than just making flat statements that tell. Examples also help to show not just tell.
Endings	A good ending will suit the purpose of the piece to provide closure on the topic but may take the reader by surprise, or leave the reader interested in hearing more.

Finally, don't forget the power you exert daily as a role model. The way you respond to students' papers will directly influence their ways of responding to others. If you comment in a positive manner, celebrating what they have done well rather than concentrating on mistakes in grammar, punctuation, or spelling, you will find your students doing the same. Your own daily interaction with students is, without a doubt, your most powerful means of modeling response!

Figure 3.2 makes further suggestions to help students become good responders within the context of an author's circle, where children share their papers in small groups.

Your students now know something about how and what to say in their response groups. As they get ready to move into their groups, you may wish to supply them with a list of questions to help them remember what to say. The sample feedback sheet in Figure 3.3 is one way to guide students until they are confident with their ability to help one another. Another way to guide students' responses is to give them specific tasks each time they meet in their groups, such as looking for "show and not tell" sentences in their writing or for sentences that need combining or shortening. The writing strategies you have taught can become the springboard to successful response groups. Remember, however, that keeping a writing group together is a lot like keeping a good relationship together; it needs constant communication and caring among the group members.

Thus prepared, your students are now ready to work in their response groups. You may assign children to groups, or let them choose for themselves. A good way to start is to have one student read a paper while others listen, sometimes called

FIGURE 3.2   Guidelines for Author's Circle

Directions to Students: You may wish to use the following questions to guide your response to your friends' papers and to help others respond to your writing.

Example for Authors:

1. Decide what kind of help you would like on your paper and tell your group.
2. Read your paper aloud to your group; you may want your group to have copies of your paper also.
3. Ask your group what they liked best about your paper; ask them to discuss other parts of the paper.
4. Ask your group to respond to the areas you said you wanted help with and discuss their advice, knowing that you will make the decision about whether you will change something or not.

Examples for Responders:

1. Listen very carefully to the author while he or she is reading his or her paper.
2. Respond to the questions the author asks and try to be helpful.
3. Point out sentences, descriptions, or other things you liked about the paper.
4. Point out one thing that might not have been very clear to you in the paper.

Some questions you may wish to use to assist your students with responding in peer groups

1. What did you mean when you said _____?
2. Could you describe that scene so we could see it and hear it?
3. What is the most important part of your story? What do you want the reader to think when he or she has finished reading it?
4. What part of the story would you like help with?
5. What part of your story do you especially like?
6. What do you want to do next with this piece?

FIGURE 3.3   Sample Feedback Questions

"author's circle." The author takes charge of this group and may begin by telling the response group what kind of feedback would be most helpful. When the reader is finished, the others respond to the writing, concentrating on making positive comments first, with questions and suggestions last. After one student has been responded to, others may take the role of author, reading their papers and eliciting input from their group. It is important for students to know that the purpose of response groups is not to count errors or look for mistakes in writing but to provide support to the writer. Because you have carefully explained the procedure, your students will know how to begin. As they all experience roles of responders and authors, their understanding and expertise in responding will grow.

Once the students are settled in their groups, you may move around the room and provide help as needed, but resist the temptation to take over or dominate the interactions. Your students will become more independent if you let them solve their own problems. In order to reinforce positive group functioning, you may wish to tape record or videotape the work of a successful group and share it with the class. In addition, you may occasionally review the attributes of a good responder or invite a successful group to share their response to a paper with the entire class. Finally, you may periodically ask students to evaluate strengths and weaknesses in their groupwork and ask them to suggest ways of improving.

A Sixth-Grade Class Works in Response Groups.   Students in Sam Garcia's sixth-grade class selected their own response groups and responded to one another following the model above. The children used some of his feedback questions and worked on papers together. Here is an example of one group working with a second language student's paper. Notice that the children first concentrate on the content rather than correctness; they also concentrate on what they like about the paper before making suggestions:

Student's Paper
I went to my grandma's house. She live in the country. We drive for 12 hours. We get on the highway to get ther. She cook so good. We

ate tamales and ice cream. She only talk Spanish but she have kind of funny acsent and my sisters and all we love to hear her talk. We love it when she tells about the old days. Like when she talk about other places.

We staying 3 days. Granpa let us help on the farm. I love to visit he's home. I help to cook and help with the animals.

Christa—11 years old

When Christa finished reading her paper, the students in her group made suggestions after Christa asked what more she should say.

> LISA: I liked the part about the food.
>
> CHRISTA: I should say more about her cooking?
>
> LISA: Yeah—like what's good about the tamales. What else did you eat?
>
> JOE: I like the part about her talking. What accent did she have? You might say that.
>
> LAURA: Maybe you could spell words like she said them, like *Roll of Thunder*.
>
> CHRISTA: That's good, but she talked different.

The group discussed the paper for about 10 minutes, pointing out other improvements such as naming what animals were on the farm. When they had finished and were ready to work on another paper, Josie volunteered to help Christa with the accent. The session with Christa ended when Martha asked her why she selected that story to tell. Christa replied: "My granma and granpa are gone, and I wanted to remember them; so I wrote this." Christa indicated that her group helped her a lot. She said that she would be able to write a clearer picture of her "granma": "You'll see and hear her now."

Peer Editing Groups

The purpose of peer editing groups is to read over final drafts to make corrections on grammar, punctuation, and spelling. Peer editing groups work well if used at the appropriate time in the writing process, *after* students are satisfied that their writing says what they want it to say. When students are still revising, it is inappropriate to concentrate on correctness, like placing frosting on a cake that contains baking soda but no flour, sugar, or eggs. However, once students are satisfied with what their papers say, then it is time to edit for correctness.

Correctness is best learned within the context of the students' own writing (Cooper, 1981). Therefore, we don't recommend giving whole-class instruction or unrelated worksheets on correctness, spelling, or punctuation. Allow students to use computers, if available, to correct their spelling. Allow them to help one another rather than playing the major role yourself. You don't need to improve your proofreading skills—they do. Therefore, make them responsible for correctness. One way to begin peer editing groups is to teach a mini-lesson on an element of grammar or punctuation and, then, post this element on the chalkboard to focus on during editing. Every so often, teach a new editing element, thus gradually building student knowledge of mechanics. In this way, students apply their mechanical skills directly to their writing, thereby using them for purposes of clear communication.

Another possibility is to make particular students experts on topics such as capitalization, punctuation, spelling, or subject/verb agreement. Then, when students have editing questions, they go to the "experts" in the class, not you. This builds self-esteem in your class and also builds independent learners. After all, your main concern in teaching should be to create independent learners, thus making yourself obsolete. Finally, when students select their own topics, when they work in response groups, and when their work becomes important to them, you will find that they are more willing to work in editing groups. Most important, when they know that their work will be published in your class, you will find a renewed enthusiasm for the work that goes into revising and editing.

THE PUBLISHING PHASE
OF THE WRITING PROCESS

One way to develop a spirit of meaningful collaborative writing is to encourage publishing projects. Some teachers like to have classroom newspapers with the students as columnists. Others have students publish newspapers for special holidays. Still others have children write newspaper articles describing calamities such as a tornado, earthquake, or war. Newspapers are easy to produce and involve children in learning different sections of regular newspapers. They can learn about creating headlines for articles they write; they can learn the difference between editorials and features; and they can learn to write sports, entertainment, and other sections. Publishing projects involve your students in collaborative groupwork as they organize, write, revise, edit, and publish. Not least important is student enthusiasm. We have seen many resistant students become very enthusiastic about writing after learning that their work would be published in the school newspaper for all to see.

Other publishing activities you may want to try include poetry anthologies, short-story collections, and individual publications of student writing. Children become very excited when they know that what they write will be read by others in book-like form. You can create a classroom library by having students publish books that will remain in your room, but you will find that students will value their published books so much that they are often unwilling to let them go. If you explain that their writing will be read by future students, you will get more cooperation. You can also ask students to donate one of their books to the school library.

Another successful publishing activity involves older students sharing their publications with younger children. Third-graders, for example, might visit a first-grade class and read their books. They might also discuss with the first-graders how they got their ideas for writing and how they developed the idea into a book. This kind of sharing creates great enthusiasm in the older students, who enjoy a real audience for their writing, and helps younger students see writing as a valuable enterprise practiced by their "elders."

Children often choose their own published works to read during quiet reading time.

Have you ever noticed that when you take a group picture, the first thing you look at when the developed picture returns is yourself? Did you forget what you looked like? Something similar happens when students publish their writing— they continually return to their own books and reread them. It's not that they don't know the contents of the book but rather that they find deep satisfaction in reviewing their accomplishments. One way we informally evaluate classrooms we visit is by noticing the number of children who line up to read their books to us. In classrooms where books are regularly published, children enthusiastically share their writing with others and demand opportunities for more publishing. If you create a publishing center and library, you will find children who are motivated to write, revise, and edit their papers.

A SUMMARY OF PROCESS WRITING

We have outlined the process approach to teaching writing, an approach that supports writing success and celebrates student accomplishments through sharing and feedback each step of the way. As students begin to see themselves as authors, they develop pride and ownership in their writing. As the process writing cycle is repeated, as students continually write for real and functional purposes, and as they learn to provide valid feedback to their peers, they grow into more proficient and caring writers. By giving children chances to work on meaningful collaborative writing tasks and by having them share their writing through publishing classroom books, you can be assured of children's involvement in the revising and editing phases of the writing process. All of these benefits are especially important for LEP students because process writing facilitates progress in written expression and promotes second language acquisition as well.

DEVELOPMENTAL PHASES
IN SECOND LANGUAGE WRITING

Second language writers, like their first language counterparts, progress developmentally as they gain control over the writing process. To become truly effective writers, they must coordinate a broad range of complex skills, including clarity of thought and expression, knowledge of different genres to suit different purposes, and the ability to use conventional spelling, grammar, and punctuation. Such coordination depends, among other things, on students' English-language proficiency, cognitive development, and writing experience. Because good writing exhibits numerous traits, because these traits vary according to the kind of writing and its purpose, and because individual development of these traits is apt to be uneven, it is not easy to characterize developmental levels. For example, one child may write very short pieces with correct spelling and punctuation, while another writes elaborate, action-packed stories without any punctuation or capitalization. Both are beginners, but neither child has consistent development in all aspects of good writing. Such variation is normal.

Despite the complexities in establishing developmental characteristics, developmental descriptions are necessary as a starting point from which to guide your teaching decisions. Thus, in this section, we discuss in detail two general developmental phases, beginning and intermediate second language writing. These phases are defined in terms of the matrix shown in Figure 3.4 and are analogous to the oral language matrix (SOLOM) you saw earlier in Figure 2.2. Though we include advanced second language writing characteristics, we restrict subsequent discussion to beginning and intermediate phases, consistent with the rest of the book. For these phases, we offer examples of student writing and suggest strategies you may introduce to help your students progress. Because you know your own students well from daily contact, you will be able to use your intuition as well as your analytical skills to decide finally which strategies will be most helpful. As a final note, feel free to use or adapt any of the strategies for any student, according to your own judgment.

In Figure 3.4, we have described beginning, intermediate, and advanced second language writing on five trait dimensions: fluency, organization, language use, style, and mechanics. Our concept of an advanced second language writer is defined in terms of an effective first language writer of the same age. In general, if a student's writing tends to be characterized by the trait descriptions listed for beginners, then we suggest that you start with strategies described for beginners in the next section. Similarly, if a student's writing tends to be characterized by

Trait	Beginning Level	Intermediate Level	Advanced Level
Fluency	Writes one or two short sentences.	Writes several sentences.	Writes a paragraph or more.
Organization	Lacks logical sequence or so short that organization presents no problem.	Somewhat sequenced.	Follows standard organization for genre.
Grammar	Basic word-order problems. Uses only present tense forms.	Minor grammatical errors, such as "s" on verbs in 3rd person singular.	Grammar resembles native speaker's of same age.
Vocabulary	Limited vocabulary. Needs to rely at times on first language or ask for translation.	Knows most words needed to express ideas but lacks vocabulary for finer shades of meaning.	Flexible in word choice; similar to good native writer's of same age.
Genre	Does not differentiate form to suit purpose.	Chooses form to suit purpose but limited in choices of expository forms.	Knows several genres; makes appropriate choices. Similar to effective native writer's of same age.
Sentence Variety	Uses one or two sentence patterns.	Uses several sentence patterns.	Uses a good variety of sentence patterns effectively.

FIGURE 3.4   Writing Traits Matrix

the trait descriptions listed for the intermediate phase, we suggest you use the corresponding strategies described for that phase. Bear in mind that your students are apt to vary in phase from one trait to another, and you will need to use your own judgment as to which strategies you will use.

Beginning Writers

Beginning second language writers, similar to beginning first language writers, are new to the coordinated efforts that go into creating a good piece of writing in English. They may find writing laborious, producing very little at first. If so, organization is not a problem, because there is little on paper to organize. If beginners do produce a great deal, logical organization is apt to be lacking. Like their first language counterparts, beginning second language writers may use inventive spelling that includes elements from the spelling system of their first language. In addition, during the beginning phase, second language writers may not have a good sense of sentence boundaries or of the conventional word order required in English. Thus, they are apt to make errors in grammar, vocabulary, and usage. In addition, they may exhibit grammatical and other infelicities common to native-English beginning writers.

When you evaluate your beginning second language writers, you need to take the time to notice and emphasize what they do well. This may not be natural or easy because errors call our attention like a flashing red fire alarm, while well-formed sentences go unnoticed as we focus on their meaning. When a child draws a picture, we don't compare it with Michelangelo's work. Instead, we delight in the accomplishment. Similarly, with beginning writers, first and second language learners alike, we need to find specific elements to praise while pointing out areas to improve. Take for example, the piece below, a beginning level student's paper referring to Bart Simpson:

> The puppy go to bart. He jump on bart. He look at bart. He see. He go.
>
> Kim, first grade

The child who wrote this paper worked laboriously to produce the final product. As a beginner, Kim uses one type of sentence only. She is able to use the present tense but has not developed the ability to use the past tense. This young beginning writer needs time and practice in both oral and written English. As a first-grader, Kim has plenty of growing time, and we suspect that she will improve steadily. Based on this writing sample, we would suggest two immediate strategies. First, additional effort during the prewriting phase of process writing might help her arrive at a more personally meaningful topic. Secondly, oral discussion of her topic combined with drawing would probably result in a more elaborated message. Because she is new to English and because she is just a first-grader, we would not require her to alter her verb tenses. Such alteration would make little sense to her at this point and would not be likely to transfer to her next piece of writing. In sum, at this point we are aiming at fluency in writing and enjoyment in self-expression.

Not all beginning writers will be so young as first-grader Kim. Quite the contrary. Beginning ESL writers vary in age, prior literacy experience, and second language proficiency. To repeat a point, the beauty of writing is that it accommodates many of the differences related to age, in that the topics are often selected and developed by the students. Thus, age and cultural appropriateness are, to an extent, built in by the students themselves through writing. Older beginning writers may bring a fairly sophisticated concept of the forms and functions of writing to the task, along with a well-developed conceptual system. Below is an example of a third-grade beginning English writer, Jorge. In this essay, Jorge attempts to describe the differences between two kinds of birds, mountain dwellers and valley dwellers, based on their portrayal in a cartoon-like picture:

> Tey are the same becaes the bofe of them haves two eggs and there head and there foot and they are not the same becaes they don't eat the same thing and ther beak and one place is the mountain and one is the valley. the end.
>
> Jorge, third grade

The assignment that led to this essay called for an expository type of writing. As a third-grader, Jorge had very little experience in writing, especially expository writing in English. He was a fairly fluent Spanish reader and had just begun instruction in reading English. Thus, the cognitive demand of this writing task was rather high. Nonetheless, he was able to convey similarities between the birds' eggs, their heads, and their feet, as well as differences in food, beak types, and dwelling locations. Nevertheless, he used little capitalization or punctuation. His single, extended sentence consists of several clauses conjoined by "and," which is a characteristic of less mature writers. Furthermore, he ends his expository piece with a narrative formula: "the end." These characteristics are indicative of beginning level writing, though more advanced than Kim's writing above. Jorge needs opportunities to write daily for a variety of purposes that he perceives to be real and important. His ability to generate ideas, even within the constraint of a particular assignment, is excellent. With opportunities to create longer pieces of writing on topics that interest him and with the chance to publish and share, it is likely that Jorge will begin writing longer essays. Organization and punctuation are two areas on which he will need to work as he prepares his writing for publication.

Strategies to Assist Beginning Level Writers

We have discussed how effective writing requires the coordination of various kinds of skills and knowledge. One way to assist beginning and intermediate writers is to provide them with temporary frameworks or supports that allow them to concentrate on one aspect of the writing process at a time. We refer to such temporary frameworks as literacy scaffolds. Just as scaffolding is temporarily provided to help workers construct a building, literacy scaffolds provide temporary frameworks to help students construct or comprehend a written message. In chapter 2, we defined literacy scaffolds (Boyle & Peregoy, 1990) as instructional strategies that help students read or write whole, meaningful texts at a level somewhat beyond what they could do on their own. In general, literacy scaffolds include predictable elements as a result of repetition of language patterns and/or repetition of routines. In addition, they are temporary and may be discarded when the student is ready to move beyond them.

Within this definition, the writing process itself is a powerful scaffold in that it breaks a complex process into smaller subprocesses, each of which is aimed at creating meaning. Other types of literacy scaffolds are described below, including dialogue journals, buddy journals, clustering, freewriting, and others. Each of these activities provides support for beginning level writers and is presented in order according to its relative difficulty. We recommend using the activities within the context of collaborative groups where the students share and respond to one another's writing.

Oral Discussion. Oral discussion prior to writing represents one kind of scaffold to literacy. When children share their ideas orally with the teacher or with their peers, they are facilitated in choosing and focusing their topic. Oral interactions help students organize their ideas and may also provide helpful vocabulary items for second language students. Informal oral language opportunities thus provide a safe arena for children to practice their language production. You don't want the children in your class to answer as one of ours did when we asked how she liked school on her first days: "I hate school," she said. "I can't read. I can't write. And they won't let me talk." You can avoid that kind of judgment by encouraging your children to talk and share orally throughout the day. We describe several activities below that promote natural use of oral language and pave the way to literacy.

Partner Stories Using Pictures and Wordless Books.   One activity that assists with children's second language development is the use of wordless books. Wordless books tell stories through their pictures only and thus offer a unique opportunity for limited English-speaking students to interact with a book. Using wordless books, children orally share their versions of stories in response groups, recognizing that the pictures might yield different interpretations. As a follow-up to wordless books, they may draw their own pictures for a book or a cartoon strip. Children may also try labeling pictures and developing a written story. Wordless books thus offer easy access to the early literacy events of a classroom for second language learners. A few wordless books you may want to try are listed below:

> ***A Short Beginning List of Wordless Books***
> Alexander, M. (1970). *Bobo's Dream.* New York: Dial Press.
>
> Arueyo, J. (1971). *Look What I Can Do.* New York: Scribner.
>
> Anno, M. (1984). *Anno's Flea Market.* New York: Philomel.
>
> Hutchins, P. (1971). *Changes, Changes.* New York: Macmillan.
>
> Mayer, M. (1967). *A Boy, a Dog, and a Frog.* New York: Dial Press.
>
> Meyer, R. (1969). *Hide-and-Seek.* New York: Bradbury.
>
> Wezer, P. (1964). *The Good Bird.* New York: Harper & Row.

Concept Books: Creating a Teaching Library.   Concept books, excellent for beginning writers, focus on and illustrate one concept or idea. For example, a child might illustrate a color, or the concepts "tall" and "short," or concepts relating to above and below. Children enjoy making their own concept books. Lisa, for example, made a book illustrating the concepts "little" and "big" by drawing and cutting out pictures to convey the ideas. One page featured a drawing of a little girl with the label "little," and, on the adjacent page, there was a picture of a big girl with the label "big." The teacher, Ms. Shirley, kept a collection of concept books that children could use to get their own ideas or to learn a new concept. Students in her class had favorite concept books and used them as models for their own books. Some of the favorites were large books to illustrate the idea of big and miniature books to illustrate the concept of small. Other favorite books were pop-up books and peek-a-boo books, where the children had to guess the concept before they could see the entire picture. Concept books build vocabulary, give second language children an activity they can do with minimal English, and create opportunities for successful participation in classroom activities.

Peek-A-Boo Stories and Riddle Books. Another effective activity for second language learners, peek-a-boo stories, are excellent for beginning level writers. Based on Janet and Allan Ahlberg's story *Peek-A-Boo!* (Ahlberg & Ahlberg, 1981), the stories allow young children to become actively involved in a nonthreatening "writing" activity. *Peek-A-Boo!* involves a repeated refrain: "Here's a little baby/ One, two, three/ Stands in his crib/ What does he see?" The page on the opposite side from the refrain contains a 3-inch-diameter hole, revealing only part of the picture on the next page. Beneath the hole is the phrase "Peek-a-boo!" When the page is turned, the entire picture is revealed, permitting the child to see whether his or her guess was correct. Children can use the repeated refrain and the *Peek-A-Boo* page to create their own first books. They write their own repeated refrain and create a page with the hole and peek-a-boo. On the following page, they can either draw their own pictures for others to guess, or they can cut pictures out of magazines to create their own book. Children then label the picture with a word, phrase, or sentence that describes the hidden picture. One child, Laura, created the following phrase: "Here's little Laura/ One, two, three/ Watching a movie? What does she see?" Behind the peek-a-boo window, Laura had pasted a picture from her favorite movie and wrote the title of the movie below the picture: "Home Alone." The peek-a-boo books offer children early access to writing stories because they are visual and because they contain repeated refrains which provide a simple pattern to build upon. Children love these easily shared stories that involve them in oral discussions of their writing. For some children, the rhyming and peek-a-boo routine become like a mantra that they will repeat for days at a time. Peek-a-boo stories prepare children for future composing and sharing activities.

Riddle books are an extension of the peek-a-boo books but adapted for older learners. Using the same format, with riddle books students create a word riddle beneath the cut out opening on the page and ask others to guess what is partially hidden. On the next page, the full picture is revealed and labeled appropriately.

Patterned Poems. Patterned poems are sentence-level scaffolds that make use of repeated phrases; refrains; and, sometimes, rhymes. The predictable patterns allow beginning writers to become immediately involved in a literacy event. One excellent resource for sentence-level writing scaffolds is Kenneth Koch's *Wishes, Lies and Dreams: Teaching Children to Write Poetry* (Koch, 1970). Full of sentence patterns that serve as springboards for writing, the book contains delightful poems written by Koch's multilingual students. Typically, children first write their own poems based on the patterns, sharing them with one another in peer response groups and in classroom publications. Two Spanish-speaking ESL second-graders with whom we worked created the following poems using the sentence patterns "I used to be. . . but now I am. . ." and "I am the one who . . ." The repetition of the pattern lends a poetic quality to the full piece of writing.

JUAN: I used to be a baby.
But now I am really big.
I used to be a karate ninja.
But now I am an orange belt.

CHABELA: I am the one who like my teacher.
I am the one who gots new shoes.
I am the one who take care the baby.
I am the one who plays on the swings.

To supplement poetry writing and reading, many teachers also introduce children to predictable literature that contains the same types of patterns and predictable features of Koch's poems. After hearing a story several times, children use pattern books as models for creating, publishing, and sharing books. Typically, they use the given patterns several times before they are ready to experiment with their own patterns and poems. Thus, the pattern offers a scaffold that students abandon naturally when no longer needed. Patterns like Koch's and pattern books offer easy and almost instant success to children's first attempts at writing in their second language.

From Personal Journals to Dialogue Journals to Buddy Journals

You will want to develop fluency in your beginning writers as a first priority. Fluency, the ability to get words down on a page easily, can only come with practice. Another word that is integrally related to fluency is automaticity (LaBerge & Samuels, 1976). Automaticity is the ability to engage in a complex activity without having to concentrate on each part of it. For example, when you first started learning how to drive a car, you had to concentrate on the steering, on the brakes, on making appropriate signals, and, perhaps, on using a clutch. At first this was difficult, but, with practice, you began coordinating all of these driving activities at once without having to concentrate on them. Writing and reading work in a similar way. For example, one child might first concentrate on making the letters, working laboriously just to write his or her own name. Only later will he or she go on to writing words and phrases. Other learners aim at getting a lot of "writing" on the page, but it will not as yet conform to conventional script.

Young beginning writers approach the task in different ways, however. One kindergartner we know, for example, filled an entire half page with carefully written scribbles. When asked what his writing was about, he replied that he did not know and returned with great sobriety to his task. We asked him two more times, with the same response, until he explained: "I won't know what I wrote about until I draw my picture." At that point, he created a fine drawing of a boy playing soccer. Writing does indeed involve the coordination of many resources, and the writing process helps students take one step at a time so that they are not overwhelmed by the task.

One of the most popular ways teachers help children develop fluency is through extensive prewriting activities, one of the most powerful being journal writing. By writing in journals daily, children develop fluency and generate ideas on which they might elaborate later. One friend of ours, who has used journals

Keeping daily journals helps students develop confidence and fluency in conveying their ideas in writing.

successfully for a long time, told us about a field trip she and her class took. The children were to take notes in their journals; one fourth-grader was overheard saying to another: "Don't look. Don't look. She'll make you write about it!" Unlike these two students, most children find journal writing nonthreatening and fun. In this section, we discuss ways in which children may use journals for developing their ideas, for sharing their thoughts and feelings, and for thinking about ideas discussed in the classroom or occurrences outside the classroom.

Personal Journals. The first type of journal you may wish to share with children is a personal journal in which the children get used to writing their private thoughts. When these journals are used, you do not comment on them unless the child asks you to do so. The children learn that the journals are for their own personal and private ideas. We recommend that you ask children to write in their journals three or four times a week at a regular time in the day. Some teachers ask children to write in their journals at the end of the day, others like them to write after lunch time or after a reading period. Whatever you decide, set a regular time aside for journals so the children come to expect and anticipate journal writing. Students can construct their individual journals by folding pieces of paper in half and decorating the cover.

Dialogue Journals. When children become accustomed to writing in their personal journal, you may want to move toward dialogue journals. First, explain dialogue journals to children (Kreeft, 1984). Tell them that they can continue to write about the same topics and ideas as in personal journals but that the difference will be that you will respond to their writing regularly. Make sure you explain that you may not be able to respond to everything they write, but if they have something special to which they want you to respond, they can mark it with a colored marker. In your responses, respond to the content, not the form, of the writing. The purpose of interactive journals is to develop fluency and authentic conversation on paper. Moreover, you are making the children's writing functional and purposeful by replying to the children and elaborating on what they have said, in the same way that parents scaffold what children say to them in early oral communication. It is only polite to respond to what people say and not correct how they say it. Similarly, in journals, concentrate on positive things you can say—encourage students to continue writing in their journals, but also let them know that some language or topics may be inappropriate for their journals if that is how you feel. If you respond positively to their journals, make suggestions about what they might write about when they have difficulty developing ideas, and encourage them continually, your children will look forward to writing in their journals and will look forward to your responses. Dialogue journals help develop fluency because they are meaningful to the children, because they are responded to, and because they give children the freedom to concentrate on what they are saying rather than on how they are saying it. Journals also help children generate topics about which they may write more extensively later. Table 3.4 lists some other types of journals you may be interested in trying.

Buddy Journals. A buddy journal is a written conversation between two students (Bromley, 1989). Buddy journals are a natural extension of personal and dialogue journals. They involve children in meaningful, self-selected dialogues about issues that concern them. Moreover, they give them the immediate feedback they require for growth as well as a real audience and purpose for their writing. After modeling responses in dialogue journals, you can introduce buddy journals to students by explaining that they will be responding to one another instead of to you. Next, assign pairs to work with one another explaining that they will have an opportunity to work with many other partners throughout the year. You might also give children guidelines for responding to the writing in the journals. Let students see that it is important to be helpful to conversation partners in the journals. You might also ask children to brainstorm potential topics to write about in their journals. Place these topics on the board and suggest that they can write about anything going on in the classroom or anything else they might want to share with one another. Two third-graders might write to one another in buddy journals while reading *Harold and the Purple Crayon* (Johnson, 1955).

JOSEPH: I like the crayon magic and how he color thing.

JIMMY: And the pies and things.

JOSEPH: There's a ''Harold and Circus'' book to read.

TABLE 3.4 Types of Journals

Journal	Purpose	Procedure
Learning log	Helps students develop sense of direction and success in the class; helps teacher evaluate student's progress; helps student articulate what is learned and ask questions for self-assessment.	After certain lessons each day you ask students to keep a daily log of their knowledge or confusions or any elaborations they may wish to make relating to the topics discussed in class. Journal is private.
Buddy journals	Students get used to the idea of writing each day; writing becomes a functional and meaningful activity, with almost immediate audience.	Students write and respond to one another about classroom topics and other topics; response is to content and not form of the message; often modeled by teacher in dialogue journal first.
Dialogue journals	Makes writing purposeful in school; gives children audience for their writing and models how to respond to the writing of others.	Journal is used daily or often; teacher responds to content or to something the child has highlighted for the teacher; writing is used as communication.
Project journals	To assist students with preparing for a project in English, science, etc; students take notes of plants growing in science in preparation for a report; they take notes of conversations in preparation for story they might write.	Students keep journal with a specific task in mind: plans for writing a story; notes for a social science paper; measurement for a math project.

JIMMY: Yeah, it has purple coloring.

JOSEPH: Let read it.

Journal writing is a valuable activity for second language children because it involves real and purposeful dialogue and because it is nonthreatening—it will not be corrected or graded. Finally, because journals build on childrens' oral interactions and provide a real audience, children see writing as a meaningful activity, one worth the extra effort it may require of them.

Improvisational Sign Language

Using a dictated story or a story children already know such as *Goldilocks and the Three Bears* or *The Parsley Girl,* children can create gestures to represent characters and actions in the story. With her second language first-graders, Sheila Jordaine asks children to share stories with the whole class before creating their own. Children first dictated a brief story, which Sheila writes on the blackboard. "Jill had a pet frog. She brought it to school." Next, they determined the symbols for each of the words. Since Jill was a member of the class, all they had to do when her name was read was point to her. They decided that bringing their hands toward them with the palms upward would stand for "had," and they made an "A" with their hands followed by petting their heads for "pet." For the word "frog," they got out of their chairs and hopped like frogs. For "she," they simply pointed back at Jill, since "she" refers to "Jill." In this way, they naturally learn anaphoric references. When they finished with their symbols, Sheila read the story, pointing to the words, while the children dramatized the story with signs. The next day, the children decided to do a "real" story, *The Parsley Girl,* to act out in signs.

The signing activity provides children with several cues for understanding stories. If the story is in a big book, the children have the words and pictures in front of them. In addition, the visual dramatization cue for comprehension gives them more information for understanding the stories they are reading. Finally, the activity involves all the children in a meaningful and functional process aimed at comprehension. Children in Sheila's class ask for improvisational signing performances throughout the year, even after they no longer need the extra comprehension support.

Life Murals

Another activity that provides a scaffold for second language children is creating life murals. Using murals, children create drawings depicting significant events, people, and places in their lives and then write about them. For example, one child represented her family by drawing a house with people outside. In another picture she drew the inside of her own bedroom, a trifle messy, to show where she spent most of her time when she was home. She also included drawings of a church and school with her friends standing outside in the rain. She drew other pictures of important toys and animals and of her grandmother, who always read stories to her. When she finished her drawing, she explained what everything meant to her partner, and her partner did the same. Finally, she wrote about her life.

Life murals make writing simpler because they are based on very personal experience. Because they are visual, children can easily get ideas from looking at one another's pictures and hearing their stories. When children have completed their murals and stories, they read them to their partners. Life murals represent an excellent way to introduce children to writing, and the drawings scaffold children's beginning attempts to compose something beyond simple entries in a journal.

Clustering

Clustering assists writers with developing vocabulary and preparing for writing (Rico & Claggett, 1980). The cluster seen in Figure 3.5 illustrates different words a child thought of when preparing to write about an experience she had had. To create the cluster, Mai simply placed her name and the word "park" in the center of the circle and then quickly wrote all the other things that came to mind. She thought of different members of her family, of friends, and of a trip she took to an amusement park. When she completed her cluster, Mai shared it with members of her peer response group by telling them about how she got very wet on a log ride at the park. In fact, "they all got so wet that they had to buy teeshirts to change into something dry."

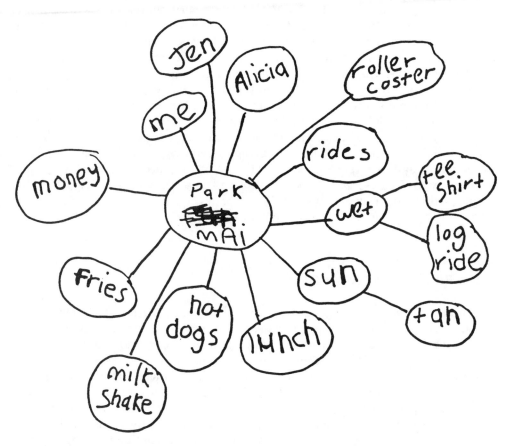

FIGURE 3.5 Student's Cluster about Trip to Amusement Park

Mai used the cluster as a prewriting strategy to begin thinking about her topic and to begin thinking about what she wanted to say. Clusters represent one of the first steps, along with buddy journals, where beginning level students begin to consider an audience for their writing. The cluster has several advantages: (1) it is easy to create and there are no rules for what can go into a cluster—students decide for themselves, (2) it fills the page and, therefore, assists psychologically in helping the student create a piece of writing, and (3) it is easy to share with others and, thus, helps the student create a story or experience orally. When second language children are ready to share their writing with their peers, clustering will help them do so.

Freewriting

Freewriting is a strategy developed by Peter Elbow (Elbow, 1973) in which writers let their words flow freely onto the page without concern for form, coherence, or correctness. In the same way that journals provide opportunities for daily writing, freewriting assists with fluency. Using freewriting, students write quickly to get their ideas down on paper. After freewriting for several minutes, students may then select a phrase or sentence they like and write about that for five minutes. They next select their favorite word, phrase, or sentence and write on it for five minutes. This process continues until students have discovered a topic or theme about which they might want to write. The freewriting assists children with developing fluency by asking them to concentrate on getting as many words on the page as possible without paying attention to correctness, and it also assists them with narrowing their topic. Through practice with freewriting, children can be freed from the constraints of having to get it right and can pay attention to generating and shaping ideas. Along with the use of journals, freewriting assists children with fluency, with automaticity, and with developing ideas. Thus, it prepares them to move to the intermediate level where they will pay more attention to refining and editing their ideas.

SUMMARY OF BEGINNING LEVEL WRITERS AND STRATEGIES

Beginning level second language learners can begin to participate in classroom literacy events upon entering the class, if you provide support. The scaffolds provided by picture books, symbol writing, concept books, and dialogue journals give students the assistance they need to participate in the classroom. These activities, shared in pairs and collaborative groups, are meaningful activities, not an assortment of skills that are abstract for students. Through these activities, second language learners grow from beginning writers to intermediate writers; from writers learning to generate ideas, to writers who shape ideas for different audiences and different purposes. They will move on from developing fluency to developing form in their writing and to revising and correcting their work. The strategies in the next section will help them develop into competent intermediate level writers.

DESCRIPTION OF INTERMEDIATE LEVEL WRITERS

While your main concern with beginning second language writers will be helping them to generate ideas and develop fluency, your main concern with intermediate writers will be to add form to fluidity in expression. That is, you will want your intermediate writers to begin developing a variety of sentence structures and organizational patterns, from narrative to letter, essay, and more. To do this, you may offer strategies that build upon the skills they learned as beginning level writers, while continuing to share good literature.

Intermediate level writers have developed a general knowledge of simple sentence types and corresponding capitalization and punctuation conventions. However, they need strategies to improve their sentences in quality, style, length, and variety. In addition, as their writing increases in length, they will need to develop organizational strategies such as paragraphing and logical ordering of ideas. At this point, spelling may be fairly standard, though, as yet, imperfect, especially if students are using more advanced vocabulary. In addition, some intermediate writers may rely too heavily on one or two sentence patterns as a conservative strategy for avoiding errors. You will want to encourage these writers to try new forms that will improve their writing and strengthen their general knowledge of English. Finally, intermediate writers may still make fairly frequent errors in punctuation, grammar, and usage. In fact, they may make more such errors than beginners because they are producing more writing—a positive sign of writing progress.

In summary, intermediate writers have developed fluency in their writing. They are able to produce a large number of words on the page, but they still need to work on organization of longer pieces of writing as well as on sentence variety, grammar, and spelling. The essay shown in Figure 3.6 provides an example of intermediate second language writing, representing the writer's best effort after working in his peer response group.

The Frist Time I saw Her

The frist time I saw her she was seven year's old and so was I. We bouth in frist grade. One day I want to take her out but my mom sed I was to young.

I try letter's and poetry so she would like me. In third grade she started to like me. In forth grade we want to see the movie avalanche at the Kabuki theater. We bought popcorn with our money. We bouth enjoy the movie because it tell you about people from diffrent contry's and how it was hard moveing to America.

I had a good time with her. I want to go out to a movie with her again.

Juan 4th grade

FIGURE 3.6 Juan's Story: The First Time I Saw Her

Juan has worked very hard on developing a topic about which he clearly cares very much. Based on the writing traits matrix, his writing exhibits elements of intermediate phase writing. Of particular note, he has organized his essay into a beginning, middle, and end. His teacher gave him special help with this. He writes with considerable fluency but retains errors in his final draft. For example, his writing exhibits minor problems with spelling and verb forms. He misspells "both" as "bouth" and "said" as "sed." However, his inventive spellings are phonetically accurate and, thus, more logical than conventional English spelling. He consistently uses an "'s" to pluralize "year's," "drink's," and "country's." He also keeps the "e" in "moveing." His spelling demonstrates substantial sophistication, requiring just a little more refinement to be perfect. A different type of error occurs with verb forms. Juan does not yet consistently use the conventional present and past tense verb markers, writing "tell" instead of "tells" or "enjoy" instead of "enjoyed." These tendencies are probably related to his developing English-language knowledge. In our experience, verb agreement of this kind represents grammatical refinement that develops late in second language acquisition. Juan needs daily opportunities to use the writing process approach. He has a lot to write about and enjoys sharing with his peers during response groups. He needs more opportunities to create finished pieces in which logical organization is needed to convey his message.

The next example illustrates an intermediate second language writer who is very close to moving into the advanced phase. The essay is a piece of expository writing, similar to the assignment required of Jorge that we shared with you earlier (p. 80). For the essay below, students were asked to compare ocean fish and bay fish based on information they could glean from cartoon-like drawings of the two kinds of fish.

> How the Ocean fish are alike to the Bay fish is that the Bay fish has same eyes like the Ocean fish. And they have same gulls as the Ocean fish. And they have same fins and 3 dots on its tail. And now how they are different is that the Bay fish have claws and the Ocean fish don't even have any teeth. An so the Ocean fish have big tails and the Bay fish have little tails. And the Ocean fish swim on the borrom of the ocean and the Bay fish wim at the top of the Bay. And the Ocean fish eat weed and the Bay fish eat little fish.
>
> Alberto, fifth grade

This essay, a first draft comparing and contrasting ocean and bay fish, exhibits thoughtful and logical sequencing. The topic has been thoroughly covered in a manner that is rather clear and concise. At the same time, the essay lacks variety in sentence patterns. In general, comparisons call for more complex sentence patterns, which Alberto was not able to produce. Instead, he uses simple state-ments, beginning new sentences with "And." To improve this essay, Alberto would benefit from a mini-lesson on sentence variety, which he could then apply in the revision process. In addition, the essay would be improved by an intro-duction and a conclusion, which Alberto could add rather easily during revision.

In the next section, we offer a variety of ideas to help improve the writing of intermediate second language writers working in collaborative groups.

STRATEGIES FOR INTERMEDIATE LEVEL WRITERS

Successful teachers of writing make sure that children have frequent opportunities to work on authentic tasks, often developing topics of their own choosing. In addition, they provide students a variety of opportunities to publish their writing in a variety of ways for a variety of purposes. Just as beginning writers work on meaningful writing tasks, so also must intermediate writers work on tasks that matter to them. Thus, the strategies we share with you are used within the context of meaningful, functional writing assignments. In most cases, your students will have selected the topics they are writing about, and they will share their writing with one another, as well as with you. Without this meaningfulness, the strategies below will become empty assignments, no better than isolated worksheets. However, when the strategies help students develop and shape their own ideas, they become functional for students.

Show and Not Tell

A telling sentence simply makes a flat generalization (Elbow, 1973). For example, a young writer might write: "The party was fun," or "She has a nice personality," or "The Thanksgiving dinner was delicious." None of these sentences provides any descriptive detail about what the writer wants to convey. Was the party fun because of, for example, the food, the games, or the people? We don't know. In contrast, showing sentences, which are easy to teach to intermediate writers, give specific information for the reader about a party, dinner, or person. It is a powerful strategy because children can learn to use it after a very brief introduction and a little practice. They can apply it to improve their writing almost immediately. The passage below, from Jean Shepherd (1971), illustrates the telling sentence: "In the morning, my father could be grumpy."

> He slumped unshaven, staring numbly at the kitchen table, until my mother set the coffee down in front of him. She did not speak. She knew that this was no time for conversation. He lit a Lucky, took a mighty drag and then sipped gingerly at the scalding black coffee, his eyes glaring malevolently ahead. My old man had begun every day of his life since the age of four with a Lucky and a cup of black coffee. He inhaled each one alternately, grimly, deeply. During this routine, it was sure suicide to goad him. (p. 130)

Showing sentences, such as the ones above, make actions specific by illustrating in detail exactly what happened. After you introduce the concept to children, ask them to identify showing sentences in literature they are reading. You can also assist them with the strategy by giving them telling sentences to rewrite with partners. The following examples below were provided by second language learners in Shirley Vance's class:

Telling sentence: The band was noisy.

Showing sentences: As the band played I felt the drummer was banging on my eardrums and the guitars yelled at me. I thought I would never hear right again.

One of the most powerful reasons to use the show and not tell strategy, in addition to its ease of learning, is that children are able to transfer this knowledge to their own writing. They are also able to use it when they are working with peer response groups. They can pick out telling sentences, and they can make suggestions for showing sentences in their own writing and in the writing of others. Giving your students a concrete strategy that immediately improves their writing empowers them and motivates them to learn more.

Sentence Combining

Sentence combining simply teaches students to combine shorter sentences into longer ones while keeping the same meaning. Researchers note that, as writers mature, they begin to write longer, more sophisticated sentences (Loban, 1968; O'Hare, 1973). Practice in sentence combining assists students in producing more mature writing. We suggest that second language students can benefit from sentence combining as well. You may use examples from students' own writing to assist them with sentence combining, or use sentence combining exercises found in books.

The essay on George Washington (Figure 3.7), by a fifth-grader in a class of language minority students, is typical of what some children do when they become comfortable with basic short sentences. Following the essay are revisions suggested by a peer response group.

The essay, of course, needs more work than just sentence combining, and the children who worked on it discovered that they needed to change the organization and to delete some of the information in order to complete their task. The following is a revised draft of the essay.

George Washington was the very first president and he had a wife named Martha. He was an orphan when he was young and was ill and very shy and polite. He was a hero in the revolutionary war and spent a horrible winter in Valley Forge. His face is carved on Mount Rushmore.

Fifth-grade group

There are, of course, many possible ways to combine the sentences. If you place some examples of sentence combining exercises on a transparency, children can try the exercises and share results. Through sentence combining, students learn to play with sentence variations and to choose the one that best suits their meaning. Moreover, children can apply the strategy to their own writing.

George Washington was the very first president. He had a wife name Martha. He had false teeth and wore a wig. His face is carved on Mount Rushmore. He died of pneumonia. He was an orphan at 15 years old. He was ill many times as a young man. He was very shy and polite. His wife Martha was a widow. He was a good leader. He was not selfish. He was a hero in the revolutionary war. He spent a horrible winter in Valley Forge.

Lettie, grade 5

FIGURE 3.7 Essay on George Washington, before Sentence Combining

An example of a teacher-made exercise is provided below.

Example:
1. The boy wanted something.
2. He wanted to buy tickets.
3. The tickets were for a rock group.
4. The rock group was his favorite.

Combination: The boy wanted to buy tickets for his favorite rock group.

Sentence Shortening

Sentence shortening, the opposite of sentence combining, assists students with changing wordy sentences into more concise sentences (Peterson, 1981). Children in the early phases of writing development often tend to write sentences that ramble on and on. You can give students long sentences to revise into shorter sentences that mean the same thing. Arturo Jackson introduces the idea to children in small groups by making a game out of sentence shortening. Using a transparency, he places a wordy sentence on the screen and challenges students to make the sentence shorter, while preserving the meaning of the original sentence. Children rewrite the sentence in their groups and then report back the number of words in the reduced version. The group that writes the shortest sentence with no loss of meaning wins. He also discusses the revised sentences with students so that they see that the shortest sentence is not always the best. A few examples of original student sentences and their revisions are shown below:

Original Student Sentence
That man who I know invented something that was entirely new. (Adapted from Peterson, 1981).

Student Group Revisions
That man I know invented something.

I know a man who is an inventor.

Original Sentence
The store over there across the street is owned by three sisters who live in the apartment above the store across the street.

Children's Revision
Three sisters live above the store across the street in an apartment.

There is an apartment above the store across the street. Three sisters live above it.

In the latter example, the student groups in the class determined that it was better to break the original sentence into two sentences. They felt that one-sentence versions didn't sound right. Arturo let their decision stand, and they learned that there are no rigid rules for rewriting sentences. They also learned to pay attention to the sound of sentences as well as the meaning. They are beginning to develop a sense of style in their writing.

Sentence Models

Sentence modeling, another strategy helpful to second language intermediate writers, is based on sentences from quality classroom reading materials or from writing produced by students themselves. You can introduce simple sentence models at first, followed by more complex models. Through the use of sentence models, students develop confidence in their ability to write with power and variety. Sentence models help intermediate level writers move from a few simple sentence structures to more complex structures, building the confidence that students need to make the transition from beginning to intermediate phases and beyond. The models below represent only a few examples of the kinds of sentences you may wish to share. When students are working alone or in peer response groups, they can try the models and immediately develop a more mature writing style.

A group of fourth-graders selected a model based on their favorite sentence in *Charlotte's Web* (White, 1952), consisting of a series of clauses that finish with a major statement (Chittenden, 1982). They then developed their own sentences from the model:

KIM: Leticia reaches in her purse, gets the lipstick, colors her lips, and gets the mirror to see how she look.

NG: Jan runs fast, opens the car door, getting in to go to the rock concert.

All twenty-six students in the class, with help from their groups, were able to write good examples of the model. Later, in their own writing, the model and different variations of the model began to appear. The children could show off with the sentence, knowing also that they could punctuate correctly. Finally, they had fun using the occasional pattern introduced by their teacher and began lifting patterns of sentences they liked from their own reading. Using sentence models gave the students confidence to experiment with other sentence models they found in their own reading. Moreover, it helped them begin to experiment and play with language.

Another more complex sentence model you may want to introduce to intermediate writers is the dependent clause in a pair or in a series. We have found that intermediate writers can do this one and gain a lot of confidence in their success. They also impress themselves and others with the model, which is particularly useful as a topic sentence in an essay or as a concluding sentence in an essay or narrative. It contains the following form (Waddell, Esch, Walker, 1972, p. 30):

If . . . , if . . . , if . . . , then *Subject Verb.*
Because . . . , because . . . , because . . . , *Subject Verb.*
When . . . , when . . . , when . . . , *Subject Verb.*

Student Examples of the Model
Because it is rainy, because it is cold, because I
feel lazy, I think I won't go to school today.

When I am home, when I am bored, when I have nobody to play with,
I watch television.

If I was rich, if I could buy anything, I would buy my parents a house.

In the last example, the writer did not want to use a series of three and saw that she could use a series of two if she wanted. Using sentence models, children begin to experiment with the sentences and learn that sentences can be organized in a variety of ways. Sentence models teach children a form they did not know before and also help them see that they have learned how to do something new. This gives them confidence in their ability to learn new English sentence structures. Using sentence models in their writing not only teaches children to develop variety in their sentences but also shows them how to punctuate.

Mapping

While show and not tell and sentence models work with form at the sentence level, mapping works with form at story levels or essay levels. A map is a visual/spatial representation of a composition or story and can assist children with shaping stories or essays they are writing (Boyle & Peregoy, 1991; Buckley & Boyle, 1981). You can introduce children to mapping by having them work in groups—later they can learn how to map by themselves. Jackie Chi introduces the strategy by giving students a familiar topic and asking them to brainstorm words or phrases for the topic. Below are some words children in a third-grade class brainstormed based on the word soap:

powder	slippery	colors	clean	sink
dirty	shiny	liquid	bathroom	kitchen
clothes	face	showers	bubbles	bar
facial	handsoap	bad taste	bath	dry

After children have generated the words for soap, Jackie asks them to think of words that go together (categories) and to place words under the category names like those below. She reminds them that they can add any new words to the list and that some of their words may not fit in any categories.

Type of Soap	*Places Used*	*Used For*
liquid	kitchen	showers
powder	bathrooms	baths
bar	machines	hands

FIGURE 3.8 Map on Soap Students Created When Introduced to Mapping

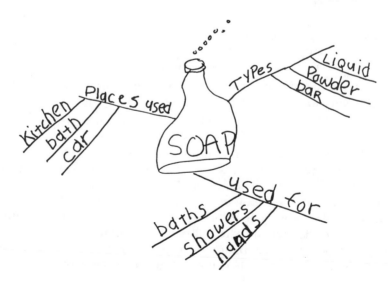

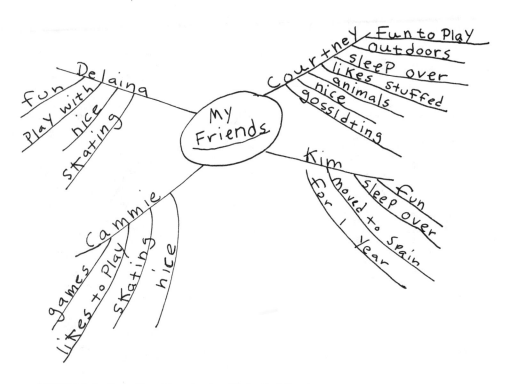

FIGURE 3.9 Prewriting Map about a Student's Friends

After they have placed their words into categories, Jackie asks students to use butcher paper and marking pens to make a map representing their words (Figure 3.8). She provides them with the simple structure in Figure 3.8 to start them out but asks them to be creative in developing maps. For example, they might want to draw pictures to illustrate their words. When each group has finished mapping, she has them share with one another. Later, she might ask children to map their own topics on a piece of paper and share them with one another. They would use the same process Jackie introduced to them—brainstorm, create categories, draw a map. When it is completed, they can use the map to write a story about themselves. Lisa, age 7, developed the map in Figure 3.9 in preparation for a piece about her friends.

The mapping procedure helps children generate ideas and think about how they might organize ideas before they begin to write. It helps them think about the content and form their story or essay will take and allows them to try out different ideas before they commit them to paper. Because mapping is less intimidating than writing a whole story or essay, children gain confidence in their ability to compose. The map and short paper in Figure 3.10 are by a student who usually struggled with writing but, with the help of the map and his response group, was able to turn in a paper that far exceeded anything he had written before. We present one of the five paragraphs he wrote.

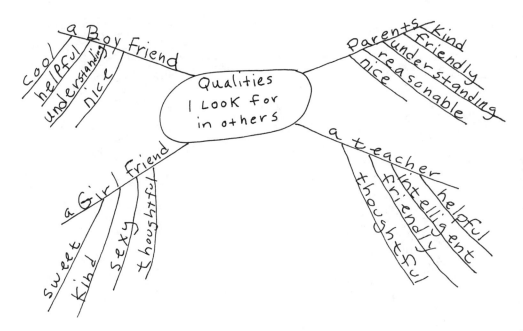

FIGURE 3.10   Prewriting Map Concerning Qualities Student Admires

This composition is about the way I feel about others. For instance, how I feel about my parents, girl friend, teachers and friend. Sertain kind of people make me sick. I don't like some people that just think that there so perfect, and so fine. I think that you have to look for alot of qualities in a parent. They have to be understanding because if your parents arent understanding you mit as well not call parents. and they must be loveing, thoughtful, and exspecialy helpful, they help you when your sick they help you when your in troble they help you ever day of your life. . . .

Keno, age 12

Summary of Intermediate Level Writing Strategies

Intermediate strategies help second language writers organize their thoughts on paper, develop specificity in expression, and utilize a variety of sentence patterns with conventional punctuation and grammar. Moreover, these strategies help students expand the array of genres they can use, from letters to stories to essays to poetry. As your second language students use the strategies, they will develop confidence and become motivated to work on revision. The strategies also guide students in evaluating the writing of others and making constructive suggestions in their peer response groups. Without specific "how to's," students will falter in response, as we learned in class one day. After peer response groups had not gone well in our third-grade class, we asked Joe to read his paper for class comment. When Joe finished his paper, Sarah raised her hand and commented:

"That's a good paper." When we asked her to be more specific, she elaborated: "That's a *really* good paper." If students are not provided specific strategies for revision, you might end up as Joe did that day: no farther ahead than if he had worked alone instead of with the group. On the other hand, if you explicitly teach children how to revise, you will give them the vocabulary to talk about writing, and you will model response to writing. The strategies we have presented have been proven to be successful with second language children and to provide them with a good start.

Assessing Second Language Writers' Progress

The best kind of assessment in any classroom comes from day-to-day informal observations of your students as they write and as they interact in their writing groups. Such informal assessment gives a much better picture of the student's overall achievement than any single paper, standardized test score, or other one-time performance sample. To accompany your observational insights, we suggest using portfolios and holistic scoring and involving students in evaluating their own writing. In this way, children become aware of their own progress. Remember that the best assessment of children's writing is going to be the writing itself, not tests concerning grammar, spelling, or punctuation, for instance. Finally, when students become evaluators of their own writing and know how and what they need to do to improve it, they will improve.

Portfolio Assessment. Portfolio assessment involves keeping students' writing in a special folder (Howard, 1990; Murphy & Smith, 1990). You will want to do this for several reasons. First, through the use of portfolios, you can assess students' growth by viewing all of their writing over the year and thereby assess your own teaching. Second, you can promote self-assessment in your students and motivate them to evaluate their own growth. Third, portfolio assessment motivates students to improve as they see their development throughout the year and helps them to see real growth when they compare what they wrote at the beginning of the year with what they accomplished by the end of the year. In summary, the keeping of writing portfolios assists students in seeing themselves as writers and assists you in evaluating your own program. Look at the two pieces of writing in Figures 3.11 and 3.12, which are separated by one-and-a-half years, and you can see that you would learn a great deal about Jorge's improvement as a writer.

FIGURE 3.11 Jorge's First Portfolio Sample: Writing about Fish

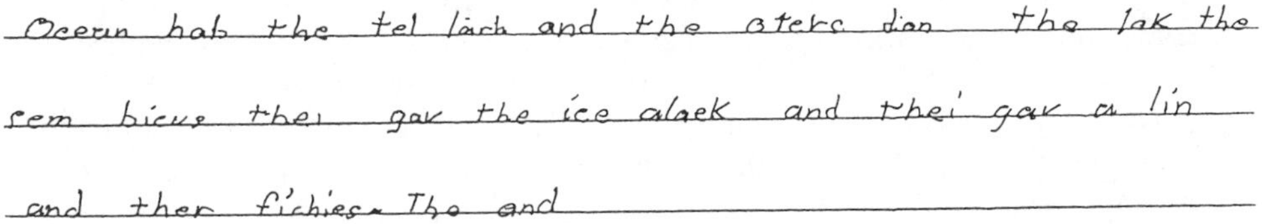
The fibis are not the sem bicus the ~~a~~ huane thet lih
Ocean hab the tel läch and the aterc dian the lak the
sem bicus thei gar the ice alaek and thei gar a lin
and ther fichies. The and

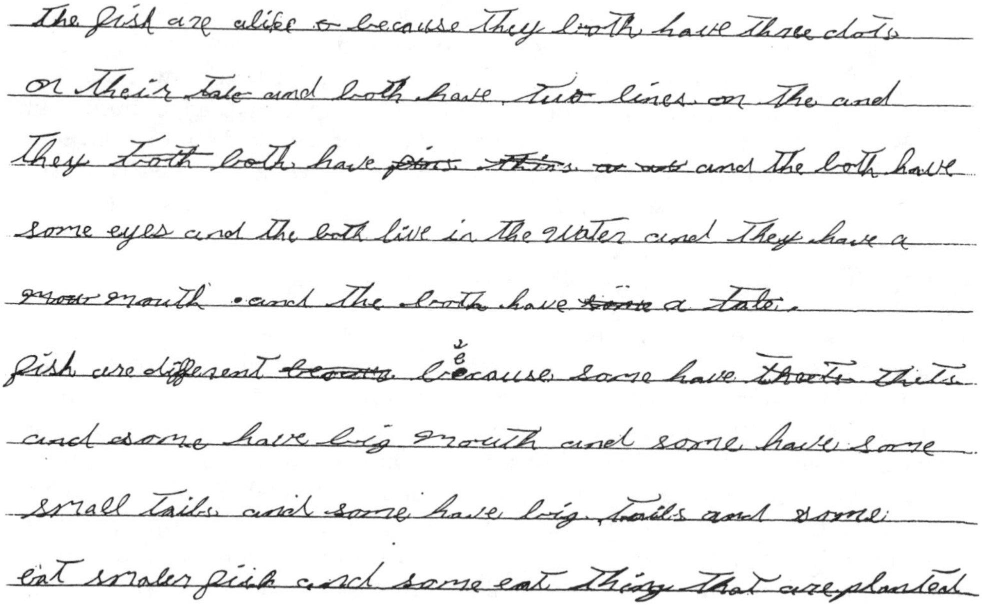
The fish are alike ~~o~~ because they both have three dots
on their tale and both have two lines on the and
they ~~troth~~ both have ~~pins~~ ~~thins~~ ~~or ws~~ and the both have
some eyes and the both live in the water and they have a
~~mow~~ mouth and the both have ~~some~~ a tale.
fish are different ~~becaus~~ because some have ~~throts~~ thits
and some have big mouth and some have some
small tails and some have big tails and some
eat smaler fish and some eat thing that are planted

FIGURE 3.12 Jorge's Writing about Fish: A Later Sample

Now imagine that you are Jorge's fourth-grade teacher and have received the essay in Figure 3.11 along with one he has just written for your class (Figure 3.12); both essays come from the same stimulus of a picture.

Clearly, the two papers might be viewed differently within the context of how far Jorge has advanced if they are found together in a portfolio. If you receive a piece of writing like Jorge's and can compare it with what he was doing last year, you can make certain decisions about what needs to be done next, about his strengths and weaknesses. You can also ask him to look at the two papers and to see his own advancement. Portfolios allow you to contextualize the student's advancement and better evaluate what is needed and what has been accomplished.

Earlier, in Figure 3.6, we shared a piece of writing by Juan (''The First Time I Saw Her . . .'') to use as an example of an intermediate writer. However, Juan's portfolio shows that he didn't write at the intermediate level when he entered the fourth grade. Below is an example of his writing in the second month of school; it will be followed by an example from the fourth month and the sixth month of school. Following the examples, we will discuss Juan's progress briefly.

Juan: Second Month Sample from Portfolio

To day it was ranning. why? The only men who can tell us is faster dan a speeding bullet. More bigger dan a penut smaller dan my hand. It middy mouse. Yes hes baaaack beeter dan ever. Faster dan ever.

He' parner jast like! But! more dumer dan middy mouse. Its supper Juan. Yes he's back more dumer dan ever. Middy mouse can't belive I he's parnter.

Juan: Fourth Month Sample from Portfolio

Dear Eney one

> To day I got up. I whast to, I took a shower. I help my brother get dress, and I got dresset too. My mom left me some money. It was five dollars in cash. I went to the story to buy my brother a pice of candey. We got on the bus we came to school and played. Her I am writing this for you.

P.S. See you later!!!

Juan: Sixth Month Writing from Portfolio

The First Time I Saw Her

The first time I saw her she was seven year's old and so was I. We bouth in first grade. One day I want to take her out but my mom sed I was to young.

> I try letter's and poetry so she would like me. In forth grade we want to see the movie Avalanche at the Kabuki theater. We bought popcorn, and drink's with our money. We both enjoy the movie because it tell you about people from different country's and how it was hard moveing to America.

> I had a good time with her. I want to go out to a movie with her a gain.

Juan, fourth grade

In the three examples, we can see Juan moving from a beginning to an intermediate level. We also see different levels of writing. In the first example, Juan uses the pattern from the Mighty Mouse cartoons to create his own pattern in writing. The pattern gives him support while he is still at a beginning level in English. In the second example, Juan writes about more mundane matters in mostly simple sentences. He makes fewer errors in his writing, but he is held back in expression by his limited English. In the third, only four months after the first sample, Juan is beginning to express himself well and in a variety of sentences. His English language ability has grown, and he shows this growth through writing. He also shares matters that are important to him, and he shares them with feeling. In a four-month period, he has moved from copied patterns, to familiar sentence models, to individual sentence structures. He writes more, he writes better, and he is well launched as a writer. Through portfolio assessment, Juan and his teacher can share his success and determine his next steps. These next steps will offer Juan more opportunities to write for different purposes and for different audiences. Moreover, he will be exposed to more sophisticated language in the stories he reads. All of these opportunities and more will assist him in becoming a better writer. If you ask Juan today what he wants to be, he will say, ''A writer.''

Students not only share portfolios with their teachers but also refer to them while working with their peers. When students have been working in peer response groups, they begin to develop questions to ask of others' writing as well as their own. As they look at their writing portfolios, they begin asking the same questions they ask of others in writing groups. What was I trying to say? Did

I accomplish what I wanted to? How would I change it? Some questions you might have students address in their own writing will reveal the strengths and weaknesses of your own program as well as the perceptions of your student writers. For example, you might ask them to think about one thing they like about a piece of writing. In contrast, you could also ask them to reflect upon one thing they did not like about their writing. Students' answers to these questions reveal the depth of their understanding and help you assist them with going beyond superficial responses to their writing such as finding two errors in a paper. Student self-evaluation is at the heart of portfolio assessment and assists you in determining what you need to do with your students.

Once students have collected a body of work in their portfolios, you can assist them with procedures for comparing their writing. Ask them to look over their writing and select what they think is the best piece of writing. In addition, ask them to select their worst piece of writing. Then, ask them to respond in writing to questions such as: Why did you select the piece? Why is it good or bad? If you decided to revise the piece, what specifically would you do with it? What have you learned about your writing by evaluating the pieces in your portfolio? What might you do differently when you write next as a result of viewing the writing in your portfolio?

Thinking and writing about the work in their portfolios helps students reflect on their writing and encourages them to share their thinking with others. Most importantly, perhaps, is the fact that students begin to see that some pieces in their portfolio are incomplete and that still others may be worthy of revisions for publication. Moreover, students tend to see writing as the development of ideas rather than the correcting of papers. Portfolio assessment helps students become reflective and self-evaluative writers. When this happens, they can use the revision and editing strategies they have learned to improve their writing and prepare it for sharing with others.

Holistic Scoring.   Holistic scoring refers to the evaluation of a piece of writing as a whole, rather than to separate aspects such as spelling, punctuation, grammar, style, or mechanics (Myers, 1980; White, 1985). When teachers assess a paper holistically, they read papers swiftly and rate them on a scale, often from 1 to 6, with 1 as the top and 6 as the bottom score. In the evaluation process, reader-evaluators agree on "anchor papers," or essays that typify each rating: 1–6. Usually, two readers evaluate each essay to increase the reliability of the score. Generally speaking, scores of 1 and 2 represent our category of *beginner,* scores of 3 and 4 represent the *intermediate* category, and scores of 5 and 6 are the *advanced* writers *with the particular group you are evaluating.* In the past, holistic assessment has been used to assess a school's or even a district's progress in writing, but you can teach your students holistic assessment and use it to help them evaluate their own writing.

Holistic scoring has several advantages over traditional methods of evaluating and grading papers in your classroom. First, you develop the anchor papers along with the students and then specify writing traits that make the papers low or high on the scoring scale. Secondly, holistic scoring helps students evaluate a paper based upon its communication of ideas rather than on correctness alone. Thirdly, holistic scoring gives children models for good writing and concentrates on what is good in writing rather than on what is wrong with a piece of writing. Children can apply these models and knowledge of good writing to their own composing, and they can evaluate their own writing holistically and think about what it needs to receive the highest evaluation. Finally, the holistic evaluation of papers by both you and your students will be very reliable. You will be surprised when students rate essays the same way you do, and you can use this evaluation process to talk about and improve your students' writing.

Procedures for Using Holistic Scoring in the Classroom.   We recommend using the following procedures for holistic assessment with your students based on Miles Myers' work (Myers, 1980). First, discuss with the students a topic they might want to write on and make sure all students can address the topic with ease. Topics such as "write a description of someone who is important to you," or "write about a favorite object you have," or "write about a person who has influenced you" are good topics because all the children can write about them. After children have selected the topic, give them a half hour or so to think about the topic and to take notes, brainstorm, or perform whatever prewriting strategy they use. Let them know that, on the following day, they will have time to write an essay on the topic. On the next day, give them time to review their prewriting notes and to think about the topic before you ask them to write.

It is a good idea to ask another teacher from another school to have students write on the same topic using the same procedures. Then, you can use those unfamiliar papers to discuss assessing and scoring the papers with your students. These papers can be used throughout the year to evaluate papers on other topics. Once you've received the papers, you can go through them and, using a scale of 1–6, select papers that you think clearly represent each score on the scale. Simply place the papers on a table and begin ranking them after reading them quickly. After you have done this with all the papers, you will want to select representative papers to become model or anchor papers that the students will use to score their own writing. Be careful that you do not select a high paper that is so perfect that no other student will be able to get a 6. Likewise do not select a low paper that is too low. Once you have selected the anchor papers, you are ready to take the papers to your students.

Give students the anchor papers and ask them to rank them from lowest to highest. If you have selected appropriate anchor papers, you will find that students will agree with your own ranking. Next, hand out copies of the other class's papers and ask students to rank them according to how they match up with the anchor papers. Tell them that their first decision is to decide whether the paper belongs in the upper half of papers (4–6) or in the lower half. After making that decision, they can decide where on the scale the paper lies. Have two students read and score each paper, with the first student placing the score on the back of the page where the second reader won't see it; later the scores will be combined to make a final score. If two readers give a paper a score two points or more apart, you will want to read it to determine the final score. In order to keep the scoring range consistent with the other papers scored by two people, you double the score you give to the paper, because your score takes the place of those of two readers. You might have students work in a group of four or five, with each group scoring all of the papers from the other class. When all the students are finished scoring, you can check to see that all groups gave similar scores to the same papers.

When students have scored all the papers, and you have shared the scores, you can ask students to perform a trait analysis on the papers. A trait analysis simply lists the qualities of a paper such as organization, vividness of description, originality of ideas, spelling, grammar, and punctuation. Before students perform this task, model doing a trait analysis with the whole class. Then, ask students to do a trait analysis of each score on the scale and share it with other groups. When you have completed this task, you can place model papers representing the scores in student portfolios and on the walls, where they can compare them with their own future papers.

Once students have ranked the papers and developed a trait analysis, they can score their own papers. In doing so, they can compare their paper on the same topic with the anchor papers and trait analysis they have developed. You will find that students can do this quite easily. Moreover they can use these same anchor papers with future papers to assess their writing. You will also find that the scores of your students will gradually begin to improve because students will have explicit ideas about improving their writing. In addition, students know which traits make a better paper, and they can apply revision strategies to move their papers to higher scores. Holistic scoring may take about five or more hours to set up and complete, but that time will be well spent because you will have students with explicit understandings of what makes a good paper. This understanding can be enhanced in their peer response groups throughout the year.

SUMMARY

We have presented research that indicates that second language writers are similar to first language writers in the ways they develop. Second language writers use their background knowledge to develop ideas and use the writing process in similar ways to first language learners. The writing process, consisting of pre-writing, drafting, revising, editing, and publishing, makes writing easier for second language writers because it breaks the writing task into manageable phases. Students, instead of having to coordinate their budding ideas with grammar, spelling, and sentence styles, can concentrate on one area at a time. Once they have gathered and organized their ideas, they can think more about correcting their writing.

In presenting the writing process, we offered examples of writing from beginning and intermediate second language writers to show what these children are able to do in writing and to illustrate how their writing reflects both written language knowledge and general second language development. We also showed the strategies that successful second language teachers often use with students who are beginning or intermediate writers. Finally, we suggested that you ask children to work in collaborative and cooperative peer response groups where they use language to share, discuss, and solve their writing problems.

Our view of teaching writing parallels our view of what parents do with developing their children's oral language. Parents whose child is first learning to speak do not criticize; instead they become jubilant in all their child's accomplishments and encourage and praise more production of language, however "imperfect." Similarly, you will want to encourage your students to express themselves in writing, viewing their first attempts, no matter at what level, as small miracles. With this encouragement, your students will gain confidence in their abilities to learn and will continue to try.

Small successes lead to larger successes and all success, when you and the students recognize it, leads to further success. Thus, assess and evaluate children's writing not in terms of comparing it to an essay by an accomplished expert; rather, view it in terms of what they can currently accomplish. Use portfolios to keep in touch with what children have accomplished and what they may need to know. Moreover, view the assistance you can give them in terms of where they are developmentally and how you can help them advance to the next level. Successful writing teachers build children's confidence, encourage them to continue to write, and point out what they have done well. They don't pay too much attention to correctness while children are learning to write because they don't want to create stuttering pencils.

SUGGESTIONS FOR FURTHER READING

Calkins, L. M. (1986). *The art of teaching writing.* Portsmouth, NH: Heinemann Educational Books.
   A thorough approach to teaching the writing process by a top researcher. Calkins presents practical strategies for developing children's writing at every stage of the writing process. The book discusses the writing process at different grade levels and makes excellent suggestions for setting writing workshops and for teaching mini-lessons. Although the book is not explicitly for ESL students, you can easily adapt the strategies for second language learners.

Frank, M. (1979). *If you're trying to teach kids how to write, you've gotta have this book.* Nashville, TN: Incentive Publications.
   This is one of the best books of writing activities and strategies for practical-minded teachers. Within the context of the writing process and the teaching of writing, Frank provides hundreds of creative activities and illustrates many strategies with children's writing.

Johnson, D. M., & Roen, D. H. (1989). *Richness in writing: Empowering ESL students.* White Plains, NY: Longman.
   Focuses on second language writers and their culture and contexts for writing. Clearly one of the best books out on ESL writing, the collection of articles by top teachers and educators of second language students contains sections dealing with the settings and contexts for writing, strategies such as peer revision and whole language, and the relationship between culture and second language writing.

Raimes, A. (1983). *Techniques in teaching writing.* Oxford: Oxford University Press.
    This book takes a different and more traditional view of teaching writing, one that is quite different from our own book. Nevertheless, the book has been used by second language instructors for many years and deserves to be read. One of the most valuable aspects of the book is the questions and answers section. In this section, Raimes answers questions on topics such as: What do I do with the errors second language students make? How will students work in groups? Who reads what students write? The book also contains specific strategies for teaching second language writers.

ACTIVITIES

1. Collect one student's writing over a period of several weeks. Collect from journals, notes, letters, stories, or any other type of writing the student may do during the period of collection. At the end of the collection period, compare the student's writing as it developed over time. You could categorize such things as the topics the student wrote about, the type of writing the student chose to do, the conditions under which the student did his or her best writing, and the kinds of development the student made in developing and organizing ideas, in grammar and spelling, or in any other aspect of writing that interests you. Report your findings to your classmates.

2. Observe classrooms where teachers approach the teaching of writing differently and evaluate the writing that takes place in those classrooms. For example, compare classrooms that use peer response groups and encourage students to select their own personal topics with a class where the teacher selects topics and spends a great deal of time correcting papers and returning them to students. What are some differences you find in the writing of the children in the two classes? What recommendations would you make to your classmates based on your observations?

3. Observe children working in peer response groups, and take notes on the kinds of questions they ask one another and on the kinds of responses that tend to lead to improved writing. Make a list to share with your class of questions and responses that seem to be most useful to young writers.

4. Observe how different teachers prepare students to work with the writing process. How is the writing process introduced? How are topics selected? How are students prepared to function in peer response groups? What is the importance of publishing children's writing in the classroom, and what are the varieties of ways teachers value and ask children to share their writing?

5. Collect writing from different grade levels so that you can compare and contrast how children's writing develops over time. For example, how does spelling develop from the first to the third grade? Do children naturally move from invented spelling to more standard spelling without a great deal of instruction, or do they need instruction in spelling in order to learn how to spell? Do children, as they develop in reading and writing, change sentence length and maturity naturally over time, or must these be assiduously taught in order for children to grow? Look at the writing you have collected from different grade levels and see what other categories you might evaluate.

CHAPTER 4

Reading and Literature Instruction for Second Language Learners

In this chapter, we discuss the reading process, compare first and second language reading, and provide suggestions for promoting second language reading through a variety of contexts and strategies emphasizing the use of multicultural literature. The following questions are discussed:

1. What does research tell us about children reading in a second language?
2. Which contexts and strategies can best assist second language readers?
3. What are the characteristics of beginning and intermediate level second language readers?
4. How is second language reading assessed?

INTRODUCTION

When Susan Jacobs was absent with the flu for a few days, her fifth-graders complained about the substitute. "She didn't know any of the rules," one child said. "She made me clean up the sinks, and it was Juan's turn," said Julia. Others complained loudly, "She didn't know anything!!!" Susan asked the children what they thought should be done about the situation. The children told her not to be absent. Knowing she couldn't guarantee that, she asked her students for suggestions to improve things if she should be absent again.

Glad to have been asked, the students eagerly suggested that the substitute needed guidelines about how the classroom functioned, and, since they knew the rules, they could write a substitute handbook. One group decided to take charge of the guidelines for cleaning the room. Another group said they would make a list of some of the general rules of behavior. "We have to talk 'bout mail boxes on our desks and that it's okay to pass notes except when something's going on." "But no airmail letters!!!" said Tina.

Thus charged, the children spent two weeks developing and refining the handbook, complete with classroom charts to make it easier for the substitute to know procedures, rules, and children's roles. Each group wrote one part of the handbook, revised it, and gave it to other groups for further clarification and revision. Finally, an editorial team edited the handbook and published it using a computer. They told Susan that all she had to do the next time she was ill was tell the substitute to read the handbook.

Because this happened early in the year, the children learned the classroom rules at a deeper level. Susan also allowed them to negotiate new rules that they thought would make the classroom work better. These new rules, added to the handbook, were to be followed by everyone, including Susan. Through the activity, children received validation for their own views on classroom management, learned the system more clearly, and became involved in a meaningful literacy event. Susan decided she would negotiate rules and create a substitute handbook with classes in the future.

You may wonder why we start a chapter on reading with an example of what seems to be a writing activity. We start this way because, although writing and reading are the focus of chapters 3 and 4, we view them as integrally related processes. When the children wrote their drafts for the handbook and considered the appropriateness for a substitute, for example, they became readers. When they shared revisions with one another, they became readers. When they shared with other groups and with the editorial team, they became readers. Though we concentrate on reading in this chapter, the emphasis will always be on reading and writing as interrelated processes working together to serve the larger purposes of communication and learning (Heath & Mangiola, 1991).

WHAT DOES RESEARCH TELL US
ABOUT READING IN A SECOND LANGUAGE?

Over the past decade, researchers have looked at how people process print when reading in English as a second language (Grabe, 1991; Carrell, Devine, & Eskey, 1988; Goodman & Goodman, 1978; Hudelson, 1981). They consistently find that the process is essentially the same whether reading English as the first or second language. In other words, both first and second language readers look at the page, sample the print, and use their knowledge of sound/symbol relationships, word order, grammar, and meaning to predict and confirm meaning. The linguistic systems involved in reading are commonly referred to as graphophonics (sound/symbol correspondences), syntax (word order), and semantics (meaning). In the process, readers make use of their background knowledge about the text's topic and structure along with their linguistic knowledge and reading strategies to arrive at an interpretation. If their interpretation does not make sense, they may go back and read again.

To see for yourself how you use graphic, syntactic, and semantic cues, try reading the passage below. We've made the task more difficult by deleting several words, and leaving a blank in their place. Think of the blank spaces as words you don't recognize. In some cases, we provide an initial letter or two as graphophonic cues.

Once upon a time, long ago and far away, there lived a gentle queen. It was the deepest and darkest 1 _____ winters, and every day the gentle queen would spend 2 h_____ afternoons sitting with her needlework at the only window in the 3 _____ . The castle window itself was framed in blackest ebony, 4 _____ anyone passing below could gaze upon the beautiful queen, 5 _____ as a picture, as she quietly worked at her 6 em _____ . One day, as she sat sewing, she pricked her finger 7 _____ her needle and three rich, red drops of blood 8 _____ upon the glistening snow below. At the sight of the red blood upon the 9 _____ snow, the gentle queen whispered: "Oh, how I wish 10 _____ a baby daughter with hair as black as ebony, 11 _____ as red as blood and skin as white as snow." And so it came 12 _____ pass that the queen gave birth to such a 13 _____ , whom she called Snow White.

Answers: 1. of; 2. her; 3. sunlight; 4. and; 5. pretty; 6. embroidery; 7. with; 8. fell; 9. white; 10. for; 11. lips; 12. to; 13. child.

Were you able to fill in all the blanks? What kinds of clues did you use to help you create a meaningful whole? Even though this passage was not titled, the very first lines provided an important clue: "Once upon a time" signals the fairy tale genre. As you read on, you needed to predict words for each blank that fit grammatically and made sense. In order to do so, you used your internalized knowledge of the syntax and semantics of English. Your implicit linguistic knowledge lets you make two essential judgments: Does it sound right, and does it make sense? In this way, you gradually created a tentative envisionment of the story. A slightly different approach would be to skim over the passage first to get a general idea of what it was about and then fill in the blanks. If you took this approach, you probably noticed that the story was *Snow White*. This information would have facilitated the task because you would have activated your background knowledge about this familiar tale. Even so, you would still make use of your knowledge of the graphophonics, syntax, and semantics of English to predict and confirm specific words to put in the blanks.

Second Language Readers

A reader who speaks English as a second language uses essentially the same process that you did to read the passage. Yet, the task is apt to be more difficult. Why? As you have probably predicted by now, the process may be the same, but the resources that first and second language readers bring to bear are different. The two most important differences are second language proficiency and background knowledge pertinent to the text being read. Take another look at the *Snow White* passage, and consider it from the point of view of an LEP student. Limitations in language proficiency will generally make it more difficult for a second language student to fill in the blanks. For example, you probably had no difficulty filling in <u>the</u> or <u>her</u> before <u>afternoons</u> in the second sentence. However, predicting words such as <u>a</u>, <u>the</u>, <u>in</u>, and <u>on</u> is often difficult for students who are still learning English. Formulaic expressions, such as "Once upon a time" and "pretty as a picture" may be unfamiliar and thus difficult to interpret fully. Thus, limitations in second language proficiency affect second language reading comprehension, causing it to be slower and more arduous.

Second Language Learners and Background Knowledge

Although second language proficiency affects reading comprehension, another powerful factor in the equation is the reader's prior knowledge of the topic of a passage or text. In the example above, you probably knew the story of Snow White. This knowledge made it easier for you to fill in the blanks. Fairy tales such as "Snow White" also follow a particular narrative structure, beginning with the formulaic opening "Once upon a time," moving through a predictable plot sequence, and ending with "They lived happily ever after." Thus, your experience with fairy tales provides you with background knowledge not only about the content of particular stories but also about common narrative forms and plot sequences. This background knowledge facilitates comprehension of written stories by helping you predict where the story is leading. To the extent that second language readers are less familiar with the topic and structure of a particular text, their comprehension task will be more or less difficult. By providing reading material on content familiar to your students, you can offset reading comprehension difficulties stemming from limited second language proficiency.

Second language students may thus experience reading difficulties related to limited second language proficiency and background knowledge that does not match the topic of a particular text. However, second language students who know how to read in their first language bring sophisticated literacy knowledge to the task of second language reading. They know that print represents a systematic code and carries meaning. If the student's home language uses a writing system similar to the English alphabet, then the transfer from the home language to English reading is fairly straightforward (Odlin, 1989). Students still need practice in English reading, but they have a substantial head start over students who are preliterate or who must learn the English alphabet from scratch.

Reading as a Psycholinguistic Guessing Game

Now try reading the passage below, observing your own process as you go along, to see if you can identify elements of the reading process we have discussed above (Buswell, 1922).

Providing students the opportunity to read in their primary language helps boost success in second language reading.

The boys' arrows were nearly gone so they sat down on the grass and stopped hunting. Over at the edge of the wood they saw Henry making a bow to a small girl who was coming down the road. She had tears in her dress and also tears in her eyes. She gave Henry a note which he brought over to the group of young hunters. Read to the boys, it caused great excitement. After a minute but rapid examination of their weapons, they ran down to the valley. Does were standing at the edge of the lake making an excellent target. (p. 22)

Because this is a passage that plays tricks with a reader's normal expectations of a text, we anticipate that you will have problems with certain words or phrases. First of all, you probably misread *bow*. We suggest that you did this because your experience with print has told you to use your background knowledge to predict what will come next. Since the text uses words such as *hunting* and *arrows,* your hunting schema has been activated, leading you to choose *bow* (rhyming with *so*) instead of bow (rhyming with *cow*). We also predict that you mispronounced the word *tear.* Your knowledge of syntax told you that the word should be pronounced *tear,* as in teardrop. English meaning is based largely on syntax or word order, leading to the difference in meaning, for example, between a *Venetian blind* and a *blind Venetian.* In some languages, such as Latin or Turkish, word order is not so important. When you came to the phrase ''Read to the boys . . .'' you had a fifty percent chance of getting it right, but may have pronounced it *read* (pronounced like *reed*) instead of *read* (as in *red*). We also suspect you may have mispronounced the word *minute* in "After a minute but . . ." because you are more familiar with the common phrase "after a minute" (as in 60 *minutes*). Finally, we guess that you hesitated but pronounced *Does* properly even though you've repeatedly seen the word at the beginning of a sentence pronounced as *does* (rhyming with *was*). No doubt you got this one right because you started adapting to the trickiness of the text and read more slowly and carefully.

The miscues or errors you made with the text further illustrate the notion of reading as a "psycholinguistic guessing game" (Goodman, 1967) in which you use your linguistic and background knowledge in interacting with print to make the best prediction you can about what you are reading. This aspect of background knowledge is particularly important when thinking of second language reading due to different background knowledge that the second language readers bring to a text.

The learning contexts we suggest for second language readers in this chapter are those in which students are hearing, reading, sharing, and responding to high-quality literature. Just as collaborative work and sharing play an important role in second language writing development, so also do they play a crucial role in second language reading development. These learning contexts will include the whole class listening to and reading fine literature, small groups of students responding to stories they read, pairs of students reading to each other, and individual students reading on their own. Just as process writing helps create a community of writers, shared reading experiences will further develop your students into a community of readers and writers.

We think of the ideal reader as an independent reader—one who responds to literature individually and shares responses with others; one who listens to other viewpoints and adjusts interpretations; and one who uses information in a literary text to support interpretations, but remains open to interpretations of others. An ideal environment for this kind of responder is one that gives children opportunities to work with each other in collaborative groups. To provide such an environment, we offer several different types of response groups that you may wish to try in your classroom.

WORKING IN LITERATURE RESPONSE GROUPS

Literature response groups are analogous to writing response groups as noted in Table 2.1. The main difference is that, in literature response groups, students discuss the work of published authors, while in writing response groups they discuss the work of their peers. Literature response groups consist of three to six students who have read a piece of literature and are ready to discuss it together. Just as we recommend that you model how to work in writing response groups, we also recommend that you model response to literature before asking children to respond in groups.

If you have modeled response to writing already, you can easily make the transition to reading response groups because the two are so similar. You may wish to remind students to respond to the content of the literature (i.e., to the problems faced by characters and situations in a narrative). They need to be flexible in their interpretations and tolerant of differing views. For example, they may find that there are several valid ways to interpret what motivates a character to act in a particular way.

At first, some teachers provide groups with response sheets to scaffold their initial response to literature. These sheets provide the children with model questions they may ask of any story. Moreover, the sheets help children begin to develop their own questions. Other teachers ask children to make up their own response sheets based on a story that the children are reading and share that sheet as a part of their own literature activity. One model response sheet developed by teachers is provided in Figure 4.1 below. It is meant to guide children's response and to prepare them for more independent interpretations of the literature they read.

The response sheet includes the following directions.

This response sheet is recommended for self-paced reading scheduled by students working in literature response groups. Expectations for your responses have been set by your class and teacher. Be ready to accept

FIGURE 4.1 Model Generic Response Sheet

1. If you did (or didn't) like the book, was there one event or character or aspect of the book that caused this reaction? What? Why?
2. Do your response group members share a common reaction to the book? What reactions are the same? What are different?
3. If you were faced with the same problems as the person in the book, would you have responded in a similar manner as the character or differently? Why?
4. How was the main character feeling when we first met him or her? Have you ever felt like the character?
5. How do you feel about the ways the main character behaves with other characters?
6. Did any of the characters remind you of anyone you have known? Yourself?
7. Do you think the author was trying to teach us something? If so, what?
8. Would you change the ending of the book? If so, how?
9. Which character would you like to have met? What would you want to say or do when you met the character?
10. Did your feelings change toward the character(s) as the story progressed? What made your feelings change?
11. If you could step inside the book and be part of the story, where would you enter, who would you be, what would you do, and how would these things change the story?
12. What things would be different in this story if it took place in a different period of time or a different place?

and respect the opinions of others in your group. You may expect the same from them with regard to your views. Your job is to help one another understand the story you are reading and to share your own views of the story. Remember there is no one single interpretation of any story you are reading; in fact there will usually be many different views of stories. You may begin your discussion with the questions listed on this sheet, but feel free to develop your own questions as your discussion proceeds.

Steps That Prepare Children to Work in Response Groups

Some of the steps teachers take in preparing children to work efficiently in response groups are as follows:

1. They read good literature to children daily and ask for individual responses informally.
2. They share with children their own responses to characters' dilemmas.
3. They help children connect the characters and situations to decisions and circumstances in their own lives.
4. They encourage different views of the literature, including views that differ from their own.
5. They share their enjoyment of stories and literary language.
6. They emphasize personal response to literature over theoretical literary analysis.
7. They teach students vocabulary to talk about literature.
8. They may provide students with a model response sheet to assist them at first.

After your students have discussed a story in their response group, you may invite them to extend their interpretations through dramatization, reader's theater, illustration, or some other recreation such as those in the following list. For example, Mary Donal sets up literature centers with materials for carrying out literature extension activities, including art materials for illustration, props for dramatization, pencils and colored markers for writing, and idea cards for further responses to particular stories.

Her students sign up for the centers at the beginning of the day. She wants all of her students eventually to try a variety of response extensions, including reader's theater, rewriting stories, and dramatization instead of illustrating the story every time. By providing centers, she guides her students while giving them choices.

When children begin to work independently with literature, they can choose from the following list to respond to it. Additionally, they may respond to the literature in their response journals, perhaps using the same questions they used in group work to focus their reading. By providing students with tools to respond to literature, we motivate them to read on their own.

Ways to Extend Response to Literature

Reader's theater	Improvisational signing
Illustrations	Response groups
Response sheets	Journals
Storytelling	Creating big books
Story maps	Developing timelines
Puppet shows	Rebus books
Egyptian hieroglyphs	Board games
Animated films	Collages
Making dioramas	Mobiles
Creating songs	Posters
Murals	Mock court trials
Book jackets	Dress up as a character
Create a radio script	Create a video

How Response to Literature Assists Second Language Learners

Literature response, whether involving the whole class, small groups, pairs, or individuals, offers second language learners the opportunity to enjoy good literature. The groups are informal and there are many chances for students to help each other negotiate the meaning of stories. As story discussion becomes routine, second language students will become familiar with ways of talking about literature, as will their first language counterparts. The oral discussions thus provide opportunities for "comprehensible input" (Krashen & Terrell, 1983) and negotiation of story meaning through social interaction. In many ways, first and second language students are on an equal footing in that they may all be new to the ways of responding to literature promoted in literature response groups.

Being able to read literature well enough to discuss it in groups, however, requires the development of both reading ability and knowledge of how to talk about it in terms of character, plot development, and so forth. In the next sections, therefore, we discuss strategies for helping students move ahead in reading ability, while developing their sense of literary elements.

DEVELOPMENTAL PHASES IN SECOND LANGUAGE READING

We view the developmental phases of second language readers as a continuum, and a fuzzy one at that. Thus, we don't see identifiable discrete stages, with crystal-clear categorization. In our experience, real children defy categorization. However, for the purposes of discussion, we offer two general categories to initially guide your teaching decisions: beginning and intermediate second language readers. For each category, we provide some general descriptions of learners at this phase and strategies to help them progress. As with writing, your task will be to help students move from one developmental phase to the next by challenging them to ever higher levels of performance. As we describe strategies for beginning and intermediate second language readers, keep in mind that only you know your own students. Thus, you are in the best position to combine our suggestions with your own analysis and intuition as you plan for your class. Therefore, feel free to use any strategy, beginning or intermediate, with any learner, according to your own judgment.

Beginning Level Readers: Characteristics and Strategies

In general, beginning level second language readers, like their first language counterparts, are just beginning to pull meaning from reading short texts. They may still be somewhat unfamiliar with the English alphabet and its unusual, if not unruly, spelling patterns. Chances are that they recognize a number of sight words, but they need more reading practice to develop a larger sight-word vocabulary. Most beginners can read simple texts such as predictable books through word recognition strategies, language knowledge, and memorization. However, they may have difficulty processing information beyond sentence-level texts. Regardless of their age, beginners need more experience with written language. If they have never read before in any language, they need frequent reminders of the many ways we use reading and writing for practical purposes and enjoyment. If they are literate in their first language, they probably have some idea of what reading and writing are for, but their literacy concepts should be broadened. In summary, beginners need to be immersed in reading and writing for readily perceived purposes. They need practice to solidify sound/symbol correspondences in English and to remind them that English reads from left to right, top to bottom. Finally, they need enough practice to move them toward being able to read simple texts independently.

Language-Experience Approach

The language-experience approach is one of the most frequently recommended approaches for beginning second language readers (Dixon & Nessel, 1983; Tinajero & Calderon, 1988). The beauty of this approach lies with the fact that the student provides the text, through dictation, that serves as the basis for reading instruction. As a result, language-experience reading is tailored to the learner's own interests, background knowledge, and language proficiency. As such, it builds on the linguistic, social, and cultural strengths and interests the student brings to school. Not least important, this approach works well for those older preliterate students who need age-appropriate texts dealing with topics that interest them.

The core of the language-experience approach builds upon stories dictated by individual children, small groups, or the whole class. As a rule, the stories are written down verbatim, after which students read them back. Students are usually able to read their own stories with minimal decoding skills because they already know the meaning. Through this approach, students learn to see reading and writing as purposeful communication about their own interests and concerns.

Moreover, they observe the process by which their own meanings, expressed orally, are put into print form. Important learning about the English writing system is thus conveyed indirectly, preparing students to write. Finally, when they read their own stories back, students are able to experience the success of independent reading. Lan Huong used the story *Swimmy* by Leo Lionni to relate her own version and then to read the story to her friends; she created a watercolor for the illustrated page of a book she planned to "write" using the language-experience approach (Figure 4.2).

While dictation itself provides a useful literacy event for beginners, the language-experience approach (cf. Stauffer, 1970; Tierney, Readence, & Dishner, 1990) provides systematic follow-up to solidify learning. For example, students may underline words in the story that are most meaningful to them, write them on a word card, and place them in their word bank in alphabetical order. In addition, students may cut their stories into sentence strips and rearrange them again to form a coherent piece. The language-experience approach thus bears resemblance to Ashton-Warner's key-word approach (Ashton-Warner, 1963) and to Freire's generative-theme approach (Freire, 1970; Freire & Macedo, 1987). All three approaches base early literacy instruction on the immediate concerns of students. Thus, as an introduction to reading, the students' own stories become

FIGURE 4.2 Lan Huong's *Swimmy* Story

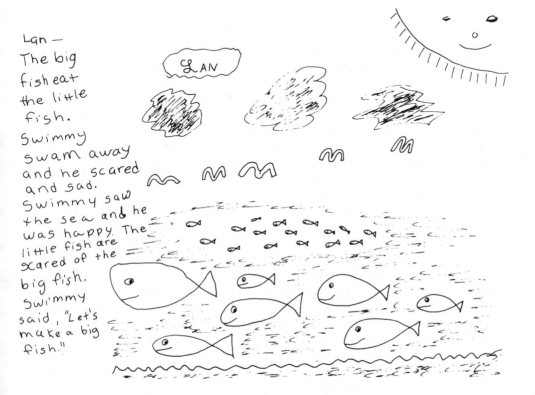

the core of instruction in composition, comprehension, word recognition skills, and general conventions of English print.

One first-grade teacher, Lydia Tanaka, sees language experience as an important part of her literature-based reading program. She reads daily to her students from big books and little books, she helps her students make their own big books based on predictable story patterns, and she responds to them weekly in their interactive journals. She also uses language-experience stories. The following example shows how.

After an earthquake the children had suffered through, Lydia decided to let the children talk about the tremor and share their feelings. She started by asking them to share in groups and brainstorm their ideas for a dictated story. She told them that they were going to create a newspaper about the earthquake, and that the front page story would be written by the entire class. When children finished brainstorming and talking in their groups, they began sharing with Lydia, who wrote their statements on the board.

CHABELA: I hear a sound first. Then it shook.

JOSE: Pictures in my house move and dishes too.

LISA: My dad looked at us. He said we better move. We got under tables.

KELLY: We turned on television.

JOE: We watched the world series and it happen.

SAMMY: Glasses broke.

Students continued in this manner until they had related the most important things about the earthquake. At this point Lydia read the group story to the children, pointing to each word as she read it. Next, the children read with her as she pointed to the words. Afterwards, she framed individual words and asked the children to read them. Then, she asked children to illustrate their story for the newspaper, working in pairs. The class would vote on one picture to be used for the front page, and the other pictures would be presented with short captions on other pages. When the groups had finished their pictures, Lydia asked them to copy the story or write their captions underneath, using large newsprint paper.

The next day, children read their story to one another and underlined words in the story they were sure they knew. These words were then copied on separate index cards to be filed alphabetically for each child. Periodically, the child's knowledge of the word bank was checked to make sure the student hadn't forgotten words once known.

Lydia's class used the original story and others to create their own newspaper about the earthquake. A computer was then used to publish the paper. Later, children read individual articles to one another and took the newspaper home to read articles to their parents and friends. The initial group sharing of a critical event allowed children to share their fears about the earthquake, helped them become involved in an initial literacy experience, showed them that the words they speak can be written, and gave them a newspaper with words they knew and could share with others.

Lydia doesn't always have events as dramatic as an earthquake, although a year later children wanted to talk about a war, but she uses whatever her students are interested in every year to develop language-experience stories. She is also quick to point out that these are not the only stories children will hear in her class. She will read aloud daily from quality literature, they will write in journals, and they will hear and act out many stories from the first day of school.

The text below was dictated by a first-grader. First she drew a picture, then started to write her story. After having some difficulty writing the story, Yukka asked a student teacher to write down what she wanted to say. We include Yukka's writing attempt along with the story she dictated.

YUKKA'S WRITING: I like horse becuss they hav lovely fer.

YUKKA'S DICTATION: They run fast. If I could have horse, he be brown.
I ride him in park. I ride him to school and I leave him on the bus.

As Yukka gains experience, her writing will be coordinated enough to keep up with her vivid imagination. Meanwhile, dictation empowers her by providing an adult scribe to get her ideas down on paper. Knowing this, Lydia will encourage Yukka to continue her own writing while, at the same time, taking her dictated stories from time to time. Language-experience stories provide but one important part of Lydia's scheme for assisting children with becoming literate in their second language. She feels that children must do much more than just read their own stories; therefore, she provides a print-rich environment full of literature to be heard and read throughout the day. This environment, supplemented with language-experience stories, will enhance the growth of children like Yukka throughout the year. By using children's experiences and language, Lydia scaffolds their learning to read and share experiences.

Literature-based Strategies for Beginning Level Readers

For beginning readers, you will need to create a classroom designed to assist them in making decisions about what to read and how to respond to their reading. This doesn't mean that you won't ever select a book for children; in fact, you may first want to select a book your entire class reads in order to model response to literature. Overall, your goal will be to assist children with making choices— about what they read, what they do with what they select, and with their own responses to literature. You will want them to share their reading with one another and to accept different responses to the same literature. However, you'll give beginning level readers a little more early direction to assure success with their first encounters with a text or story. We have selected several literature-based strategies, sequenced from simpler to more complex, that work well for beginning level readers. These strategies all fit the criteria for literacy scaffolds discussed earlier, by working with meaningful and functional communication found in whole texts, by making use of repetitive language and discourse patterns, and by supporting students' comprehension beyond what they could do alone. All of these strategies are meant to provide temporary support to beginning level students who will drop the scaffolds when they no longer need them.

Patterned Books.   Patterned books make use of repeated phrases, refrains, and sometimes rhymes. In addition, patterned books frequently contain pictures that may facilitate story comprehension (Heald-Taylor, 1987). The predictable patterns allow beginning second language readers to become immediately involved in a literacy event in their second language. Moreover, the use of patterned books meets the criteria for literacy scaffolds by modeling reading, by challenging students' current level of linguistic competence, and by assisting comprehension through the repetition of a simple sentence pattern.

One popular patterned book is Bill Martin's *Brown Bear, Brown Bear, What Do You See?* (Martin, 1967). The story, amply illustrated with colorful pictures, repeats a simple pattern children use to begin reading. In one first-grade class, for example, Rosario Canetti read *Brown Bear* to a group of nine children with varying English proficiencies. Having arrived recently from Mexico, four of the children were just beginning to learn English as a second language. After hearing the book read once through, the children responded to the second reading as follows:

ROSARIO READS: Brown Bear, Brown Bear, What do you see?
  [*Rosario turns the page and children see a picture of a red bird.*]
CHILDREN REPLY: Red bird!
ROSARIO READS: I see a red bird looking at me!
  Red bird, Red bird, what do you see?
  [*Rosario turns the page and children see a picture of a yellow duck.*]
CHILDREN REPLY: Yellow duck!
ROSARIO READS: I see a yellow duck looking at me.
  Yellow duck, Yellow duck, what do you see?
  [*Rosario turns the page and children see a picture of a blue horse.*]
CHILDREN REPLY: Blue horse lookin' at me.

The story continued in this way as other colorful characters were introduced: a green frog, a white dog, a black sheep, a goldfish, and finally pictures of children and a teacher. As a group, the children began to elaborate their responses to include the full pattern: "I see a _____ looking at me." A few children, however, just mouthed the words, participating in the story in a way that was comfortable for them with the support of the group.

After reading several patterned stories to the group, Rosario gives her students opportunities to read the books to each other during self-selection activity time. She also invites them to create their own big book versions of the story or to tell each other the story using flannel board pieces or their own drawings.

One group of Chinese first-graders in Audrey Fong's class created their own big book after hearing the patterned story of the "Meanies." In the story, the question repeated is: "What is it that Meanies do?" This question is followed by an answer repeated three times: "Meanies drink their bath water (in normal voice). Meanies drink their bath water (louder). Meanies drink their bath water (shouting in disgust)'' and the final phrase: ''That's what Meanies do.'' Using the pattern, the children created their own book: ''What is it that Goodies do?'' A part of the story is shown below without the illustrations the children drew:

What do Goodies drink?
     Goodies drink 7-up.
     Goodies drink 7-up.
     Goodies drink 7-up.
That's what Goodies drink.

In the book, Meanies eat old bubble gum. The children created their own phrase:

What do Goodies eat?
Goodies eat cake and ice cream.

Audrey Fong's kindergarten class

After becoming familiar with the story and language patterns in books like ''Meanies,'' children create their own illustrated books following the pattern. In the early stages of second language acquisition, students may use both their first and second languages. Later, as second language proficiency develops, they may focus their efforts increasingly on English. Patterned books' most important function is to offer immediate access to meaningful and enjoyable literacy experiences in the child's second language. That may explain why we've seen small second language children carry predictable books around with them all day like security blankets. A partial list of some other patterned books that have proved successful with second language learners include the following:

Allard, H. (1979). *Bumps in the Night.* Garden City, NY: Doubleday.

Barrett, J. (1970). *Animals Should Definitely Not Wear Clothing.* New York: Atheneum.

Brown, M. (1947). *Goodnight Moon.* New York: Harper & Row.

Carle, E. (1977). *The Grouchy Ladybug.* New York: Crowell.

Charlip, R. (1971). *Fortunately.* New York: Parents' Magazine Press.

de Paola, T. (1978). *Pancakes for Breakfast.* Orlando: Harcourt Brace Jovanovich.

Flack, M. (1932). *Ask Mr. Bear.* New York: Macmillan.

Galdone, P. (1975). *The Gingerbread Boy.* Boston: Houghton Mifflin.

Hoban, R. (1972). *Count and See.* New York: Macmillan.

Hutchins, P. (1968). *Rosie's Walk.* New York: Macmillan.

Keats, E. J. (1971). *Over in the Meadow.* New York: Scholastic Press.

Kent, J. (1971). *The Fat Cat.* New York: Scholastic Press.

Martin, B. (1967). *Brown Bear, Brown Bear, What Do You See?* New York: Holt, Rinehart and Winston.

Mayer, M. (1968). *If I Had* . . . . New York: Dial Press.

Polushkin, M. (1978). *Mother, Mother, I Want Another.* New York: Crown.

Sendak, M. (1962). *Chicken Soup with Rice.* New York: Scholastic Press.

Illustrating Stories or Poems.   Illustrating stories or poems they have read provides another way to develop second language children's response to literature. Students can make a published book of a short story, folktale, or poem and create pictures that illustrate the literature. This activity is used by Judy Bridges because all of the children, even those who speak little or no English, become involved in the illustrations. Thus, the activity immediately integrates a child into the collective activities of classroom response groups. The illustrations also assist the children in expressing and defining their own individual responses to the literature and prepares them for verbally sharing in response groups when their language is more developed. When children develop illustrations together, they help one another with a basic understanding by illustrating key events. Because they are shared easily, the illustrations provide a communication channel beyond words for assisting comprehension and response to stories.

Shared Reading with Big Books.   Big books, oversized books used to present literature to groups of children in an intimate and joyful way, simulate the kind of lap-reading that may take place in the children's homes (Holdaway, 1979). If children have been read to in this way, they move readily from lap-reading to large-group shared reading with big books. If they haven't been read to often at home, the large-book experience provides an interesting, nonthreatening introduction to reading. Because the books are oversized, you can share them with all the children in a more personal way than a smaller book would allow. As a result, all of the children become group participants in this delightful and engaging literacy event.

Shared books use predictable patterns that children memorize easily after two or three readings. Then they can "read" the books themselves or to each other, demonstrating a good deal of literacy knowledge. Finally, you can use oversized books to share stories and discussions with children; to point out certain words in the stories that might be difficult to decode; to help them become familiar with reading from left to right, top to bottom; and to assist them with recognizing oral and written versions of the same word.

To use shared reading with big books, you will need to develop a small collection of oversized books. Many are available commercially. You and your students may also create your own big-book versions of your favorite stories using large tagboard for each page and securing the page with ring clasps. Either way, select stories that are predictable at first, as these are well loved by all children and easy to understand and remember. When you introduce the story, be sure to read the title and the names of the author and illustrator. When your students create exact remakes of a story, they will include the author's name, too, but they will be named as the illustrators. If they write new episodes based on a

These first-graders put in a lot of effort preparing to present a choral reading of a favorite book to the fifth-graders. Their rehearsals had a real purpose, motivating them to perfect their reading through repetition and practice.

particular pattern, they will be credited with authorship. In this way, reading and writing are integrated, and important learning takes place.

When Thalia Jones introduces *Animals Should Definitely Not Wear Clothing,* for example, she starts by asking children to imagine what different animals would look like if they wore clothes. Sometimes, she starts by letting the children draw a picture of an animal wearing clothes to support their thinking and discussion and to help involve students who barely speak English. If necessary, she shows a picture or two of animals wearing clothes to help them start drawing. After this introduction to the topic and title, she reads the story using a pointer to underscore the words from left to right. She reads each word clearly and naturally and gives children time to look at the pictures of each outrageously bedecked animal. She leaves time for laughter, too, especially after their favorite picture, the one of the hen whose newly laid egg is caught in her trousers! When the story is over, Thalia allows children to read small-book versions of the story in pairs. At times, small groups listen to a tape of the story as each child follows along in the book. Finally, she invites children to make their own individual or group books based on the story. Children then make their own big books using pictures of animals wearing clothes, labeling each picture with a sentence that models the pattern in the original Big Book and often competing with one another to see who can create the most absurd illustration. As the weeks go by, Thalia occasionally rereads the big book and the children's own patterned books. All of the books are kept on hand in the classroom library, where they are available as choices during free reading.

Big books, full of rhythm, rhyme, and interesting sequences, motivate children to see reading as fun and interesting. If you are careful to select books with predictable patterns and imaginative language, your students will call for the stories again and again. Their initial engagements with print will be joyful and fun, motivating them to want to read more.

Directed-Listening-Thinking Activity (DL-TA).   The Directed-Listening-Thinking Activity (DL-TA) provides a scaffold by modeling how experienced readers make predictions as they read. Using DL-TA, you ask questions throughout a story, guiding children to make predictions and to monitor these predictions as subsequent text is provided (Boyle & Peregoy, 1990; Stauffer, 1975). Usually you ask more questions at the beginning of the activity, encouraging children to generate their own questions as the story proceeds. Eventually, students incorporate the DL-TA questioning procedure as a natural part of their independent reading.

Lisa Joiner uses DL-TA with her second language children early in the year as a part of the regular classroom time used for listening to stories; thus, the activity becomes a listening activity at first for her students. She likes to introduce the concept by using Crockett Johnson's magical crayon story *Harold's Circus* (Johnson, 1959). In the story, a little boy, Harold, encounters problems that he is able to solve by drawing something with his purple crayon. For example, he falls into deep water and draws a sailboat so that he can float away safely. Lisa makes overhead transparencies of the pages in the book in order to share it with the whole class. Before reading the book, she asks children to fold a large piece of paper in quarters and hands each child a purple crayon. Then, she asks them to think about what they might draw with the crayon if it were magic and could make anything they drew become real. After the children share their ideas, she introduces the book by saying:

> LISA: The story I'm going to read to you today is about a little boy named Harold, who has a magic purple crayon. Harold gets into little troubles at the circus and sometimes has to get out of trouble by drawing something with his magic crayon. What kinds of things do you think might happen to Harold at the circus?
>
> NG: Tiger eat him.
>
> JUAN: A elephant steps on him.
>
> TERRI: A snake swallow him.

The discussion goes on until most of the children have shared their own ideas. The children have fun seeing who can think of the worst thing and say "aaaah!!! ugghh!!!" after each new comment. The discussion ends with a fat lady sitting on Harold and everybody laughs. At this point Lisa quiets the children and introduces the DL-TA strategy.

LISA: I'm going to ask you to draw what you think Harold will draw to get out of trouble. So listen carefully and, when I ask you to, draw a picture of what you think Harold will draw next. [*She reads the text on her overhead pointing at the words as she says them:*]

LISA: One moonlit evening, mainly to prove to himself he could do it, Harold went for a walk on a tightrope. [*The picture shows Harold drawing a tightrope.*] It is easy to fall off a tightrope and Harold fell. By a stroke of luck, a comfortable-looking curve appeared beneath him. [*The picture shows Harold drawing a curve.*]

LISA: [*Speaking to the children.*] I want you to draw what you think that curve was. Remember this is about a circus. Draw your guess on the upper-left-hand corner of your folded paper.

The children draw their pictures and share them with partners before Lisa reads on and shows them the picture of what Harold drew—an elephant. Most of the children drew other things, so they laugh when they see that the curve Harold started to draw became the trunk of an elephant. Lisa continued to read the story, and the children got better at guessing and drawing pictures as they caught on to how the story worked.

Through DL-TA activities like this, Lisa's children become actively involved in understanding a story that is shown to them on the overhead. They learn how to make predictions when reading, finding out that, as they do so, they get better at understanding what they read. They also see that reading stories like this can be fun, and they frequently ask Lisa to read stories like it again. At first, they are only interested in "Harold" stories, but, later, they ask for other stories too. This activity is very sheltered in that pictures accompany the story, and the children themselves respond by drawing. In this way, they are involved through pictorial means in the higher-level processes of story comprehension. They also learn to use drawings on a folded piece of paper to make their own stories and to have others guess what might be on the next page. The stories become little mysteries that they share with one another.

During the DL-TA, Lisa avoids making judgments about students' predictions, so students learn that it is acceptable to make predictions that may be inaccurate. In addition, they learn that, by making predictions, even incorrect ones, they are more likely to get involved in the action and understand the story. Moreover, they learn that good readers may make inaccurate predictions but that they improve as the story progresses. Finally, the children have fun making predictions with stories, as active, rather than passive, involvement engages them in story comprehension and in predicting and monitoring for their understanding while reading.

Reader's Theater. Many teachers like to use reader's theater in their classrooms to assist children in responding to literature. Reader's theater is an excellent activity for beginning second language readers as well (Busching, 1981; Sloyer, 1982). Beginning readers read and dramatize a script from a story they have read. Intermediate readers, as we describe later, create their own scripts to read and dramatize. For beginning second language students, select stories that have several characters so that more children can participate. In addition, the stories should be somewhat brief and have a simple structure with a clear beginning, middle, and end. Many folk tales are excellent for introducing reader's theater because they meet all of these requirements. For example, a story such as "Cinderella" has clear examples of character roles and requires several different parts. In addition, it has a clear beginning, middle, and end, with the slipper fitting only Cinderella's foot. A side benefit of "Cinderella," as well as other fairy tales, is that variations exist among different cultures. This allows children to act out and understand different Cinderella stories. Some teachers like to use story maps (described in a later section) to assist students in determining the variations in different versions of a folk tale.

Once an appropriate story has been selected, you may make performance suggestions such as diction, dramatization, and expression. Because students have had a chance to rehearse and because they read from the script, they are able to read well during the performance. A good starter story for reader's theater is *Why Mosquitoes Buzz in People's Ears* (Aardema, 1975). The rhythm and rhyme of this delightful cumulative tale are compelling, and the moral of this African tale speaks to us all. Your students might want to create masks for the various animal parts in the story before they perform the script. Figure 4.3 shows part of such a script.

Once children have been introduced to the idea of reader's theater, they can act out other scripts of favorite folk tales or other stories. Let them select from the many stories that they have heard in your class or from a book or movie they know.

One third-grade class, after consulting with their teacher on their script, performed the story of "The Three Little Pigs" in front of the class. Later, the teacher told them that there was a book that presented the wolf's side of the story, *The True Story of the Three Little Pigs by A. Wolf* (Scieszka, 1989), and that maybe they would like to read that script. When they read the story, they were excited and presented it to the class.

When children do reader's theater, they have to analyze and comprehend the story at a deep level in order to present it again to the class, and they have to assess their understanding with others. They also have to determine the tone of voice for the various characters and orchestrate their reading performance into a coherent dramatic production. In short, they have to respond to the story,

FIGURE 4.3   Partial Reader's Theater Script

Adapted from Why Mosquitoes Buzz in People's Ears.

NARRATOR: One morning a mosquito saw an iguana at a waterhole.

MOSQUITO: Iguana, you will never believe what I saw yesterday.

IGUANA: Try me.

MOSQUITO: I saw a farmer digging yams that are almost as big as I am.

---

accept various interpretations from their peers, and offer an effective presentation to the class. Reader's theater gives power to children over story interpretation. Later, as these beginning level students become intermediate level students, they will write their own scripts from favorite stories.

Story Mapping.   Story mapping is an example of a scaffold because it helps children use story grammar or the basic structure of a story for comprehending and composing stories. For example, many children's stories have a basic skeletal structure consisting of a major character or two, a goal the character wishes to achieve, an obstacle that makes it difficult to achieve the goal, and a resolution of the conflict between the goal and the obstacle. In the words of novelist John Gardner, "In nearly all good fiction, the basic—all but inescapable—plot form is this: A central character wants something, goes after it despite opposition (perhaps including his own doubts), and so arrives at a win, lose or draw" (Gardner, 1983). The simple story map in Figure 4.4, which is based on this skeletal structure, provides a four-part sequence for students to fill in (Boyle & Peregoy, 1990; Schmidt, n.d.).

Using the story map, one group of five second-grade ESL learners produced several story maps after their teacher read "The Three Little Pigs" to them. The children's responses are reproduced in Figure 4.5. Since this was the children's first experience with story mapping, the teacher involved the whole group in creating the maps together. In the process, the children first chose the Big Bad Wolf as the character to map, producing "The Big Bad Wolf wanted to eat the pigs, but they boiled him in hot water, so the pigs lived happily ever after."

Another version produced by the group resulted in "The three little pigs wanted to build strong houses to be safe from the wolf, but the wolf blew the houses down, so they boiled the wolf in hot water." Through the process of mapping the story, the children were able to focus on the different perspectives of the wolf and the three little pigs. By the time they created the second map, they had arrived at the type of analysis for which the story map aims.

Students may use the simple story map to focus their attention on important parts of a story. When they use story mapping, it soon becomes evident to students that stories have several characters whose goals often conflict, leading to interest and intrigue as the plot develops. Even a story as simple as "The Three Little Pigs" can be mapped in a variety of ways following the story map model. By sharing and discussing their maps, children deepen their story comprehension and gain awareness of how stories are structured, which assists them with subsequent reading and writing. Once introduced, story maps help children not only to understand and to remember key elements of a story but also to create an outline for writing their own stories.

FIGURE 4.4 Story Map Skeleton

Someone	Wants	But	So

Someone	Wants	But	So
the wolf	wants to eat pigs	but they boil the wolf in water	so the pigs live happily ever after
the pigs	want strong houses to be safe from the wolf	but the wolf blows all but one house down	so the pigs boil him in water and live happily ever after

FIGURE 4.5   ESL Second-Graders' Map of "The Three Little Pigs"

Finally, the story maps provide a starting point for children to share their individual responses to the values and events they perceive in their transactions with the text (Rosenblatt, 1978, 1983, 1984). Through these transactions, second language learners can discuss various views and experiences presented in a story. Ultimately, these responses lie at the heart of literature study, and the maps provide a scaffolding for children's explorations and transactions with stories. A different kind of story map was used by Lianna for the story *Bedtime for Frances* (Hoban, 1960) and is shown in Figure 4.6.

FIGURE 4.6   Lianna's Map Based on *Bedtime for Frances*

Intermediate Level Readers: Characteristics and Strategies

Intermediate second language readers will come to you with a rather large sight vocabulary and the ability to comprehend various kinds of texts, such as stories, letters, and simply written news and magazine articles. Generally, they are apt to speak English well enough to negotiate meanings orally with their peers during literature response groups. They have a fair amount of automaticity in their reading so that they also are able to read with a degree of fluency. They read extended texts but have some difficulty dealing with texts that contain new vocabulary. They will generally need less assistance than beginning level students and less contextualization of lessons with visuals and other scaffolds. Nevertheless, you will want to provide them with the strategies used with beginning readers in addition to the new ones presented in this section.

Cognitive Mapping Strategies. Similar to a story map or a life map, a cognitive map is a graphic drawing summarizing a text. Intermediate level readers can use maps to assist them with comprehending and remembering what they have read, and they can use mapping as a prewriting strategy to generate a plan for their compositions (Boyle & Peregoy, 1991; Buckley & Boyle, 1981; Hanf, 1971; Ruddell & Boyle, 1989).

While story maps assist children by scaffolding comprehension and memory of a simple story such as a folk tale, cognitive maps also assist students with comprehension and memory of more complex stories containing many characters, settings, and plots. To introduce cognitive mapping for narrative texts, we suggest you follow procedures similar to those you used to introduce mapping as a prewriting strategy. Another good way is to draw a map on the chalkboard or use a mobile-like map such as the one in Figure 4.7 showing the characters, setting, and plot. Once students have a clear understanding of the categories, you can ask them to generate information from a story they have read to be placed in the map, or you may choose a story that all the children are familiar with to introduce mapping for the first time.

After practicing group mapping, children can begin to create individual maps to summarize information from their reading. The map shown in Figure 4.8 was developed by a fifth-grader on the folk tale "Beauty and the Beast." Many teachers use maps as a part of their individual reading programs. Because maps help students organize and remember stories, they prepare students to share in their literature response groups.

You will notice that the map in Figure 4.8 differs from the prototype used to introduce the concept to children. That is because children quickly move away from the prototype after they have a clear understanding of what the process is about. They make maps with concentric circles, triangles, ladders, and of different artistic shapes to illustrate concepts in their stories. Because mapping is easily learned and easily shared, because it is visual and spatial, second language teachers and their students find it a particularly useful strategy (Northcutt & Watson, 1986).

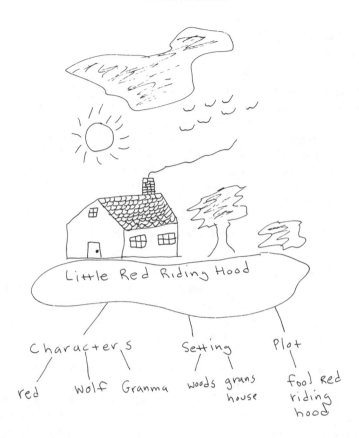

FIGURE 4.7   Mobile Map Illustrating Story Parts

Directed-Reading-Thinking Activity (DR-TA).   Directed Reading-Thinking Activity (DR-TA) is carried out in the same manner as the DL-TA (Stauffer, 1975). The only difference is that students read the text themselves silently after having made predictions during oral discussion. The activity is actually directed by the teacher, who invites predictions and confirmations on one portion of text at a time and then tells students how many paragraphs to read in order to find out whether their predictions were correct. This activity provides support at the beginning of a story to help readers get into the text. It also provides students with a model of active questioning during reading. Soon readers carry out the prediction process without teacher participation.

Leticia Palomino models DR-TA using the overhead projector and an index card to cover parts of a story. Uncovering the first paragraph, she asks students to read and predict what they think will happen next. She starts with simple stories such as "The Magician's Apprentice" below and teaches students to ask questions beginning with who, what, when, where, and why. Who are the characters in the story? What happens in the story; what are the problems faced by the characters? When does the story take place? Where does it take place? How will the problems be resolved? What will happen next? Below is a partial script of

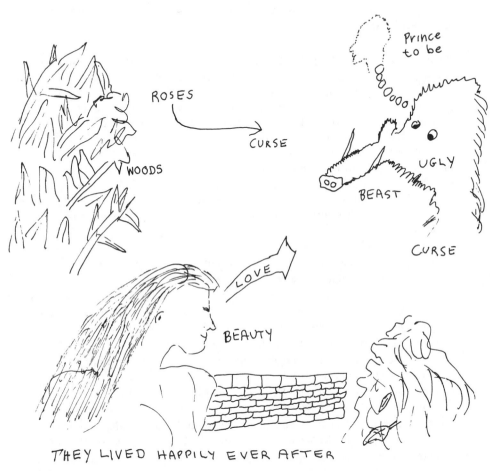

BEAUTY and the BEAST

ROSES

CURSE

WOODS

Prince to be

UGLY

BEAST

CURSE

LOVE

BEAUTY

THEY LIVED HAPPILY EVER AFTER

FIGURE 4.8 Map Student Created after Reading "Beauty and the Beast"

Ms. Palomino's students working with "The Magician's Apprentice." First read a part of the story that we have transcribed (Boyle, 1990) and then note the approach she uses to introduce the DR-TA strategy to her children.

The Magician's Apprentice

Once upon a time there was a little boy named Julio who wanted to be a magician. He read about magicians and watched magicians on television and bought magic tricks. When he became a magician, there was one trick he wanted to perform. He wanted to make a tiger disappear. One day a circus came to the boy's town. The great Magica the magician was with the circus. Magica was especially known for one trick. She could make a tiger disappear right in front of the audience.

The little boy could not wait to go to the circus. That night he had a dream. He dreamed that the magician would teach him the tiger trick. The next day he was very nervous about going to the circus.

Ms. Palomino began by reading the title and asking the children what they thought would happen in the story.

CHILDREN: Magic tricks! Juggling! Balls in air! Disappearing things! Rabbits get lost!

TEACHER: Do you know what an apprentice is? [*The children stared at one another and waited for the teacher.*] That's what they call somebody who helps a person who is very good at what they do. Somebody who has experience. Like a good plumber might have a helper or a carpenter has a helper. Helpers are people who are learning to do something, and they are called an apprentice. So what do you think a story about a magician's apprentice will be about?

CHILDREN: 'Bout man helps magicians? About people helping magicians.

TEACHER: I'm going to read parts of the story and ask you questions. When I do, you guess about what you think will happen next in the story. OK? [*She begins reading after the children nod their understanding. She uncovers only the sections of the story she is reading.*]

TEACHER: Once upon a time there was a little boy named Julio who wanted to be a magician. Class, what do you think will happen to Julio in this story?

CHILDREN: Helps a magician. Rabbits disappear.

TEACHER: Julio read about magicians and watched magicians on the television and bought magician tricks. When he became a magician, he thought, there will be one trick I will do. What trick do you think Julio will do?

CHILDREN: Elephant disappear! Ball floats. Card tricks.

TEACHER: He wanted to make a tiger disappear. One day a circus came to Julio's town. What do you think Julio will do when the circus comes to town?

CHILDREN: He'll go to the circus. He'll ride on a elephant. He'll see motorcycle riders. A magician. [*Other children seem to agree with the magician idea.*]

TEACHER: The great Magica the magician was with the circus. Magica was especially known for one trick. What trick do you think Magica was known for?

CHILDREN: Tricks. Tigers disappear. Tigers disappear!

TEACHER: She could make a tiger disappear right in front of the audience. [*Children laugh.*] The little boy could not wait to go to the circus. That night he had a dream. What did Julio dream, class?

CHILDREN: About the circus. About the magician. About tiger tricks.

TEACHER: He dreamed that the magician would teach him how to make a tiger disappear.

Ms. Palomino continued to read the story and the children's guesses became more enthusiastic and more accurate. Notice that she did not correct children if they predicted incorrectly. In fact, she encouraged all guesses and made a point of showing students that it really is not as important to guess correctly as it is to make plausible predictions and to check them against the text as new information appears. In this way, children gain experience in predicting and monitoring their comprehension as more mature readers do. After some practice with the DR-TA strategy, Ms. Palomino reminds children to make predictions in their independent and group reading activities. She starts their independent reading with stories that are amenable to making predictions and monitoring comprehension and then moves them to more difficult texts, where it may be a little more difficult to make predictions but even more important to do so.

Literature Response Journals.   Literature response journals are personal notebooks in which students write informal comments about the stories they are reading, including their feelings and reactions to characters, setting, plot, and other aspects of the story; they are an outgrowth of learning logs and other journals (Atwell 1984). You may wish to let students decide how often they will write in their journals, or you might set a schedule for them. The choice really depends on the purpose. For example, if several students are getting ready for a literature response group, you might suggest that students comment at the end of each chapter and finish the book by a certain date. On the other hand, if the response journal is based on voluntary, free reading, you may wish to leave the choice entirely up to the student. As a middle road, you might want to give students some general guidelines such as suggesting that they respond once a week or after reading complete chapters.

To help students get started in their response journals, it is useful to provide sample questions they can consider while they are reading, such as: "What do you like about the book or characters in the story?" "How do you feel about some of the decisions characters make in the book?" "Would you make different decisions?" "What do you think the main characters should do at a particular point in the story?" In other words, the questions you suggest to students should invite their personal reactions and responses to the experience of the story rather than aiming at literary analysis. That can come later. The purpose of the journal is to encourage dynamic, experiential, and authentic involvement with literature. The example below shows a few brief responses by Sammy, a third-grade intermediate level reader, to a story he selected to read individually.

> The story about "The Japanese Fairy Tale" about a very ugly man of long long ago. He ugly becuss he give his pretty to the princess. He loveing her very much to do that. I wouldn't do that I don think so.

You or your other students may respond to the journals. If you do, be sure to respond to the intent, not the grammatical form. You might ask an occasional question about the literature or a character in the story or what might happen next. Or you might share a similar response to a piece of literature you have read. Whatever your comment, encourage the students in their search for meaning in the literature. To manage your own responding time, you might ask students to highlight sections to which they want you to respond. In this way, literature response journals may become interactive. Some questions you can give students to assist them with responding to the stories they are reading include the following. These questions can be used for journals, response groups, or independent reading.

1. What would you tell characters in the story to do if you could talk to them?
2. What was the most exciting or interesting part of the story for you?
3. Why do you think the author wrote the story?
4. If you wrote this story, what parts would you change?
5. Would you recommend the story to others? Why?
6. What way would you like to respond to the story? Mural, map, summary, etc.?

Developing Scripts for Reader's Theater, Films, and Videos.   When second language students attain the intermediate level, they are ready to go beyond the reader's theater activities that asked them to read, interpret, and act out scripts provided for them. At this point, they can begin to develop and write scripts of their own, based on the stories they are reading. Developing their own scripts requires them to pick out the most important events in a story according to their own interpretations. In addition, they must identify the most important characters in a story as well as the conflicts and problems they face. Finally, students must interpret the resolution of these problems. After these choices are made, they need to determine the dialogue that they will use for their script. You may want to have the students create maps of the stories before they develop their scripts; the maps will help them make decisions about major events and the dialogue that goes with them. In order to create scripts, students must know a great deal about story structure. Thus, reader's theater at the intermediate level requires substantial sophistication.

Students must be sophisticated in their understanding of character motivation and conflict, and they must be able to show this sophistication in the scripts they write. They must have sophistication concerning the conflicts characters face and interpret these for their script. Finally, they need to understand the resolution of the story, its meaning and ramifications for various characters, and they must portray this in their script. Developing a reader's theater script provides students with a purposeful and meaningful activity for interpreting stories and involves them in activities that will enhance their comprehension of stories. Because they must negotiate meaning when developing scripts and because they act out the dramatic script, second language intermediate readers benefit from reader's theater, an activity that integrates oral and written language with a dramatic flair.

Adapting Stories into Plays and Scripts for Films and Videotapes.
Another way you can involve students in meaningful and motivational reading and writing activities is to have them adapt stories into scripts for making animated films or for interpreting stories from television. Animated films require children to develop a story first and then create a storyboard for the film. Storyboards are cartoon strips created by animators to determine the sequence of events both visually and with dialogue. Once they have developed the story, they create a storyboard for the film, somewhat like a cartoon drawing sequenced to tell the story. Once children have developed the storyboard, they are ready to create cut-out or clay characters to be moved on backgrounds for the animated effect. They then make the film, adding dialogue and music to the finished piece of animation. Just as reader's theater required students to interpret stories at a

sophisticated level and provided different channels for assisting students with negotiating meaning and developing scripts, so also does the animated storyboard and film provide built-in sheltering to communication.

Scripts for Interpreting Television Plays.   Another activity that provides children with "reading" a story and developing a script is television writing. This activity involves taping a short scene or two from television and asking students to create dialogue for the scene(s). The students may want to select and tape their own scene from favorite television shows for the script, but it also works if they don't know what the original scene is about. Students then watch the scene until they are familiar with it and create their own dialogue to fit with what is happening in the scene. Finally, students plug a microphone into a VCR, dub the dialogue into the tape, and then play it back for their classmates to see. The activity works best if you have more than one group working on the same scene. They then can have fun comparing different versions based on the same video scene. Because the scene is visual, it provides an additional channel of communication for LEP students. Perhaps most important, script development of this sort is highly motivating, and thus can promote functional and fun involvement in a multimedia literacy event.

ASSESSING SECOND LANGUAGE READERS' PROGRESS

Assessing second language reading is an ongoing process requiring a variety of information sources. Daily observations while students read in class provide one important source. The advantage of in-class observations is that they focus on students' reading in natural, routine situations involving authentic literacy tasks. These informal assessments will tell you much more than a myriad of standardized tests. Nothing takes the place of a perceptive and observant teacher who knows students and watches for their progress throughout the year. To augment your observations, you may wish to use individual assessment procedures from time to time to document student progress or to understand better a student experiencing reading problems. We describe several individual assessment procedures you can use, including miscue analysis and line-by-line reading procedures. However, your best reading assessment opportunities will grow out of day-to-day classroom observations and interactions with students as they negotiate meaning through print. A teacher who responds to the teachable moment easily takes the place of all the standardized tests and reading labs in the entire school district.

Assessing with Materials Children Bring to Class

One excellent and valid way to assess children's reading abilities is to ask them to bring something to the class to read. This casual approach to assessment is nonintimidating and affords you an opportunity to see what the child selects. Moreover, from this approach you might discover whether the child has anything to read at home or whether the child reads at all outside of the school environment.

When using this approach, make sure the child understands that she can bring anything she wants to school: a TV guide, a record label, a comic book, a magazine, or anything else. When they have brought in their selection, ask them to read it aloud. As they do so, evaluate their performance with their self-selected materials in comparison with materials you've heard them read in class. If the children do quite well with self-selected materials and poorly with school materials, you can begin to select materials more appropriate to their interests and level of reading efficiency. If they do poorly with self-selected materials, you will have a better idea of their proficiency and of how you can assist them with becoming better readers. Be careful not to make judgments too quickly when assessing children, however. Assess them with various materials from school and from home, and assess them informally each day to gain as much knowledge as possible before you draw conclusions about children's reading abilities.

Informal Assessment

Informal assessment procedures may be used with individual students to evaluate their reading. They differ from standardized tests in that they are individually administered to evaluate performance on specific reading tasks. If administered periodically during the year, they establish a profile of progress. We feel strongly that the informal assessment procedures presented here and elsewhere are the ones that will help you to determine how your students are doing. As noted above, we also suggest that the best informal procedure for assessing students' reading and writing is to watch children daily as they approach various reading, writing, and oral language tasks and accomplish authentic reading activities throughout the day. The informal procedures presented in the following sections, therefore, represent strategies for assessment that will augment your daily informal assessment in the classroom.

Miscue Analysis

Miscue analysis is a reading assessment tool that focuses on the reader's errors or "miscues" made during oral reading (Goodman, 1973; Goodman & Burke, 1972). Rather than carrying the onus of a terrible mistake, miscues provide a valuable source of information about how the reader is processing print. Some kinds of miscues actually indicate good comprehension. By analyzing a reader's miscues, it is possible to evaluate strengths and weaknesses, and thereby determine what kind of instructional assistance might be appropriate. By studying the kinds of deviations a reader tends to make, you can infer which reading strategies children use and which ones should be taught to help them improve. Because miscue analysis is based on oral reading, teachers need to separate oral pronunciation style and/or errors from reading errors. While the miscue analysis reveals the process of comprehending, a measure of overall comprehension of the text is also needed. This is accomplished by asking the reader for a summary, an oral retelling, of what was read.

Miscue Procedure (based on Goodman & Burke, 1972)

1. Select a child whose reading you wish to assess. Then choose a reading selection at about a grade level above what the reader usually deals with in class. The selection should be about 500 words in length and should be a meaningfully complete piece. Use your own judgment if you think the selection should be shorter.

2. Gather and prepare materials for tape-recording the oral reading.
   (a) a copy of the reading selection for the child (original or copy)
   (b) a tape recorder and blank tape
   (c) a copy of the selection for you to write on (triple-spaced)
   (d) notes on the selection that you will use to probe the child's spontaneous retelling of the piece (i.e., what you think are important parts to remember in terms of characters, plot, theme, setting)

3. Find a quiet place to record the session. Start by telling the child that you are going to tape-record his or her oral reading in order to help you learn more about how second-graders (or whatever) read.

4. Turn the machine on "record" and ask the child to read the passage out loud all the way through. Tell the child: "Here is something I want you to read for me out loud. I can't help you read it, though, so if you come to a word you don't know, try to figure it out and then read on. When you have finished reading, I will ask you to tell me all you can remember about what you have read." After the reading is finished, ask the child to tell you all he or she can remember. Then follow up with questions as needed to see if the child can retell all the parts you considered important.

5. At the end, let the child listen to his or her voice just for fun.

6. Later, listen to the tape to analyze the miscues.

The coding system in Figure 4.9 defines and illustrates how to mark miscues children may make while being informally assessed.

An example of one child's oral reading and miscues is shown in Figure 4.10. Juanita, an eight-year-old second-grader, was asked to read a passage and the questions following it. The passage (Karlsen, Madden, & Gardner, 1976) is marked according to the information in Figure 4.9.

After reading and answering the questions, Juanita retold the story. What can we learn from her reading and retelling? How can the miscue analysis combined with comprehension questions assist you in determining a reading program for Juanita? Let's analyze Juanita's performance and make some decisions for assisting her.

Interpreting Miscues. Juanita had trouble pronouncing the name *Barbara,* but this didn't impede meaning. She pronounces *lived* in a nonstandard way, but this "mispronunciation" is appropriate because this is how she pronounces the word in her oral language. Again, the "error" is not one that stands in the way of meaning. The same is true of her pronunciation of "lov—ed"; when she was asked what that meant, she answered: "It mean she like baseball." For Juanita

1. **Insertion:** the child inserts a word not in the text; place a caret where the insertion is made and write the inserted word above it.

   Example: The cat was *also*^ in the kitchen.

2. **Omission:** the child leaves a word out; circle the word the child omits.

   Example: Many people find it (difficult) to concentrate.

3. **Substitution:** the child replaces one word with another; place the child's substitution over the replaced word.

   Example: The *dog* doll was in the little girl's room.

4. **Word Supplied by Tester:** child can't get word and tester supplies it; put supplied word in parentheses.

   Example: Joe ran to *(school)* school.

5. **Word Missed then Corrected by Reader:** child says word wrong then immediately corrects it; place missed word above word and place a check by it.

   Example: The *rat ✓* cat is sleeping.

FIGURE 4.9 Recording Miscues

baseball and softball are the same thing. Juanita also pronounces the Spanish word "chocolate" (cho-coh-lah-tay) for chocolate; clearly she is understanding the passage. When we get to the last sentence, however, we find that she has trouble with words that do impede comprehension. She says "grace" for grass and "lunched," for laugh. In the retelling, it becomes clear that at that point she is confused. Nevertheless, even the miscue of "lunched" for laughed indicates a degree of comprehension up to this point. She matches the word laughed with a word "lunched" which matches laughed syntactically and is contextually appropriate given the previous information concerning lunch.

FIGURE 4.10 Miscue Analysis Passage

Bar-bar-Barbára lee-ved   *lov-éd*
Barbara lived in a big city. She loved to play softball in the park on Saturday morning. Every

cho-coh-lah-tay
Saturday for lunch, she'd buy a hot dog and chocolate milk. One day, Barbara asked her father

grace   *lunched ✓*
how chocolate milk was made. "The cows eat chocolate grass," her father said. Barbara laughed

Reet
and said, "Right!"

Based upon this analysis, we can see that Juanita has many strengths as a reader. First, she reads for meaning and tries to make sense of the passage. Second, she is able to pronounce most of the words according to her oral language equivalents. She misses a few words in the text but, with further reading, will probably learn these on her own because of her quest for meaning. Indeed, in the line-by-line discussion below, we will illustrate that very fact. Through the miscue analysis, we are able to gain a great deal of information about Juanita, information that will help us know whether she needs special assistance, whether she is reading for meaning or just for pronunciation, and whether we need to intervene in her progress as a reader.

Sometimes the information you obtain from a reader will be very different from the information about Juanita. For example, you might find a student who pronounces every word perfectly but does not comprehend the passage well—a student who seems to be "barking at print." Miscue analysis is a powerful tool for you to use with students to identify their reading behavior and develop an appropriate program for reading. The line-by-line approach below, when used along with miscue analysis, may add significant information that is not always available using miscue analysis alone.

Line-by-Line Protocol

One new procedure used in research to assess children's reading comprehension involves oral line-by-line reading (Fillmore & Kay, 1981; Langer, Bartolome, Vasquez, & Lucas, 1990; Peregoy, 1989; Wong Fillmore, Ammon, Ammon, DeLucchi, Jensen, McLaughlin, & Strong, 1983). The line-by-line procedure is administered individually. Passages are presented one line at a time, and the subject is asked for interpretations and predictions concerning the text after each line of reading. When the next line of text is presented, the child goes back and reads from the beginning of the text in order to have the whole of the text available to comprehend in spite of the interruptions caused by questioning. For analysis, miscues are marked and the child's comprehending strengths and weaknesses are noted on the basis of the line-by-line questions.

We conducted a line-by-line reading study (Peregoy, 1989) of six children learning English as a second language using the text below (Karlsen, Madden, and Gardner, 1976): two beginners, two intermediate, and two advanced speakers of English as a second language. Slashes indicate where the child paused for questioning of the line-by-line reading.

Pat noticed it at the last possible moment./ It was good that she had,/ because she had almost stepped on it./ It was the most beautiful shade of blue she had ever seen./ Pat decided that it must have fallen out of one of the nests in the tree above./ She bent down to look at it and saw that it had not broken./ "Oh good," she said. "Maybe if I leave it alone, it will still hatch."/

The text was presented to students in the following format:

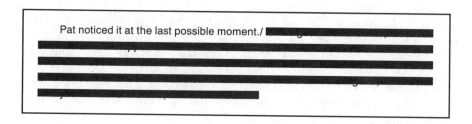

After the first line of text, subjects were asked for the meaning of the word *notice*. Next, students were asked, "What did Pat notice?" referring to *it* in the text. Following the line "it was good that she had," the children were asked, "It was good that she had *what?*" Following the line "it was the most beautiful shade of blue she had ever seen," subjects were asked about the meaning of *shade*. The procedure continues with the adult asking appropriate questions throughout the text to check children's ability to predict and comprehend text as well as to incorporate new information into their schema to assist in understanding the text.

Many subjects in our research were able to guess that the mystery topic of the passage was either a bluebird or a blue egg by the time they had read the line "it must have fallen out of one of the nests in the tree above." The word "hatch" generally gave the final clue that it was an egg that had fallen from the tree. However, other subjects did not know the meaning of the word "hatch" and were unable to get the full meaning of the passage. Thus, most children were successful to some degree using the procedure; we believe that the element of repetition in the procedure allows for a more sophisticated view of what a reader can do unassisted than a miscue alone would provide. We discuss these views below.

The analysis of the line-by-line reading shows examples where lack of vocabulary and lack of sensitivity to syntax lead subject in erroneous directions in constructing meaning of the passage for the beginning and intermediate English proficiency subjects. However, most subjects were able to arrive at the meaning of the text by the end of the passage. This was true even for the lowest English proficiency subject, who seemingly understood none of the passage until the third line, "because she had almost stepped on it." The fact that most subjects were able to answer the comprehension questions correctly on this passage is probably due (1) to the repetition in reading, since as each line was added the child read from the beginning of the passage, and (2) to the questioning involved in the line-by-line procedure. The line-by-line results also showed that low English proficiency subjects were able to successfully construct the meaning of the passage as a result of the questioning technique involved. This finding is a reminder that certain instructional techniques can facilitate reading comprehension and that there is an important difference between independent reading level and instructional reading level. Furthermore, our findings suggest that there are several advantages to asking children to repeat lines of reading and to adopt questioning practices modelled in the line-by-line procedure.

Of particular interest, we found that the repetition and questioning in the line-by-line procedure seemed to assist the lowest English proficiency subject in comprehending the text. As a result, they demonstrated higher reading comprehension than they would have if they had read the entire text once as in traditional miscue analysis. When children had an opportunity to read passages and words over again, they often corrected miscues they hadn't noticed the first time they read. Indeed, we frequently found that children would mispronounce certain words the first three or four times and then say the word correctly on the fifth time. After doing so, they would add this new information to their understanding of the passage and would use the word correctly from that point on in the passage.

In addition to helping students correct word-level miscues, the line-by-line procedure allowed children to adjust their envisionment of passages they were reading by asking them to predict what would happen next and by allowing them to monitor that prediction. We found that, after using the procedure, children were able to read normal texts using the same kind of prediction and monitoring procedure. In doing so, they usually improved their comprehension of texts, which we measured by their ability to answer comprehension questions and by their retellings, which were more accurate and more elaborated. We feel that the line-by-line procedure adds a new and powerful addition to our ability to evaluate what children can really do in their reading.

Advantages of the Line-by-Line Procedure.   The line-by-line procedure has many advantages: (1) the repeated reading aspect allows the reader to correct aspects of word pronunciation that may have been missed on a first reading, (2) the questioning procedure assists students with comprehension by modeling a procedure that mature readers use, and (3) the procedure chunks text for the students and, thus, models another mature reading process. By combining miscue analysis with DR-TA-type procedures and repeated reading, the line-by-line procedure gives a deeper analysis of second language reading processes.

Child Self-Assessment

Throughout our book we have emphasized placing children in charge of their own learning. They are responsible for their own writing and work in writing response groups to shape their narratives. Similarly, they take charge of their reading literature in literature response group. Moreover, we shall see how children set purposes and monitor their comprehension in chapter 5, yet this kind of self-assessment has often been a missing element in the past. Now, however, there are many writers and researchers who build child self-assessment into their programs (Heath & Mangiola, 1991; Yochum & Miller, 1990).

You may be surprised at how much information children, even young children, can give you about their own reading abilities. They are often able to tell you the kinds of words that give them difficulty or the kinds of reading they find frustrating. We believe in asking children regularly about their interactions with any text they are reading. There are several advantages to this approach. First, children often know more than you or any test will reveal about their reading; you only need to ask them. Second, asking children can save you the time of using any elaborate methods to discover children's reading abilities. Finally, and, perhaps, most importantly, asking children about their own reading processes helps them become more aware of what they are doing and of what strategies or procedures work for them under what circumstances. For example, they may discover that they can read narrative texts rather quickly, but that they need to slow down with more complex expository text. They learn that one adjusts speed of reading and reading strategies according to the demands of the tasks. This metacognitive aspect of reading may be the best gift you can give them in their development as readers. We strongly recommend asking children first; by doing so you place them in charge of their own advancement without abrogating your own responsibilities.

SUMMARY

In chapter 4, we began with a description of the reading process of second language learners, emphasizing the interplay of linguistic knowledge, background knowledge, and reading strategies. We then provided a rationale for literature instruction, followed by specific contexts and strategies for implementing literature study with beginning and intermediate second language readers, using appropriate literature and other reading materials. We emphasize children selecting their own books and responding to these books in literature response groups. We also suggest a variety of ways in which students can legitimately respond to literature that go beyond the usual discussion of stories; activities that allow second language children to draw pictures that depict major themes and scenes in stories they are reading, that give them opportunities to dramatize stories in reader's theater or puppet shows. We emphasize variety in response to meet the needs of all children regardless of their language proficiency.

Finally, we described assessment procedures for second language reading development. Through using informal observations, portfolios, and line-by-line procedures you can become an expert "kidwatcher" and can assist children in making regular advancements in language and literacy (Goodman, 1978). In addition, by assisting children with self-assessment, you help them take charge of their own learning and assist you with making instructional decisions.

Our belief, presented throughout the chapter, is that children need frequent opportunities to read self-selected literature. You can assist children best by constantly sharing good literature with them and by sheltering the literature and activities involving the whole class. One of the most powerful ways to assist children with different cultural backgrounds is to give them choices in their reading and in their responding to literature. They will choose experientially and culturally appropriate materials for themselves, and they will let you know what they like and what they have difficulty with if you create a secure classroom, a classroom where second language children are involved in decision-making, in choosing to be silent when they wish to, in taking control of their own learning, while trusting your guidance.

Finally, excellent literature is the core of all excellent reading programs. Literature is a human and humane experience because through good books, children may explore their own natures, become aware of potentialities for thought and feeling within themselves, acquire clearer perspectives, develop aims and a sense of direction, and compare their values with the values of characters they meet in books. Literature is the only subject in school that is fully and honestly involved in exploring what it means to be human; it is the written history of human experience.

In a sense, when we read, we discover not only the world around us, but also ourselves. Through literature, we can extend our experiences, compare our ethical concepts, relieve emotional frustrations, discover beauty and grandeur in our language and in ourselves, and nourish our imaginations. The goal of every literature program should be to enhance these experiences for children and to give them the ability to read literature with enjoyment and understanding and to nurture a need for further reading. Literature is an intensely personal experience, and it is with this experience that the classroom should be mainly concerned.

For all children, including second language children, literature not only extends experiences and gives chances for comparing values, but also plays an important role in expanding the language of readers. Through literature, children become aware of the delight and magic of words; through poems, short stories, riddles, books, and jokes children can learn about the full range of language use. In our best literature exists the finest use of our language. Thus, an excellent reading program for second language learners consists of the best literature. Anything less than the best is a disservice to children. As Mark Twain said, "A man who reads poor literature has no advantage over a man who doesn't read at all."

SUGGESTIONS FOR FURTHER READING

Carrell, P., Devine, J., & Eskey, D. (1988). *Interactive approaches to second language reading*. Cambridge: Cambridge University Press.

A thorough discussion of second language reading research is found in this collection of articles written by researchers and practitioners of reading. The sections in the book suggest its comprehensiveness: Interactive Models of Reading; Interactive Approaches to Second Language Reading—Theory; Interactive Approaches to Second Language Reading—Empirical Studies; Implications and Applications of Interactive Approaches to Second Language Reading—Pedagogy.

Dixon, C., & Nessel, D. (1983). *Language experience approach to reading and writing: LEA for ESL.* Hayward, CA: Alemany Press.

The book presents a clear and thorough discussion of the language-experience approach for second language learners, both readers and writers. It is particularly valuable because it contains views of how to use the approach with students at different developmental levels. It also contains a good example of one teacher's class where language experience is being used.

Peterson, R., & Eeds, M. (1990). *Grand conversations: Literature groups in action.* New York: Scholastic.

The book discusses the author's philosophy concerning literature-based programs and presents valuable information about setting up and sustaining literature response groups. The seventy-nine-page book is one of the most valuable resources for teachers who want to set up literature response groups.

Tierney, R., Readance, J., & Dishner, E. (Eds.). (1990). *Reading strategies and practices: A compendium* (3rd ed.). Boston: Allyn & Bacon.

This is a book containing everything you wanted to know about reading instruction. Although it is not aimed specifically at second language learners, it contains complete information about most of the best reading strategies used in classrooms. More than sixty strategies offer ways to assist response to literature and drama, ways to build vocabulary, approaches to cooperative learning, and teaching comprehension. This is the best book of its kind.

ACTIVITIES

1. Assess a student in reading using a reading miscue inventory combined with the line-by-line procedure. List the student's specific strengths and weaknesses (e.g., What are the student's decoding skills when reading in context? What is the level of comprehension?). Finally, discuss the kind of program, procedures, or strategies you would suggest for the student.

2. Observe children working in literature response groups. What are the advantages of creating literature response groups? Are there any disadvantages or weaknesses with which a teacher needs to be concerned? What would you do differently from the classroom you observed in order to implement literature response groups?

3. Develop a reader's theater script for a story in elementary school, and discuss how you will use reader's theater with younger or older elementary students. Observe how drama is used in the classrooms you visit: what does drama add to children's abilities to respond to literature?

4. Working with a second language child who is limited in English, develop a series of language experience lessons. How does the child, within the context of language experience, develop as a reader over time? Does the child seem more or less enthusiastic about reading than a child who has been immersed in literature only? What are some of the shortcomings of a literature-based or language-experience approach to teaching reading?

5. Observe several classrooms in which teachers feel that literature is central to students' learning to read. What are the variations in the ways different teachers implement literature programs? What are the views of the teachers, stated or unstated, toward literature study? What role does the teacher play—expert, facilitator, equal participant in exploring literature? What effect do these different views of literature study have on the children's response to literature?

CHAPTER 5

Reading and Writing across the Curriculum

In this chapter, we address the following questions:

1. What does research tell us about content instruction for second language learners?
2. What characteristics of narrative and expository text structure are useful for students to know and why?
3. What kinds of contexts and strategies can assist students to use reading and writing in English as a learning tool?
4. How can students be assessed in content area reading and writing?

The sea is a radiant water galaxy. It's a world of its own in a special way. Under its foam crested surface, there exists a universe of plant and animal life. With the tiniest microscopic beings to the most humungus creature that ever lived, the sea is alive!

Thus opens *Our Friends in the Waters* (Kids of Room 14, 1979), a delightfully written and informative seventy-nine-page book on marine mammals: sea otters, whales, dolphins, seals, sea lions, walrus, manatees, and dugongs. What's different about this book is that it was conceived, written, and illustrated entirely by a fourth/fifth-grade class. It's a book by kids for kids! The work that went into this book is remarkable. The reverent wonder expressed in the opening paragraph is unmistakable. How did it all come about?

As explained by the children, the class expressed curiosity about marine mammals, and their teacher, Lynda Chittenden, followed their wonder by facilitating a year-long research project that culminated in the delightful publication. Living near the Pacific coast, the class was able to take a number of field trips. They visited a seal rookery, spent two days watching gray whales migrate south, and observed dolphins in training. They also put their imaginations to work to sense from within what it would be like to live as a marine animal in the water. One child's conclusion: "Today I learned how important it is to have blubber. Our class went swimming in a 40 degree pool. I did learn that I COULD swim in that temperature. But, I couldn't even breathe the first time I jumped in. Gradually I got better. I could swim two laps without flippers. But I still don't see how a whale could live in 33 degree water, even with layers and layers of blubber" (Steig Johnson's learning log quoted in *Our Friends in the Waters,* Kids of Room 14, 1979, p. 16).

Sparked initially by general interest, the class was spurred on by the fascinating information that began to accumulate. The more they found out, the more they wanted to know. Manatees and dugongs, it seems, were the animals that gave rise to the mermaid legend and were probably what Christopher Columbus was referring to in his diary when he mentioned sighting "three mermaids" in the Caribbean! Thus engaged in the pursuit of knowledge, the class read books, invited marine mammal experts to visit their class, and wrote in learning logs to keep track of their growing body of knowledge. Finally, they organized their findings and put them all together in seven co-authored chapters that tell "with facts, stories, pictures, poems and dreams the lives of most marine mammals from a kid's point of view" (Kids of Room 14, 1979, Preface, p. 9).

We share this extended example with you because it illustrates what we consider the epitome of good learning and teaching. The Kids of Room 14, through their project, enlighten us as to the possibilities and potentials children can achieve by taking charge of their own learning with the facilitative guidance of an excellent teacher.

Let us take a look at the project in terms of what it might offer LEP students. As we do so, we want to illustrate that most of what you or I readily recognize as excellent teaching with first language speakers incorporates strategies that facilitate optimal learning for LEP students as well. The key to success lies with finding ways for all students to participate and contribute to the learning enterprise, even if their English language competence is as yet limited.

The marine mammals project provided several avenues of learning that we consider highly beneficial to LEP students. First of all, the project emerged from the expressed interests of the students. Thus, it built upon prior knowledge and more importantly, upon the curiosity and concerns of the students themselves. Secondly, the teacher and the class were able to generate a variety of ideas leading to field trips, providing direct experiences for learning about marine mammals. Third, the teacher herself guided students in processing and keeping track of the information they acquired through oral class discussions, individual written learning logs, and question posing to further the learning process. Finally, when the class decided to put their findings and illustrations into a book, each chapter was written collaboratively by pairs or small groups of students. Students used process writing with peer response groups to elaborate and refine their writing, keeping in mind the question: "Will other children who have not had the same experiences, understand everything we've learned about these most wondrous of animals?" To complement the text, some children made line drawings to illustrate the chapters. Poems and song lyrics were added from all student journals and learning logs, giving depth of feeling to the book's overall informational message. In other words, a variety of writing and drawing was published, accommodating individual strengths. Within this type of project, all students can contribute: native and non-native English speakers alike. The theme cycle approach used by this teacher enhanced the children's learning to select and organize materials for their own needs in synthesizing information for themselves, and, most importantly, in becoming independent learners.

In summary, the marine mammals project incorporated six elements that create optimal content learning for second language learners:

1. *Meaning and Purpose:* the topic was meaningful to the students; they selected it and helped shape its development.
2. *Build on Prior Knowledge:* learning was built on prior knowledge and direct experience such as field trips.
3. *Integrated Opportunities to Use Language and Literacy for Learning Purposes:* oral and written language was used to acquire knowledge and present it again to others.
4. *Scaffolding for Support:* scaffolds were provided, including group work, process writing, and direct experiences for learning.
5. *Collaboration:* students collaborated to build knowledge and organize it for summarizing in a book.
6. *Variety:* variety was built in at every step, with oral language, reading, writing, field trips, class discussions, guest speakers, and other avenues of learning provided.

An important assumption that we make in this book is that all language skills: listening, speaking, reading, and writing are best developed when students are using those skills to achieve communication goals that are interesting and meaningful for them. This assumption holds true for both first and second language development. When students are involved in projects such as the marine mammal study, they integrate and practice an astounding number of important social, linguistic, and academic skills related to their own learning: posing questions; gathering data through reading, interviewing, and direct experience; discussing findings with peers; evaluating formats for presenting findings; organizing and summarizing information for oral, written, and multimedia presentation; and so on. Through the integrated use of these skills, further social, linguistic, and academic development takes place. Our concern with second language learners is to help them participate fully, while stretching their language and literacy performance to their next developmental level.

In this chapter, then, we focus on assisting second language students in reading and writing longer, more complex material that becomes increasingly predominant in the upper elementary grades, middle school, and high school.

By our definition, second language students who are reading and writing longer, more complex pieces in English are intermediate or advanced in English language proficiency. For these students, we offer a wide variety of strategies, scaffolds for support, to assist them as they pursue complex information and ideas relevant to their interests and purposes. The strategies may be used in conjunction with theme cycles or units or with single subject instruction in science, social studies, literature, or any other area of study. As the teacher, you may select from the strategies, as needed, to help an individual student, a small group, or the whole class.

If you have non–English speakers or beginners in your class, they are not likely to be reading and writing long, complex English stories or essays. Nonetheless, it is important to involve them as much as possible in your instruction, because their participation will promote both social integration and second language development: top priorities for newcomers. Sheltering your instruction will improve beginners' chances of understanding the general ideas of your instruction and will facilitate language development. However, for older beginners, sheltering alone will not provide full access to the complex information taught in the upper grades. Supplementary instruction in the students' primary language may be needed to preview and review complex concepts you are covering in class. As we present various strategies in this chapter, we will highlight ways to involve beginners in your day-to-day instruction.

The remainder of this chapter offers: (1) strategies you may select from before, during, and after reading to promote reading comprehension; (2) strategies that integrate writing into the process of academic learning; (3) an example of an integrated thematic approach to content study incorporating selected comprehension and composition strategies; and (4) a review of assessment procedures. First, however, we provide background information on key issues related to helping students read and write longer, more complex pieces as part of their academic learning. In particular, we review the concept of sheltered instruction, describe classroom applications of research on text structure and metacognition, and discuss ways to estimate the difficulty of a text for particular students.

WHAT DOES RESEARCH TELL US ABOUT READING AND WRITING ACROSS THE CURRICULUM FOR SECOND LANGUAGE LEARNERS?

As students move beyond the primary grades, they are expected to read and write about increasingly complex topics in increasingly sophisticated ways. In particular, they must move beyond pattern books and simpler stories to longer literary works and expository prose found in textbooks, magazine articles, encyclopedias, and newspapers. All students, including second language learners, can benefit from assistance in dealing with expository texts and complex literature, both in reading and in writing (Singer & Donlan, 1989). In addition, LEP students may need assistance related to their English language knowledge (O'Malley & Chamot, 1990).

Research is, as yet, limited on second language children's abilities to read, write, and learn from texts, expository or narrative. Instead, most research and discussion falls under the broader category of "sheltered English instruction"—instruction designed to be understandable to students with limited English proficiency while at the same time appropriate to the student's age and academic level (Northcutt & Watson, 1986; Schifini, 1985). As noted earlier, sheltered instruction serves two purposes: (1) subject matter learning and (2) second language development related to academic work. In other words, sheltered instruction is both comprehensible and cognitively demanding in that content is not "watered down." This goal is not easy to achieve without primary language instruction when students arrive in the upper elementary grades, middle school, or high school. However, for students with an intermediate knowledge of English, sheltered English instruction can be effective.

Sheltered instruction aims to facilitate both language and subject matter learning by building on students' prior knowledge, making use of concrete materials and direct experiences, creating opportunities for students to collaborate on learning tasks, and providing explicit strategies to help students use oral and written language for learning (Chamot & O'Malley, 1986). As you can see, our criteria for teaching second language students include all of these features. To these we add the use of thematically organized instruction with student choice built in to create motivation and purpose, while providing a single, meaningful theme to which all reading, writing, and other learning efforts relate. However, sheltered instruction may be successfully implemented in traditional, "single subject" areas such as mathematics, science, and social studies (Chamot & O'Malley, 1986; Crandall, 1987; Northcutt & Watson, 1986; Schifini, 1985). In developing instruction, second language acquisition experts typically incorporate learning strategies that have proven successful with first language students, modified to meet the needs of second language students in terms of English language proficiency and prior experience.

BACKGROUND INFORMATION ON STUDENTS' INTERACTIONS WITH TEXTS

Because this chapter focuses on helping students read longer, more complex texts, this section presents background information on some characteristics of longer texts and ways readers interact with them. We present research and theory on: (1) aesthetic and efferent stances toward a text, (2) text structure in relation to comprehension and composition, and (3) metacognition. In addition, we discuss how to match students with texts they must use for academic purposes. These are rather complex topics, but they are important because they provide the basis for the reading and writing strategies recommended later.

Aesthetic and Efferent Interactions with Texts

Louise Rosenblatt, in presenting her transactional view of literature response, discusses two attitudes or stances readers may take when reading: efferent and aesthetic (Rosenblatt, 1978, 1984). *Efferent* comes from the Latin word *effere,* meaning "to carry away." When the reader takes an efferent stance toward a text, the central purpose is to carry away information; and this is what we commonly do with expository texts. When we read an article or essay, for example, our major concern is to carry away the information or argument the author is presenting. Rosenblatt defines *aesthetic* reading as aimed at experiencing or feeling a piece of writing. Readers usually set aesthetic purposes when reading literary texts; they are interested in the problems faced by the characters, the way characters face the problems, and identifying with the characters and situations in a story. Their primary concern is not to carry away information about a particular type of government or about biology, though that may occur.

To illustrate the two purposes, Rosenblatt offers a "pure" example of efferent reading: a mother reading the antidote on a bottle of poison after her child has swallowed from the bottle. The mother's only concern is with carrying away the information that will save her child. To illustrate the aesthetic purpose, Rosenblatt suggests we imagine a father reading to his son from *Alice in Wonderland.* When the rabbit says, "I'm late, I'm late, for a very important date," the boy objects: "Rabbits can't tell time and rabbits can't talk." The father replies, "They do in this story!" The boy missed the aesthetic purpose of the story, taking instead an efferent stance, in which the textual information contradicted his knowledge of the real world (Rosenblatt, 1983). These purposes do not mean that a reader cannot gain aesthetic experiences from an essay or that a reader cannot carry away specific information from a story. They simply mean that the primary stance when reading essays and narratives is often different. As Dewey once said (Rosenblatt, 1983): "Just because a China tea cup is beautiful, does not mean that it cannot have the pragmatic purpose of carrying tea."

One of the first things readers must do when approaching a text is to know whether they are to take a largely aesthetic or efferent stance. As the teacher, you can facilitate student success with reading by explicitly stating what you expect them to gain from a text and what you want them to do with what they have read. This holds true for narrative as well as expository texts, whether the stance is aesthetic or efferent. Theme cycles offer the advantage that students set the purpose themselves and select written materials accordingly, with teacher guidance.

Effects of Text Structure on Comprehension and Memory

An important feature of longer, more complex expository texts is their organization or sequencing of ideas and arguments, often referred to as text structure. One familiar expository text structure, frequently found in textbooks, is the attributive pattern, which states a main idea and then lists supporting details. In the attributive structure, words such as *first* . . . , *second* . . . , and *third* . . . typically signal the organization of the list; or words such as *in addition, also,* or *moreover* may tie the list together. Two other expository text structures include problem/solution and cause/effect. Both of these differ in turn from the basic narrative structure summarized by the "someone/wants/but/so" narrative sequence discussed in chapter 4. These ways of organizing information and ideas are standard conventions that have evolved and become accepted as appropriate for English (Connor & Kaplan, 1987). There are other ways to structure arguments and ideas, and, in fact, what is considered appropriate text structure in other languages differs from the patterns to which we are accustomed in English. Our discussion focuses on English.

Awareness of text structure is important because research indicates that readers use their knowledge of text structure to store, retrieve, and summarize information they have read (Meyer, Brandt, & Bluth, 1980). In other words, text organization has a profound effect on comprehension and memory (Bartlett, 1978; Meyer, Brandt, & Bluth, 1980). As students gain familiarity with text structure patterns, such as compare/contrast or problem/solution, through reading and writing, the patterns form templates that permit predictions of the words and ideas to come, thereby facilitating comprehension. The template also helps students remember the information in the text by providing a conceptual net for keeping the information in mind. In addition, when students become aware of different text structure patterns, they can use them to structure their writing. Thus, helping students become aware of text structure will help them become more effective in both reading and writing.

As you familiarize yourself with different text structures, you may call children's attention to the organizational patterns of their texts, thereby helping them read and remember more efficiently. Some research suggests that different cultures structure texts in rather different ways (Connor & Kaplan, 1987; Hinds, 1983a, b). Therefore, explicit explanations regarding the conventions of English text structure may be important for older second language learners who have reached substantial literacy development in their home language prior to immigration. In fact, explicit instruction on text structure is apt to be beneficial for most students, native and non-native English speakers alike.

Cohesive Ties/Signal Words.   An important aspect of text organization is the use of "signal" words and phrases, called cohesive ties, that indicate how arguments and ideas relate to each other both within paragraphs and across paragraphs and larger sections of text. Cohesive ties act as signposts to help the reader navigate the text. One way they help is by pointing out the overall structure of a text. For example, words such as *first, second,* and *third* signal to the reader that the author is providing sequenced ideas, of similar weight, to support a main idea. *Moreover* and *in addition* indicate equal ideas, while *nevertheless* and *nonetheless* indicate minimization or negation of previous statements (Halliday, 1975). Table 5.1 categorizes several cohesive ties according to their signpost function: time order, additive, cause/effect, conclusive, and minimization or negation of previous information.

Some cohesive ties can be very difficult for second language students to understand due to their abstract quality. After all, cohesive ties do not refer to objects, people, actions, or concepts. Instead, they convey relationships between complex ideas expressed in phrases and clauses. To get a feel for the difficulty they may present, try defining a few for yourself, such as *nevertheless, moreover,* and *notwithstanding.* Other cohesive ties are more concrete in meaning, such

TABLE 5.1 Cohesive Ties

Time/Order	Additive	Cause/Effect	Conclusive	Changing
soon	in addition	as a result	consequently	nonetheless
when	moreover	because	in summary	despite
finally	also	since	therefore	however

as *first, second, third,* and *finally.* One way to help older students comprehend cohesive ties is to provide a bilingual dictionary so that they can find corresponding terms in their native language. This solution is limited, however, because relational words do not always translate directly into other languages. However, dictionary translations provide one way to start. A more useful approach is to show students how to use cohesive ties in their own writing. In this way, the student offers the meaning, while you help the student convey that meaning effectively through cohesive ties.

Students can use their knowledge of cohesive ties together with their knowledge of text structure to assist them in comprehending and remembering the information in a text. With these basic structures in mind, children will be ready for the strategies such as mapping and DR-TA, which will assist them with learning from texts. Moreover, the same knowledge of text structure assists children with writing expository prose. By learning how authors organize information, children can begin exploring compare/contrast, attributive, and other structures in their own writing. Similarly, they can begin to use the same cohesive ties good writers use as signposts to guide their readers.

Figure 5.1 gives examples of different text structure patterns, the types of texts in which they are likely to occur, the cohesive ties or signal words that they typically contain, and one teaching strategy that you might use to assist students with the particular text structure (Singer & Donlan, 1989). Not all texts come in the form of a "pure" structure such as these. However, you can use the chart to help you identify and share text structures with students. As noted earlier, knowledge of these structures also provides students with a starting point for structuring their own writing.

Headings and Subheadings.   Headings and subheadings are another aspect of text structure that children can use to become more proficient readers. For example, students can use headings and subheadings to preview a text to gain a general sense of its content. Children can read headings to assist them in making predictions about the content of a text. Research indicates that children and older students often ignore headings entirely. However, students can enhance their comprehension by reading and using headings and subheadings (Bartlett, 1978). Thus, you will want to explain their usefulness to your students, and we will share strategies to do this.

Type of Rhetorical Pattern	Text Occurrence	Signal Words	Teaching Strategy
Temporal Order (Sequence)	History texts	First, second, third	Make a timeline
Example: The American revolution came first, then the French revolution, and last, the Russian revolution.			
Attribution (List)	Narratives	First, in addition	Make a list
Example: He bought the car because it has exemplary features. First, it has four valves per cylinder. In addition, it has split rear seats. Last, but of greatest importance to his wife, it has maroon upholstery to match the exterior color.			
Adversative (Compare-Contrast)	Science, math, social studies, history	However, nevertheless	Construct similarities and differences
Example: Computers can only carry out the activities for which they have been programmed. However, the latest generation of computers can modify their own programs according to interactive information they receive from computer users. They are therefore becoming similar to man's ability to learn from his experience.			
Covariance (Cause and Effect)	Science, history	because, as a result, consequently	State cause and effect
Example: The tectonic plate theory explains the cause of earthquakes. They are the result of the movement of plates on which the continents rest.			
Response (Problem-solution Question-answer)	Social sciences	problem is, solution is, question is, answer is	Identify problem and solution
Example: The question asked repeatedly by Senator Baker at the Watergate investigation was, "What did the President know and when did he know it?" The answer to the question led to President Nixon's threatened impeachment and resignation.			

FIGURE 5.1   Text Structure Patterns

SOURCE: *Reading and Learning from Text,* 2nd ed. (p. 128, box 5.3) by Harry Singer and Dan Dolan, 1989, Hillsdale, NJ: Lawrence Erlbaum Associates. Copyright 1989, by Lawrence Erlbaum Associates. Reprinted by permission of the publisher.

Teaching Text Structure: One Classroom.   In teaching text structure for reading and writing, one teacher we know, Leticia Alvarez, places a drawing of a train on her bulletin board such as the one in Figure 5.2. Leticia explains that one good structure for an essay is like a train. Each section of the train stands for an important part of the essay. For example, the engine of the train knows where it is going just as the first paragraph of an essay tells the reader where

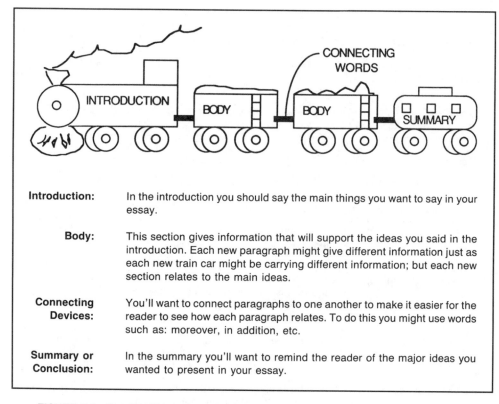

Introduction:	In the introduction you should say the main things you want to say in your essay.
Body:	This section gives information that will support the ideas you said in the introduction. Each new paragraph might give different information just as each new train car might be carrying different information; but each new section relates to the main ideas.
Connecting Devices:	You'll want to connect paragraphs to one another to make it easier for the reader to see how each paragraph relates. To do this you might use words such as: moreover, in addition, etc.
Summary or Conclusion:	In the summary you'll want to remind the reader of the major ideas you wanted to present in your essay.

FIGURE 5.2   Relating Essay Organization to a Train

the essay is going. The engine is linked to the car behind it just as signal words help link one paragraph to another in an essay. Similarly, each car in the train carries new cargo just as each new paragraph in an essay carries new information. Finally, the caboose in a train looks toward where we've been, just as the final paragraph in an essay tells the reader where he or she has been. We have seen children refer to the train analogy while discussing one another's compositions, and we have heard them talk about the words they will use to link one paragraph to another. In a very concrete way, Leticia has taught her children how to develop very sophisticated essays. Later, she may teach students other structures to use for both reading and writing.

Literary Structure

As students progress through school, the stories they read will be longer and more complex than the patterned books and short narratives they encountered early on. Thus, a more sophisticated knowledge of literary structure may benefit students in understanding and remembering narratives. In chapter 4, we shared the someone/wants/but/so outline as a simple structure young children could use to understand and retell simple stories, but a more detailed way to display narrative content becomes appropriate as students begin to read more complex stories (Buckley & Boyle, 1981; Boyle & Peregoy, 1991). The map in Figure 5.3 provides a more sophisticated template for summarizing the literary elements of such stories.

Discussion of Story Elements.   To add depth to children's appreciation of literature, they need to know the basic elements of most stories: the *setting, characters, conflict,* and *denouement.* The setting is simply where the action takes place. In more complex narratives, the setting may change often and may even carry symbolic meaning such as good or evil. The characters (protagonists) are usually people or animals in the story. In longer narratives, characters have time to develop and change, whereas, in short stories, characters often remain static. Thus, in longer stories, we may ask children to look for changes made by characters. The conflict or problem usually consists of a situation the character is trying to resolve. In short narratives there is often only one conflict, but, in longer narratives, there may be many conflicts and problems to be solved. The solution or denouement consists of the way the situation is resolved.

Metacognition and Learning from Text

Metacognition means "thinking about thinking." In research on comprehension and problem solving, metacognition refers to the act of reflecting on one's own thought processes so as to consciously guide the outcome. In reading, metacognition includes the ability to monitor one's own reading processes, as well as the ability to take strategic steps to remedy the situation when one's reading does not make sense. Readers need to be aware of the demands of a reading task in

FIGURE 5.3   More Complex Outline of Story Parts

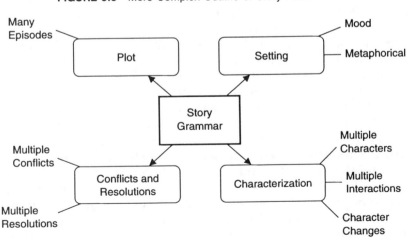

order to make choices about the strategies they will use. Metacognition is knowing when and how to use strategies to assist in comprehension and composition (Baker & Brown, 1984).

The strategies students need to know in studying texts, described in detail later, involve both retrieval and comprehension of information and remedying problems they may have with understanding texts. Specifically, students need to use strategies to preview texts, to ask questions, to preview headings and subheadings, and to organize information for memory. In addition, students need self-monitoring strategies to help them when they are having problems with achieving their goals in reading. These self-monitoring strategies include setting a purpose for reading, evaluating whether the purpose is being met, and revising goals or remediating their own interactions with texts. For example, students need to recognize that they may have to read a math text more slowly than a narrative text or that they need to recognize when they are not understanding a text. Recently, there has been a great deal of concentration on the direct teaching of metacognitive strategies to help students recognize text structures, ask questions of texts, and recall information (Palinscar & Brown, 1984; Ruddell & Boyle, 1989; Boyle & Peregoy, 1991; Nolte & Singer, 1985).

Matching Students and Texts

In any class, students vary in their ability to read academic material independently. It is axiomatic in teaching that variation among students increases with each grade level. Such variation is further accentuated when students vary in English language proficiency. Whether you are collecting materials for theme cycles or teaching a standardized curriculum, it is important to obtain a variety of resources to accommodate varying levels of reading ability and English language proficiency. For example, if your class is studying European exploration of the New World, it is important to supplement any textbook you may use with filmstrips, audio-cassettes, and short, simple, illustrated articles on exploration of the New World. In addition, this topic calls for the use of maps, perhaps student-made maps to post on the bulletin board. The supplementary materials offer a variety of ways for students to access information on the topic. In addition, they build background knowledge that may facilitate students' success in reading more difficult material.

One way to match students with texts, then, is to allow them to select from materials of varying difficulty. You will want to be available to encourage them to try more challenging texts when appropriate. At times, you may want to evaluate directly how your students handle written material from a textbook. If so, you may wish to try the procedure described below, the group reading inventory (GRI).

Evaluating Students Interaction with Text Using the Group Reading Inventory (GRI).   The group reading inventory (GRI) (Vacca & Vacca, 1989) allows you to evaluate students' reading based on your text and the kinds of assignments you require. Though intended for group administration, the GRI can also be adapted for individuals. The GRI has the advantage of assessing students on a typical reading of your text, allowing you to get immediate information on

Concepts	Reading Skills
1. The North is industrialized, and the South is agrarian.	Compare/contrast the two sides. Details of differences.
2. Differences between wars of the past.	Details of differences. Vocabulary terms.
3. Involvement of different states in the war.	Reading a chart and graph. Extracting details and major ideas.

FIGURE 5.4 Concepts Identified and Their Related Skills

their interactions with your text. This information can be used to guide you in adapting your use of the text so all students can be successful.

The first step in developing a group reading inventory is to choose a passage similar in content, length, and complexity to the readings you may require of your class. Next, select the key concepts you would want students to know after reading the passage. With each concept, determine the reading skill required to understand the concept. For example, the skill might be understanding vocabulary in context or identification of a main idea and its supporting details. Similarly, the skill might be to understand a cause/effect relationship or a compare/contrast relationship. Or you may want students to understand a graph or chart that illustrates an important concept in the selection you are using. Finally, make up a GRI based on the concepts and skills you have identified. An example of some concepts from a reading on the American Civil War and the GRI is presented in Figures 5.4 and 5.5.

FIGURE 5.5 Sample Group Reading Activity (GRI) Based on the Civil War

---

Directions for Students: Read pages 32–37 in your book and answer the following questions:

Word Meanings: Briefly describe or explain the meaning of the following words used in pages 32–37: 1) emancipation; 2) writ of habeas corpus; 3) border states; 4) blockade.

Comprehension—Compare/Contrast Relationships: Read pages 35–36 and answer the following questions:

1. How did the North and South see the causes of the war differently?
2. How were the lifestyles of the South and North different?
3. What advantages did the North have over the South in the war?

Details: Find the information for the following questions in pages 35–36:

1. Identify three labor-saving devices that helped make the North more wealthy than the South.
2. Give two examples of the Southern view of slavery.

The brief example of a GRI in Figures 5.4 and 5.5 is based on the key concepts identified in a chapter. In conjunction with your GRI, you might also ask students to outline the information in the chapter using the headings and subheadings or to write a short summary of the pages read. When the students have completed their GRI, you can then evaluate their ability to interact with your text. You can determine how much time needs to be spent discussing vocabulary terms or how much time you need to spend modeling ways to determine main ideas in texts using headings and subheadings. The GRI has the added advantage of being a study guide that students can use to develop purpose and monitor their own comprehension of the reading tasks in your class; it provides a scaffold for their reading. We recommend giving GRIs throughout the year, as an ongoing informal evaluation procedure.

Evaluating Your Own Interaction with One Text.   At this point, we would like you to try the brief exercise below to evaluate your own efferent reading processes. Read the passage below and answer the questions without referring to the text (Right to Read, 1972).

> The Echmiadzin is a monastery in the Armenian S.S.R., in 40″ 12′ N., 44″ 19′ E., the seat of the Catholicus or primate of the Armenian church. It is situated close to the village of Vagarshapat, in the plain of the Aras, 2,840 ft. above the sea, 12 mi. west of Erivan and 40 mi. north of Mount Ararat. The monastery comprises a complex of buildings, surrounded by brick walls 30 ft. high, which with their loopholes and towers present the appearance of a fortress. Its architectural character has been considerably impaired by additions and alterations in modern Russian style.
>
> On the western side of the quadrangle is the residence of the primate, on the south, the refectory (1730–35), on the east the lodgings for the monks, and on the north the cells. The cathedral is a small but fine cruciform building with a Byzantine cupola at the intersection. Its foundation is ascribed to St. Gregory the Illuminator in 302.
>
> Of special interest is the porch, built of red porphyry and profusely adorned with sculptured designs somewhat of a Gothic character. The interior is decorated with Persian frescoes of flowers, birds, and scrollwork. It is here that the primate confers episcopal consecration by the sacred hand (relic) of St. Gregory; and here every seven years he prepares the holy oil which is to be used throughout the churches of the Armenian communion. Outside the main entrance are the alabaster tombs of the primates, Alexander I (1714), Alexander II (1755), Daniel (1806), and Narses (1857), and a white marble monument erected by the English East India company to mark the resting place of Sir John Macdonald Kinneir, who died at Tabriz in 1830 while on an embassy to the Persian court.

Questions to Be Answered without Referring to the Text:
   1. What direction is Mount Ararat from the monastery?
   2. What was the avocation of St. Gregory?
   3. What are the five types of architecture mentioned in the passage?

Answers: 1. southeast; 2. architect; 3. Romanesque, Gothic, Byzantine, modern Russian, Persian.

Did you answer correctly? If not, it may be because you did not know why you were reading the passage. If students don't know why they are reading a passage, they will not monitor their understanding appropriately, and they may remember unimportant details rather than key information. One of the ways teachers prepare students to read texts is by clarifying the purpose, pointing out what students must do with the information. For example, if we had asked you to read the questions prior to reading, your purpose would have been clearly focused. Once students are prepared for a passage, they are ready to assess their own interactions with the text based on their purpose for reading. Finally, they will be able to organize key information for memory.

Summary

In this section, we have discussed current theory and research that informs teaching decisions when students must read and learn from longer, more complex texts, both literary and expository. We described the difference between efferent and aesthetic stances toward a text; elaborated on a variety of text structures, narrative and expository; explained how awareness of text structure facilitates effective reading and writing; and defined metacognition in relationship to students' monitoring and evaluating their own reading and writing. Finally, we discussed issues related to matching students and texts to maximize learning. All of these discussions provide the theoretical and practical underpinnings for the reading and writing strategies presented next.

STRATEGIES TO PROMOTE
READING COMPREHENSION

Many students read texts passively, waiting for information to present and organize itself for them. Proficient readers, however, know what they are looking for, engage their background knowledge while reading, and monitor achievement based upon their purpose (Ruddell & Boyle, 1989; Boyle & Peregoy, 1991). In other words, they are thoughtful about reading, using metacognitive processes every step of the way. Figure 5.6 depicts a variety of strategies to help students to become actively self-aware and proficient when reading for academic purposes. The strategies are grouped according to whether they are to be used before students read a text, during reading, or after reading. In the *prereading* phase, a purpose for reading is established and background knowledge is developed to enhance comprehension; *during reading,* readers monitor their comprehension based on purpose by asking questions of the text; in the *postreading* phase, students boost their memory through writing and organizing information. During all three phases, student are encouraged to be metacognitively aware of their reading. In addition, they are taught to use text structure to assist comprehension. Because vocabulary plays a key role in reading comprehension, vocabulary strategies are offered for all three phases.

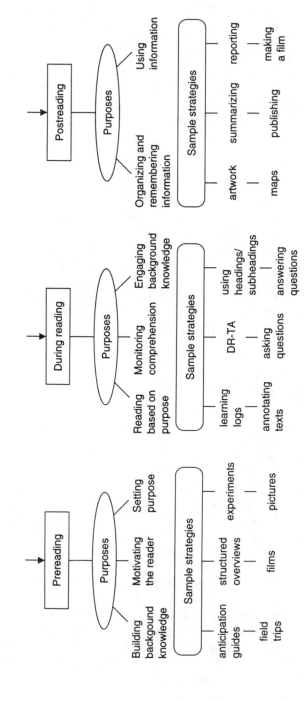

FIGURE 5.6 Model of Reading/Writing in Content Areas

In chapters 3 and 4, we discussed different strategies for beginning and intermediate second language learners. In this chapter, we drop this distinction because the strategies used for both groups are virtually the same. Of course, there are important differences between beginning and intermediate students. One way to accommodate these differences is by providing supplementary texts of varying difficulty along with audiovisual materials. Another way to accommodate beginners is to spend more time on a particular strategy or to combine strategies. Remember to choose strategies that (1) make use of pictures, graphs, dramatization, and other paralinguistic cues to meaning; and (2) incorporate peer support to help beginners glean information from texts. These criteria ensure integration and involvement of newcomers.

PREREADING STRATEGIES: DEVELOPING MOTIVATION, PURPOSE, AND BACKGROUND KNOWLEDGE

The strategies we describe for the prereading phase serve several purposes. First, they motivate student interest and build background knowledge on the topic of the text the students are to read. Students may have little or no knowledge of the text topic, or they may have misconceptions about the topic that can be clarified during the prereading phase. In this way, students are better prepared to read an assigned or self-selected text (Hawkes & Schell, 1987; Herber, 1978). Second, during the prereading phase, students clarify their purpose for reading a particular text. If you have assigned the reading, you'll want to explain to your students why you have selected the material, what you expect them to gain from it, and what they are to do with the information later. In theme cycles, your students have selected their own purpose and already have in mind why they are seeking certain information. The third purpose of prereading strategies is to help students gain a general idea of the text's organization and content by perusing the headings, subheadings, table of contents, and so forth.

Direct and concrete experiences facilitate learning for anyone but are essential for LEP children. Thus, if we are trying to teach about whales, the best way would be to visit the ocean when whales are present. If that is not possible, we could show a film about whales or make use of photographs and pictures. All of these are concrete experiences that enhance children's understanding of their reading about whales. The most important thing to give children, however, is a chance to develop their knowledge of a topic *before* they read about it, through such activities as class discussions, field trips, and films.

Teacher Talk: Making Purposes Clear

Were you ever in a class when the bell rang, and everybody was leaving, and the teacher shouted out, "Read chapter 5 and answer the questions at the back of the book for homework." Even worse, were you ever simply told to read a chapter without having any idea what the chapter was about, or why you were reading it, or what you needed to know after reading the chapter? We have found that children are often unable to state why they are reading a text or what they are supposed to do with the information later. Lacking clear purpose, they are likely simply to read the words and forget about them.

As the teacher, you can prepare students for reading efficiently by using a few simple and straightforward techniques. One important technique, obvious as it may seem, is to state clearly to your students why you want them to read a particular passage and what they will do with the information later. Sometimes this only requires a few words, and, at other times, it may require a short talk, but we maintain that children should not be given an assignment without knowing its purpose and what they are expected to know when they have finished reading. Without this background, they will end up as you may have with the monastery assignment—not getting the point of the reading or remembering haphazardly. We maintain that no assignment should be made without making explicit what you expect of students who have read the text. One of the easiest ways to accomplish this is to simply tell students your expectations and provide them with the background knowledge they will need to get the information, whether it is efferent or aesthetic in nature.

Field Trips and Films

One of the best things you can do to build background knowledge and vocabulary on a topic is to take your class on a field trip where they will experience directly your topic of study. A visit to a primeval forest, a planetarium, a business or factory, a nursery, or a butcher shop builds students' schema for a topic. In addition to field trips, or in lieu of one, you can create excitement with a good film or even with simple pictures or transparencies. A good film involves children visually in a topic and contains narration that builds concepts and vocabulary. When children have a visual image of a subject that they carry to their reading, they will be better prepared to understand a text and much more motivated to endure a difficult one.

Simulation Games

Simulations re-create real-life experiences as closely as possible, just as the bridge-building project, mentioned in chapter 2, involving "companies" in designing, building, and testing bridges is a simulation of real-life bridge-building. When students play the roles of senators and members of Congress, taking a bill from inception through various committees until it finally is voted upon, they are recreating the realities of Congress. Simulations thus provide students with direct experience through role-play. As a result, simulations build background knowledge that will help students comprehend texts discussing how bills are passed. Thus, simulations provide the appropriate background knowledge for students to understand difficult and abstract texts, and they also help motivate students to read.

Simulations may be of particular help to second language students, because they provide direct experience for learning, thus engaging in nonverbal channels of information. At the same time, the building of background knowledge verbally and nonverbally during simulations develops concepts and corresponding vocabulary in context. Thus, simulations may be especially helpful to students who have difficulty with complex texts. In the past, simulations were often used at the end of a unit of study. However, current research on second language readers indicates the importance of building background knowledge prior to reading texts on new and unfamiliar topics (Carrell, 1984). Simulations offer a powerful way to do so.

Experiments

Another way to develop background knowledge as a prereading strategy is to involve students in experiments related to a theme or topic. For example, in a science unit on plants, children can experiment with growing plants. They may discover that roots will always grow down, seeking water and the earth, while shoots will try to reach the sunlight, even when the plants are placed upside down in a jar. Children can also chart the growth of carrots or potatoes, giving them different kinds of nutrients to test their effect. Students may keep journals, learning logs, or drawings to record growth for reporting later. Such experiments prepare students to read about plant growth, to use the knowledge acquired through their experiments, and to comprehend their texts better. Whether it is an experiment in science, an estimation project for mathematics, or an oral history project for social science, experiments and research build background knowledge for reading, provide motivation, and enhance comprehension.

Developing Vocabulary before Students Read a Text

All of the preceding strategies for building background knowledge also offer students concrete opportunities to acquire new vocabulary in the context of direct experiences through field trips, simulation games, and experiments. However, it is not possible to provide direct experiences for all vocabulary. Sometimes it is necessary to teach vocabulary separate from direct experience. Whenever possible, it is helpful to illustrate meanings with pictures or diagrams. In addition, it is helpful to teach semantically similar words in a way that shows how they are related, rather than simply presenting a list of words to be memorized. If, for example, you were teaching the *bow* of a boat, you would teach the *fore, aft, mast,* and other nautical terms at the same time. This gives students a category or cognitive net to hold similar words and makes the words easier to remember. As we have stated before, when information is meaningfully organized, it is easier to remember.

One of the simplest ways to assist students with vocabulary before they read a text is to discuss critical terms before asking students to read. Another is to ask students to brainstorm or cluster around a familiar word to help them expand the word's meaning. For example, if students were going to read about the desert, you might ask them to think of all the words that relate to desert. One class we observed came up with words such as *hot, wind, dry, sand, cactus,* and *scorpions.* The teacher wrote the words in a cluster on the board. The students also discussed each word so that they were prepared to read the text with a better understanding. In this case, the vocabulary activity activated important schema for their reading.

Another way to organize prereading information is to create a map or structured overview of a concept. In this case, the key word is placed in the center of the map, with supporting categories placed on extensions from the center. The map provides a context for understanding the word. For example, a map might have the word *giraffe* in the center. On the extensions might be such categories as "what the giraffes look like" or "food eaten by giraffes." Underneath the extensions would be details describing the category. In this way, children get a more complete view of what the category "giraffe" means before they read about it. In short, you might select key words or words you anticipate children having difficulty with before they read the text. You will thus have a better assurance of their successfully engaging the text materials.

Structured Overviews

Structured overviews are visual displays of information, similar to flowcharts, that provide readers with a basic outline of the important points in a book, chapter, or passage. Presented on an overhead projector, on tagboard, or on butcher paper prior to reading, structured overviews preview and highlight important information and interrelationships of ideas and corresponding vocabulary (Readance, Bean, & Baldwin, 1981). Similarly, by providing a hierarchy of ideas in a text, structured overviews give readers an idea of the relative importance of ideas and provide categories to assist comprehension and memory of key concepts. The following structured overview presents an organized scheme of the different parts of the U.S. government. Look at the overview in Figure 5.7 to see how it might assist a student preparing to read a chapter on the U.S. government and how it might help a reader organize information.

FIGURE 5.7   Structured Overview of U.S. Government

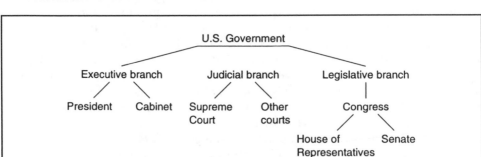

Directions: Consider the following questions, based upon headings and subheadings from chapter 5, before you read. Try to predict how the chapter will answer each of the questions and check your predictions when you read the chapter.

---

1. What is meant by content area instruction?
2. How is reading and writing used for learning in content areas?
3. What is the importance of text structure in content reading?
4. What can be done as a prereading exercise to prepare students to read a difficult text?
5. How can teachers assist students during reading?
6. What is the role of postreading in content area instruction?

FIGURE 5.8   Preview Guide of This Chapter

Preview Guides

Preview guides can also help give children an overview of the important ideas within a text because they help them determine how to preview for reading (Vacca & Vacca, 1989). Typically, a preview guide shows children how to read the titles, headings, subheadings, and summaries contained within a book. By reading these, children gain a sense of a text's content and begin to set a purpose for their reading. By reading a summary, for example, your children become aware of what they should know *before* they begin reading a text. The preview guide in Figure 5.8 teaches children how to preview a chapter and assists them with setting a purpose and monitoring their comprehension.

Anticipation Guides

You can create anticipation guides to prepare students for a story or text. Anticipation guides motivate students and help them predict what will happen in a text (Ausubel, 1968; Holmes & Roser, 1987). A typical guide invites students to state an opinion or predict something about the main ideas or themes in a story or essay before they read it. After reading, students compare the views they held before and after reading. The guide below (Figure 5.9), based upon *The Great Gilly Hopkins* (Paterson, 1978), illustrates how an anticipation guide both motivates students to read a passage or book and assists them with setting a purpose and monitoring for purpose during reading. Notice that the guide also provides children with some background knowledge about the text they are about to read. Though we list anticipation guides under prereading, you can see that they provide support during and after reading as well.

Summary

Prereading strategies build background knowledge, create motivation, and help students establish a purpose for their reading. Based upon your view of what students need to be successful readers of a complex text, you may choose

Directions: Before reading *The Great Gilly Hopkins,* answer these questions, which are part of the book's experiences. After reading the book, answer the questions again to see if you still have the same opinions. Answer the questions: strongly agree, agree, agree somewhat, strongly disagree.

Before Reading	*After Reading*	
_____	_____	1. Having to move constantly from one foster family to another would make me very angry.
_____	_____	2. Most people are not prejudiced toward people who are handicapped or fat or toward African Americans.
_____	_____	3. Prejudice comes from being ignorant.
_____	_____	4. People can overcome their ignorance and prejudice.

FIGURE 5.9   Anticipation Guide for *The Great Gilly Hopkins*

anticipation guides, preview guides, structured overviews, or less elaborated methods to assist students with comprehension. Finally, when students establish a purpose for reading, they are prepared to monitor their interaction with a text. Self-monitoring assists students with assessing their own success rather than relying solely on the teacher to evaluate their interactions with a passage.

DURING-READING STRATEGIES: MONITORING COMPREHENSION

During-reading strategies help students monitor their comprehension based upon the purpose they have set for reading (Leal, Crays, & Moetz, 1985). They need to ask themselves: "Did I find what I was looking for?" If they have a clearly set purpose, then they will be able to determine their success while reading. They can use the structure of their texts to assist them with finding information based upon their purpose. For instance, they can use headings and subheadings to ask questions they think will be answered in a passage. Thus, if they read a heading that says: "The Three Causes of the Civil War," they will know to look for three causes. If they only find two, they will recognize the need to reread. When students know what they are looking for and what they will be doing with the information later, they will be better able to evaluate their own reading.

If students have not established a purpose for their reading, they will not be able to evaluate whether they have been successful readers. When they check their understanding based upon the purpose they have set, then they are monitoring their comprehension. If the purpose for reading is to obtain a football score in the newspaper, they will know they have been successful when they have found the score. If, on the other hand, they are interested in who scored the touchdowns, they will be looking for different information and may, therefore, scan the print differently. Thus, the purpose established for reading a chapter in your classroom will determine how the student will monitor his or her comprehension during reading.

Most of the during-reading strategies center around questioning strategies, some which are modeled by you and others that help children develop self-questioning abilities. These *active comprehension* strategies (Nolte & Singer, 1985) model questions for children (Stauffer, 1975), help students ask questions of each other (Palinscar & Brown, 1984), and teach self-questioning strategies after some background knowledge has been provided (Singer, 1978; Yopp, 1987). All of the strategies below attempt to model some form of self-questioning to assist children in monitoring what they are learning as they are reading (MacDonald, 1986). We present several strategies that assist with purpose-setting and self-assessment, beginning with vocabulary instruction and continuing with using headings and subheadings to form questions to be answered during reading.

Using Headings and Subheadings

Headings and subheadings not only help students establish specific purpose in reading, but also guide students in monitoring comprehension during reading. Research shows that you can boost your students' comprehension and retention substantially if you simply make sure that they read the headings and subheadings and formulate questions about them (Meyer et al., 1980). Students sometimes feel they can plow through a text more quickly if they don't bother to read headings. However, they will find that if they read the headings in texts, they will be able to turn the heading into a question and answer the question when they read the text. For example, if the text heading states: "Three Environmental Dangers of Deforestation," students will create the question: "What are the three environmental dangers?" or "What does deforestation mean?" The question will create their purpose for reading, and they will know that if they only find two dangers in the subsequent paragraphs, then they will have to look for a third danger. By using headings in their reading, students can check whether they have been successful readers. This checking comprehension based on purpose is called "monitoring comprehension." When you teach students how to turn headings into questions, you help them to monitor their understanding and to become independent, successful readers.

Directed-Reading-Thinking Activity (DR-TA)

In chapter 4 we discussed another questioning procedure, DR-TA, with narrative texts (Stauffer, 1975; Peregoy & Boyle, 1990a; Peregoy & Boyle, 1990b). DR-TA can also be used with expository text. Because expository texts normally contain headings and subheadings, it is sometimes easier to determine when and where to ask key questions. When Lucinda Lim introduces DR-TA with expository text to her sixth-graders, she uses the following steps. First, she models the procedure with a short reading. Next, she shows students how to create questions using headings and subheadings. She then asks students in groups to make up questions based upon headings and to answer them in their groups. Finally, she asks her children to report their questions and answers and to compare them. After some practice in groups, she asks students to use the procedure on their own. She often places beginning level students in heterogeneous groups or places them with an advanced level student to assist them with difficult reading. In this way, the advanced student needs to articulate the meaning of a text clearly and thereby gains a sophistication about the text. At the same time, the beginning level student gains access to a difficult text. Figure 5.10 is a brief edited transcript of Lucinda's introducing DR-TA to her class with a text about the "History of Soap."

In this brief transcript in Figure 5.10, we can see that Lucinda has prepared her children to read the article on soap. First, she has activated their background knowledge about soap by simply asking some questions. Second, she has shown them how to anticipate and predict what an article might be about by using headings. She has also shown them that it is appropriate to make guesses about something they will read. Finally, she has prepared them to monitor their understanding.

Thus, DR-TA combines aspects of prereading activities and questioning procedures to assist children's comprehension.

Vocabulary Strategies during Reading

Students often need strategies to help them comprehend unfamiliar words they may encounter while reading. Two strategies discussed by Tierney, Readence, and Dishner (1990) in their excellent resource book, *Reading Strategies and Practices: A Compendium,* are *contextual redefinition* (Cunningham, Cunningham, & Arthur, 1981) and *preview in context.* Both strategies attempt to assist students with comprehending and acquiring vocabulary within the context of their reading. For convenience, we combine features from both strategies to suggest a way to help your students use their background knowledge and the text context to gain a better understanding of their reading. First, you select words you consider

FIGURE 5.10 Edited DR-TA Transcript

TEACHER:	We're going to read an interesting article about the history of soap. What do you think we'll find in the article?
CHILDREN:	About different kinds of soap. Like bubbles and watery. Bars of soap.
TEACHER:	One of the headings, you'll notice, says "Cleaning before Soap." How do you think people got clean before soap?
CHILDREN:	They probably jumped in the river. They didn't get very clean; they smelled. [*laughter*]
TEACHER:	Another heading says "Life without Soap"; what do you think our lives would be like without soap?
CHILDREN:	Joey would smell. [*laughter*] We'd all smell. [*laughter*]
TEACHER:	When you read the article, see if your guesses about soap are like what the article says, and make your own guesses using the other headings. Remember, if you are guessing you'll have your best chance of understanding what you are reading, even if your guesses are not always right.

important to the understanding of a particular passage. Next, you create several sentences using the words to give your students a chance to predict the meaning of new words in context. You might show students how to use the specific context of the words to gain knowledge about them. For example, surrounding words can give clues to meaning; headings or subheadings can hint at the meanings of words; or, often, authors paraphrase technical words in common phrases to assure their readers will understand. When students become aware of the ways authors help them with new vocabulary, they will be more successful in their interactions with texts.

Finally, students can view the words for which you have created sentences in the passage that you have asked them to read. At this point, you might ask them to make guesses about the words and to check with their peer groups or verify their guesses in the dictionary. Later, these words will be used in a postreading phase to ensure that students know the words and will remember them. Using some form of contextual vocabulary instruction gives students the capability of becoming independent readers who can rely on their own use of strategies to gain meaning from print.

Jigsaw Procedure

Jigsaw, introduced in chapter 2, is another group strategy for assisting comprehension of all students in a class (Johnson, Johnson, & Holubec, 1986). Using jigsaw, teachers make students responsible for one another's learning; help them with identifying purpose and important concepts in a text; and assist them with reporting information gained. Steps for using jigsaw in a class include the following:

Step 1: Place students in groups of three; each student has a number of 1, 2, or 3.

Step 2: Students who are 1s become responsible for reading a certain number of pages in a text; likewise for numbers 2 and 3.

Step 3: Students read the section for which they are responsible.

Step 4: Groups of 1s get together too for an "expert" group; they share information and decide how to report it back to their main or "base" groups (the groups consisting of the original 1, 2, and 3); 2s and 3s do the same.

Step 5: 1s report information to 2s and 3s in base groups; 2s and 3s do the same.

Step 6: Some teachers like to have a brief whole-class discussion on the sections that they have read.

Using the jigsaw procedure, you place the responsibility for purpose-setting, questioning, and comprehension-monitoring on the shoulders of your students. Moreover, all students take responsibility for one another's learning. When students present information to their base group, they present ideas and answer questions about the text for which they are responsible. Similarly, when it is their turn to hear from other members, they will ask the questions to clarify their own thinking. The approach, good for all students, is particularly useful for students who might otherwise struggle with content texts because of limited knowledge of English. They will be able to read, question, and understand on their own but will also be able to share their reading and understanding with other students in the "expert" groups. They will also be assisted by other students in their "base groups" and tutored wherever necessary. Because the Jigsaw procedure makes each student in a base group responsible for the comprehension of all students in the group, second language students can rely on much more support than they might receive in many content classes. Through the constant negotiating of meaning and through the continuous use of oral language each day in class, students gain optimal access to comprehensible input for further language and concept development. Jigsaw provides all children with a maximum amount of support for reading in the content areas. While this support is provided mainly in the during-reading phase, it is also provided in the postreading phase because students are also asked to organize their information for reporting to their base groups.

Learning Logs

Journals and learning logs are discussed more fully later, but we want to point out their utility now as an excellent learning tool in the during-reading phase. Learning logs require students to formulate questions about what they are learning or what might be difficult while they are reading (Calkins, 1986). Using learning logs, students may write specific notes concerning a passage in a text, a formula or experiment, or a period of history. As you review student logs, you can identify concepts that you may need to clarify. In addition, learning logs provide an excellent and natural way to evaluate a student's progress. Most importantly, learning logs provide students with a way to both assess their own learning and get help from you. One student's learning log shows how a student can create a dialogue of learning with the teacher:

> JOSH: I don't understand about photosynthesis. How does the light make air? How do plants help us live and breathe?
>
> TEACHER: This is a very difficult idea. Many students are having some difficulty with it, and I will be going over it tomorrow. We'll be going over it in groups where we'll share questions to help us make the ideas clearer. Then maybe it'll be clearer to everybody.

Summary

The primary responsibility of students in the during-reading phase is to assess or monitor their comprehension based upon their purpose for reading. During-reading strategies also help students keep track of information they may want to present later to others. As a final step, students must consider how they will organize the information so that it will be remembered. The postreading strategies below will help them do just that.

POSTREADING STRATEGIES
FOR ORGANIZING AND REMEMBERING

If students have developed background knowledge for a text, set a purpose for reading, and monitored their comprehension during reading, then they must next organize the information so that they can remember what they have read. If information is not organized in some way, it will not be adequately remembered (Bruner, 1960). Thus, *postreading activities* help students organize and remember the information they have gathered in reading. The strategies below—semantic feature analysis, mapping, rehearsing, summarizing, and writing—will assist students with remembering important information.

Vocabulary Instruction in the Postreading Phase

One method used for reinforcing important concepts and terms after reading is semantic feature analysis, which is a graphic method of listing and analyzing the essential traits that define members or examples of a particular category or concept. For example, given the category "pets," one might list dog, cat, hamster, fish, parakeet. To analyze the essential traits of these pets, a traits list must be generated such as land, water, wings, fur, legs, fins. The final step in the semantic feature analysis is to create a chart and check the features that apply to each member of the category (Figure 5.11).

After the matrix is set up, children and teacher together check off the traits for each pet. In the process, vocabulary items are reinforced, while categories are analyzed and explored. An additional step is to invite students to add other pets to the list, for which the feature analysis is carried out. Students may also come up with other traits to analyze, such as whether the animals are carnivores, herbivores, or omnivores.

FIGURE 5.11   Sample Chart for Semantic Feature Analysis

CATEGORY: PETS				
Traits:				
land	water	wings	legs	fur
Member: dog cat hamster fish parakeet				

Type of Government	Elections	Freedom	Number of Rulers	Powers	Free to Assemble	Free Speech	Other
Monarchy							
Democracy							
Dictatorship							
Oligarchy							

FIGURE 5.12 Semantic Feature Analysis of Government

The semantic feature analysis can be especially helpful in illustrating abstract relationships among complex concepts, as shown in Figure 5.12 on government. After reading and study of various forms of government, students may work in groups or as a class to list each type of government and establish a list of traits such as freedom to assemble, the right to hold elections, the number of leaders, and so forth. Next, students fill in the chart, analyzing each type of government according to the traits listed in the chart. In this way, students are able to reinforce the meaning of words such as oligarchy, monarchy, democracy, and dictatorship, while developing insights concerning similarities and differences among them.

Other visual strategies that help students assimilate special vocabulary are mapping, clustering, and structured overviews. Each of these strategies helps students expand their knowledge of new technical terms and understand them in the context of related terms, thus creating a kind of cognitive net for keeping the information in long-term memory. Briefly stated, vocabulary is best taught within a meaningful context, whether you are learning words for a better understanding of government or a better understanding of literary writing. You will want to assist students with special vocabulary terms before they read, with strategies for understanding words during reading, and with strategies for solidifying their new vocabulary knowledge after they have completed a text. Since vocabulary knowledge plays a major role in reading comprehension, vocabulary strategies play a central role in your teaching.

Rehearsing to Organize and Remember Information

Rehearsing refers to the reformulation or presentation again of information to oneself or to others. Have you ever studied with someone else? If you have, you rehearsed the information you knew by sharing it with another person. When

Having rehearsed the information during small-group work, this student is well prepared for her oral presentation on her home country, Haiti.

you repeated what you knew and listened to others present what they knew, you were rehearsing the information. Rehearsing information goes beyond simple memorization and repetition. Having an audience requires you to organize the information so that it is easier to understand. You can also rehearse information culled from a text by talking to yourself or repeating the information aloud. Rehearsing information is necessary for memory, whether by repeating orally, paraphrasing in writing, or creating a map. Rehearsing requires a deeper level of processing than just reading and assuming that you will remember the information. The mapping strategy, presented next, facilitates rehearsal by organizing information visually and spatially to make it easier to obtain and recall.

Mapping

Mapping is a powerful strategy for assisting students with organizing and remembering information. In addition, because maps are both spatial and visual, they assist second language readers with sharing information and with sharing their own visual interpretation of the information they have obtained from reading (Buckley & Boyle, 1981; Boyle, 1982; Ruddell & Boyle, 1989; Boyle & Peregoy, 1991). A map may simply represent information using headings and subheadings as presented in the text, or it may synthesize the information according to the

- Student places title in center of map and places headings on extensions from the center.

- Student places information found under the extensions for headings.

- When map is complete, student checks for important information and reviews the map. If important information is left out, the student places the information under appropriate headings.

- Map is studied for a few minutes and is reviewed a few days later for memory. If student forgets something in map, he or she checks the text for verification.

FIGURE 5.13   Developing a Map

readers' deeper understanding of the topic gained by reading the text. Procedures for developing and using a simple map are presented in Figure 5.13, followed by an example in Figure 5.14.

The map in Figure 5.14 on ''Soap'' illustrates how one student developed a map using the headings and supporting details. The student was able to remember the information presented in the chapter ''History of Soap'' in some detail even a few weeks later.

The map in Figure 5.15 was developed by a group of students who had been studying the U.S. Constitution. After reading a chapter and developing a map such as the one on soap in Figure 5.14, the students then attempted to develop a map that went beyond the information, showing relationships among the basic concepts discussed in the text. Their map on the Constitution was their first attempt to synthesize the information they had derived from the activities in the class unit.

FIGURE 5.14   Map of Chapter in Book

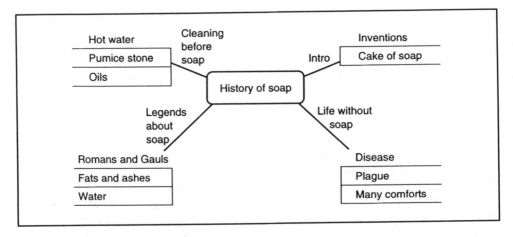

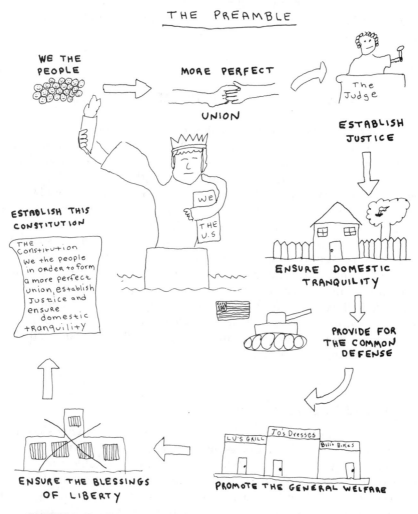

FIGURE 5.15 Group Map Illustrating the U.S. Constitution

The maps help students organize key concepts in a text and their inter-relationships. Mapping thus requires students to reconstruct information and organize it for memory.

Summary

The purpose of postreading strategies is to assist with understanding and retention of important information. Most of the strategies, therefore, involve organizing or restructuring information gathered in order to make it easier to remember.

We have shared several strategies that assist with organizing and restructuring information such as mapping, rehearsing, and various writing strategies. These strategies call for a deeper level of processing information because they require students to present information to others in a coherent manner.

WRITING ACROSS THE CURRICULUM

Writing is another powerful strategy that promotes discovery, comprehension, and retention of information (Calkins, 1986). In recent years, teachers have begun to use the writing process and its various phases as an integral part of their content instruction classrooms. They have found that writing helps students clarify their thoughts and remember what they have learned. Similarly, you will find that you can evaluate and assist your students' learning by reading learning log entries, journals, and notebooks. Recent research has supported the use of writing in content areas by showing that students who write tend to understand more and remember more. We recommend that you ask second language students to write in logs and journals, to write in notebooks, to summarize and comment on their own learning, and to perform hands-on research projects that are reported in writing. We believe that journals and learning logs are an excellent way to begin involving students in writing in content areas, and we have found in our own research that even kindergartners can write in journals and evaluate their learning (Peregoy & Boyle, 1990a).

Journals and Learning Logs

Table 5.2 illustrates the kinds of journals you can use in various content areas: dialogue/buddy journals, notebooks, learning logs, and response journals (Kreeft, 1984; Rupert & Brueggeman, 1986). In addition, the table notes the general purpose of the journal type along with an example of its use in different content areas. While the types of journals are not always mutually exclusive, they give you a feel for the variety of roles journal writing can play in content areas.

In most cases, you will want to respond to the students' journal entries about once a week. As mentioned in our previous discussion of journals, your comments should concentrate on the content of the journals, not on grammar, punctuation, and spelling. For example, you might clarify a concept over which a student indicates confusion or you may simply give students support for their entries. Journals provide excellent opportunities for students to write daily, to develop fluency, to clarify ideas, and to monitor their own learning. Moreover, writing down information assists memory. You may remember a time when you made a grocery list but found when you entered the store that you had left it behind. Nevertheless, you remembered much of your list because you wrote it down; writing had assisted your memory just as writing will assist your students' memory.

TABLE 5.2 Journal Writing across the Curriculum

Journal Type and Purpose	Science	Language Arts	Mathematics	Social Science
Dialogue/Buddy: to share with another	Explain to teacher or to friend what is happening in class and what is understood	Share with another about a story or poem being read; sharing other aspects of class	Let teacher or friend know how class or assignments are going	"Discuss" information pertaining to topics in class
Notebook: take notes to assist memory	Write down information pertaining to an experiment in class	Take down conversations overheard for use in a story to be written	Keep notes about math concepts	Write down key information discussed in class
Learning Logs: discuss and process information from class	Write down notes about what one understands in the class and about what might seem unclear	Write down key concepts from class such as definitions of concepts: setting, theme, characterization	Try to explain math concepts for oneself or perhaps for another; clarify or try to apply a new concept	May take notes on causes of "Civil War" or other key ideas; asks self to identify and clarify ideas
Response Journals: to respond openly and freely to any topic	Might respond to feelings about scientific experimentation or use of animals as subjects of biogenetics	Make any comments on characters or conflicts presented in a story being read	Respond to math in any interesting way; such as ask questions about why people who would never admit to being illiterate will seemingly brag about their math ignorance	Respond to politicians' handling of peace after World War I or about attitudes of pilgrims toward Native Americans

Developing Topics and Student Self-Selection of Topics

We generally support the view that students, whenever possible, should select their own writing topics. That is, if your class is studying plants, students should be allowed to select topics that interest them within the context of plants. Additionally, if students are going to do research, they should select and shape their own topics for research. However, we also recognize that you may have important topics you want all students to write about. When this is so, we recommend that you create "context-enriched" topics, which we define as topics that embed abstract concepts in real-life experiences, allowing students to use their own experiences as part of your assigned topic. The following examples should clarify this process.

Recently, we met a teacher, Joe Allyn, who wanted his students to know something about world economies. Instead of assigning his students to write a paper on "the economy of Peru," Mr. Allyn gives them the following situation: "You are a travel agent, and you intend to take a group of vacationers to a country. In order to attract enough people for the trip, you will need to prepare a brochure. In the brochure, you will explain the various sights and major cities. You will also need to advise people on how much money they will need and on the clothes they will take, based on the climate. Your travelers will also want to know the kinds of items they might buy and where the best buys are found. Finally, they will need to know how much to expect to pay for hotels, for meals, and what kinds of tips, if any, they should give to waiters. Your brochure should have an attractive cover and should contain any other pieces of information you feel travelers to your country should know." Joe then lets students pick a country, work in peer response and revision groups, and share research on the country with one another. He then has a travel day in which each group tries to entice their classmates to "travel" to their country; students use their brochures along with pictures and short films of the country.

The context-enriched topic Joe created has several advantages over traditional assigned topics. First, the students selected their own country. Second, they had an audience for their writing—other travelers and the students in their class. Third, they had a "real" assignment, one that people actually perform in the world. Finally, the activity involves group collaboration and research. For second language learners, activities might range from doing research on their own home country to drawing pictures for the brochure, to adding personal knowledge of travel in another country they may know well. Most traditional writing assignments can be changed into context-enriched assignments by allowing students to use what they already know to create something new. We give one more example below from an English class to describe further the expressive approach to writing in content areas.

Noel Anderson asks her students to select a topic of their own or to use one of her suggested topics after reading a novel. Here is one context-enriched topic she gives to students as a possible writing assignment. "You are Tom Sawyer, and your raft has been carried away in a time warp. Select one of the situations below or create one of your own, and write a letter to Becky about what you experienced and what you think of your experience."

1. You find yourself in the school cafeteria where the students are having a food fight.
2. You find yourself on the fifty-yard line of the Super Bowl.
3. You find yourself in the middle of a crowd at a rock concert.
4. You find yourself in the middle of a class where the book *Tom Sawyer* is being discussed.
5. Select your own situation.

Noel finds that her students enjoy not only the topics she creates but also the ones they create for themselves, including some that are modeled after her own and others that are totally original. The opportunity to create their own situation instead of writing an abstract character sketch is particularly useful to second language learners because they can start with a familiar situation to use as background for explaining a less familiar character such as Tom Sawyer, for instance. These questions, furthermore, can be answered individually or in collaborative groups and model for students questions they might wish to ask.

Photo Essays: Combining Direct Experience, the Visual Mode, and Writing

Photography has great potential for stimulating student interest in school projects, and it forms the basis of the photo essay, a method using visuals to organize thinking prior to speaking and/or writing (Sinatra, Beaudry, Stahl-Gemake, & Guastello, 1990). In essence, students choose a topic for which they take a set of photographs, or they bring in photos already taken. Then, they organize the pictures in a sequence that will support their discussion of the topic reflected in the photos. After oral discussion, students write and publish their photo-illustrated essay. We have seen this approach used successfully at both the elementary- and secondary-school level with students of varying language proficiency.

In Ms. Guadarrama's third-grade class, for example, children brought in photos of their families, including pictures of themselves. They organized their pictures on construction paper in the order they would tell about them during sharing time. Ms. Guadarrama and her assistant went around the room to listen to the children describe their pictures, helping them reorganize the pictures if necessary for sharing with the class. The children then pasted the pictures onto the paper and orally shared their stories with the entire class. The next day, the children used their photo essays to organize the writing of their stories. The written story was then stapled beneath the photo essay, and the final products were posted around the room for everyone to look at and read. In this activity, the photos not only supported children's writing but also supported reading as students took time to read each other's stories.

In Mia Taylor's sixth-grade class, students were invited to work in pairs to develop a photo essay related to their family, school, or neighborhood. Because

Ms. Taylor often used whole-class photo essays as a follow-up after field trips, her students were familiar with the general idea. For the pair projects, Ms. Taylor asked her students to (1) choose a topic and brainstorm how they would develop their ideas through photography; (2) check with her to get approval for their topic and plan; (3) take the pictures; (4) organize their pictures into a "storyboard," and (5) write the story, with the final product to be published complete with photo illustrations.

Students' photo essays addressed a variety of topics, including how to make tamales from scratch, a visual inventory of a shopping mall, and a day in the life of a laundromat operator. These photo essays were primarily organized around chronological or spatial sequences. In addition, the photo essay may be set up for classification, as was the case with a pair of students who photographed and analyzed different kinds of businesses in their neighborhood. The procedure also lends itself to thematic organization. Two girls, for example, prepared a photo essay on "the problems of being twelve." In this case, the girls presented a photo of themselves in the center with the caption, "Problems with Being Twelve." They then presented a wheel of problems, with a photo attached to each spoke depicting problem areas: indecision over hair and make-up, too young to drive, boredom, too much housework, and so forth. The organization of the photographs thus offered a concrete form of semantic mapping.

In summary, the photo essay provides students with the opportunity to use direct experience and photography around a chosen theme. They are able to manipulate the pictures as a concrete way of organizing their ideas for writing. In the process, they use a great deal of visually supported oral language. Finally, they write the essay and produce an illustrated product for others to read.

Written and Oral Collaborative Research Projects

When entering Fernando Nichol's class, you will sense that he does things a little differently. All four walls of his classroom are covered with books, and, this year, 3-ft. × 3-ft. airplanes are hanging from the high ceilings. In one corner, a rocking chair with a serape hanging over the back faces a large carpet. Each semester, Mr. Nichol's second language students use the books in his class to do research projects that require reading/writing and oral language use. They use Fernando's chair to present their findings to the rest of the class and use the tables around the classroom to work collaboratively on their research topics. Usually, while studying a general topic such as "The Civil War," students select a subtopic such as "The Role of Slaves," to explore more fully and share their findings with their peers. These written research projects involve collaborative reading and writing and students need to be fairly proficient in English to be totally involved in them. Other teachers use oral history projects to engage students in research and sharing of knowledge.

Oral history projects involve students in selecting a topic of interest, researching the topic by reading and interviewing knowledgeable individuals, and reporting the information orally and in writing. For example, Lee Tzeng asks his students to select a topic that relates to what they are studying and to conduct an oral research project. In one case, students decided to do a project on World War II. They had read about the war in their class and had seen several related films. A number of students had relatives who had participated in the war, and they decided to interview their relatives and others in their own neighborhoods who could talk about their war experiences.

To get started on the project, students discussed the types of questions they wanted to ask and the purpose of their project. They determined that their purpose would be to get a personal view of the war and its aftermath. Next, they created questions and discussed how to conduct a good interview. Joe placed them in teams of three, with each member being responsible for one part of the interview: one would be responsible for asking questions, another would tape record the interview and take notes, and the third person would think of some extra questions that might be asked at the end of the interview.

After completing interviews, students transcribed them. This required them to listen carefully and to work together on mechanics, spelling, and punctuation as they transcribed. After transcribing, they next wrote a narrative describing the individual they had interviewed, using Studs Terkel's work as a model (Terkel, 1974). They then refined their written narratives in peer response and editing groups.

Next, each group created a chart with each individual's name and a summary of important elements from the interview. After finishing their charts, they examined them for categories or questions they might suggest. One category that emerged was racial discrimination in the army. One African-American man, for instance, shared his experience of all-black troops that were headed by white captains. He said that he and his fellow troopers liked to slow down their work, acting as if they didn't understand the orders if the white captain treated them unfairly or without respect.

As a result of their initial analysis, the students began asking questions about different groups of soldiers. What was the effect of the war on African Americans as opposed to Japanese Americans, for example? What did this mean in terms of job availability for each group? How were Italian Americans and German Americans treated in the war? After students made these generalizations, they created a book about World War II that they disseminated to the people they interviewed as well as to others in the community. The oral projects represent one ideal type of research because students selected their own topics, decided on important questions, and carried out the topics on their own. In addition, students were involved in oral and written composing, transcribing, revising, and editing a research report on a relevant topic. When the students were ready to publish the results of their research, they could refer to the chart Lee Tzeng provided to assist them with clear interview reporting (see Table 5.3).

The oral interview topic above was used for social science, but we have seen students perform the same kind of oral projects in math, science, and other areas. In mathematics, one class asked business people how math was used in their jobs and what aspect of math would be most important for students to know. Another class interviewed gardeners and nursery owners to gain information about plants. Wherever we have seen oral projects used, we have seen a great deal of enthusiasm from students and teachers alike. The projects tend to involve students at the

TABLE 5.3 Elements of Good Reporting

Element	Description
Opening	At the very beginning state what your topic is and how you will develop it (e.g., state that you have interviewed World War II veterans from different ethnic groups to learn about their different or similar experiences).
Background Information	Give readers the background information they will need to know to understand your report. For example, explain the attitudes of Americans toward different ethnic groups at the time of the war. This might help explain why some troops were segregated from others or treated differently.
Reporting Interviews	When reporting the interview of a specific person, give background information on the person that may be important to the reader's understanding of the interviewee.
Summarizing Information	Use your interview charts to find categories of responses that might be similar or different among the interviewees. Remind the readers what your purpose was and state your findings.

deepest levels of oral discussion, critical thinking, reading, and writing. Moreover, they tie learning to real people, real problems, and real life. In so doing, they tend to override subject-matter boundaries, creating integrated knowledge across several traditional disciplines of study.

THEMATIC UNITS: PROVIDING A CONTEXT FOR ESL STUDENTS

The thematic unit "Plants in Our World," described below, illustrates how LEP students can use oral and written language for learning academic material. Special attention is given to assuring a variety of ways students can participate. Ms. Carroll's class of fifth-graders has twenty-nine students, including two newcomers and five intermediate ESL students. The native languages of the ESL students are Spanish, Russian, and Cantonese. Ms. Carroll has no aide. However, an ESL teacher provides all seven ESL students with language development on a pull-out basis.

The unit activities take place between 1:30 and 3:15 each afternoon, after sustained silent reading. Students have a ten-minute recess at 2:30. Ms. Carroll provides her students the time from 2:45 to 3:15 to complete any unfinished work. If they are caught up, they may read or choose a game with a friend. Students often use this time to complete projects undertaken during thematic instruction.

Introducing the Topic and Choosing Study Questions

Ms. Carroll has chosen to develop a unit of study on "Plants in Our World," a topic for which she is responsible according to the state science framework. She teaches this topic each year but with some variations, depending on her students' interests and curiosity. In accordance with her own philosophy and the state's guidelines, she makes sure all of her students have opportunities in the processes of scientific inquiry—observing, communicating, comparing events and objects, organizing information, relating concrete and abstract ideas, inferring, and applying knowledge. She is aware that these processes involve critical thinking, and that as her LEP students engage in these processes, they will have opportunities to develop cognitive-academic English language skills. The careful and precise ways of thinking, talking, and writing about scientific data are fairly new to all her students, native and non-native English speakers alike.

In addition to making use of the inquiry approach to science, Ms. Carroll is concerned that certain basic information about plants be understood by all her students, as outlined in the state framework. In particular, she wants them to be able to describe the parts of a plant and how each functions to enable plant growth and reproduction. She also wants her students to know the basic needs of plants and to understand and appreciate how plants have adapted to various climate and soil conditions, leading to the remarkable diversity of plant life on earth. Throughout her science and social science curriculum, she weaves the philosophical thread of the interrelatedness among all living things and their environment.

This year, for plant study, Ms. Carroll opened the unit by asking students to look around the room to see what was different. Several students pointed out that the room was decorated with potted plants—two ferns, an ivy plant, and a variety of cactus plants. Ms. Carroll then initiated a discussion on plants, inviting the class to name as many kinds of plants as possible. As students volunteered names of plants, she wrote them on a large piece of butcher paper. In this way, Ms. Carroll activated and assessed her students' background knowledge and started a vocabulary list developed in the context of class discussion of the topic.

Next, she asked the class to peruse the list and look for plants that were similar in some way and thus might be grouped together. She then created a map of the students' collective thinking, reproduced in Figure 5.16. Next, she invited the class to work in groups of four to discuss the question: What would our lives be like without plants? Students discussed the question for about ten minutes and then shared their ideas with the whole class.

This introduction helped students focus on the general theme, plants. For those few students who were unfamiliar with the word "plant," the oral discussion with mapping established the concept and its label. As students listed all the specific plants they could think of, the concept was elaborated and additional vocabulary was generated. For all students, the listing and categorizing activated background knowledge about plants to prepare them to discuss the question: What would our lives be like without plants? As students discussed this question, Ms. Carroll was able to get some ideas about what the students already knew about plants. For example, several groups suggested that our food supply would have to come from animals instead of plants. Then someone pointed out that some animals eat only plants, so they could not provide a food source if there were no plants. Another group mentioned the importance of plants for the air, but they didn't know what the effect would be if there were no plants. From this discussion, Ms. Carroll commented that her question had led to more questions than answers! She asked the students to help her list some study

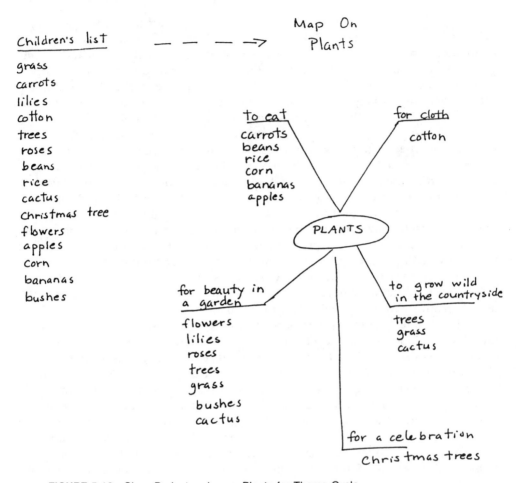

FIGURE 5.16   Class Brainstorming on Plants for Theme Cycle

questions for the unit on plants. The class settled on the following questions, which were posted on the bulletin board.

1. How are plants used by people?
2. Plants give us so much. Do we give them something?
3. What kinds of plants grow in the rain forests?
4. What would the air be like without plants?

To get started on the first question, students were asked to make note of anything they used that day that came from plants. This was a homework assignment, and they were encouraged to ask family members to help them add to the list if possible. These lists would be compared the next day in class and posted on the bulletin board. Based on the lists, the class established six categories of things used by humans: food, clothing, medicine, shelter, tools/implements, and aesthetics. Students volunteered for study committees to specialize in finding out more about how plants are used in each category.

Ms. Carroll felt that the second and fourth questions could not be answered without first providing background information on plants, including how they grow and reproduce, what they need to survive, how they make food from sunlight and chlorophyll, and how they give off oxygen and other elements as by-products of photosynthesis. She explained to the class that they would be learning some basic information about plants that they could use to help them answer these questions.

For the third question, on the rain forests, Ms. Carroll foresaw rich learning possibilities, extending beyond just plant life into the delicate balance among all earthly things: living and nonliving. A study of the rain forests would provide her students a fine opportunity to understand and appreciate how plants adapt to their environment and how they form a part of a larger ecosystem, another topic designated for study in the state framework. She decided to leave the rain forest question for last, preparing her students for its complexities with direct study of plants in class and in the surrounding community. This would also give her some time to gather resources, as this was the first time she had undertaken a study of the rain forests. She explained her thinking to the students, and asked them all to be on the lookout for information on rain forests in the form of news articles, television specials, or books they might come across in their research on plants. She established a small classroom corner for these resources and immediately began filling it with books, maps, and other materials that her students could peruse in their free time.

Organizing Instruction

To begin the study of plants, Ms. Carroll established two parallel projects for students to work on: (1) human uses of plants, with six research committees; and (2) plant observation and experimentation to lead to understanding of plant parts, functions, and life needs. Each research committee was to gather information on its topic with the goal of sharing its findings through a poster display, including a short written report, pictures, and objects. Each group was given a section of classroom counterspace or a table. The six displays would remain for two or three weeks to give everyone a chance to enjoy and learn from them, creating an impressive tribute to the gifts of the plant world.

For the first week of plant study, Ms. Carroll set up the following schedule:

Week 1: Introducing the Unit and Getting Started

Monday: Whole Class: Potting plants

Ask class what typical plant needs to grow. List on chart. Illustrate with simple drawings, pointing out plant parts and functions.

Set up experiments with groups of four or five, manipulating variables indicated by students such as water, plant food, sunlight, and soil.

Each group pots two identical plants and grows them under different conditions. Each day they will observe and record plant size, color, turgor, and other health signs in their science logs.

Tuesday and
Wednesday:

Ms. Carroll meets with plant-use study groups to establish goals and plans to help them get started. She meets with three groups each day. While she meets with them, the other groups carry out activities she has set up for them at five science activity centers:

1. Parts of plant and functions: Drawing and labeling for journal.
2. Herbs and spices: Classification by plant part; geography of where grown; history of uses and trade.
3. George Washington Carver and his research on the many ways to use peanuts.
4. Filmstrip on the life cycles of different kinds of plants: Conifers, deciduous trees, wild grasses.
5. Discussion, listing, and classifying of plants used for food. Group leader needed. List plants used for food. Classify according to plant part. Make a group chart to display the classification.

Thursday:

Groups work on plant-use projects. Groups work at centers. Ms. Carroll is available to assist as needed.

Friday:

Students take a field trip to the nursery to find out what kinds of plants are sold, who buys them, and how they are cared for.

During the first week of the unit, Ms. Carroll has followed a highly structured schedule to build basic background knowledge and get students launched in group study. During subsequent weeks, students assume greater responsibility for independent work. Ms. Carroll adds several more plant-study experiments and reminds students to record results in their science logs. In addition, students work independently on their group projects. At the end of the third week, all six groups set up their poster displays. At this point, Ms. Carroll reminds students of the questions they posed at the beginning of the unit. The class, satisfied with the amount of information they accumulated on how people use plants, know that their rain forest interest will be studied next. However, their second and fourth questions have not yet been answered.

Ms. Carroll explains to the class that they have come up with good questions that require thinking about their current knowledge of plants. She also explains that these questions require using their imaginations to figure out some answers. She suggests that students talk in their groups and write down ideas to address the questions: "What do we give plants?" and "What would the air be like without plants?" She reminds her students that questions like these have many possible answers and that the students should use what they know about plants as the basis of their responses. The ideas generated by each group will be posted for each question.

Instructional Modifications for LEP Students

Ms. Carroll has not changed the essence of her teaching style to accommodate her LEP students. She has always organized instruction around topics and themes, and, in recent years, she has found ways to let students pose questions of their own and choose certain directions of study. These changes in her teaching, motivated by discussions with colleagues and occasional workshops, have aimed at improving instruction for all of her students. Although the essence of her teaching remains much the same, she now scrutinizes her teaching plans with an eye toward maximizing participation among her LEP students.

For the unit on plants, she used three strategies to this end. First, she introduced the topic with more sheltering than she might have if the students had all been native English speakers. For example, she made sure to have a variety of plants in the classroom on the first day of the unit to make her verbal reference to plants unmistakably clear. She did this specifically for the two non-English-speaking children in the class. She also made sure to illustrate some of the words she wrote on the board. These sheltering techniques, though unnecessary for many of her students, enriched her teaching and added interest for the entire class.

The second strategy she used was collaborative grouping. She allowed students to cluster in interest groups around the plant-use categories. However, she balanced the groups in terms of number and social support for students with very limited English language knowledge. The two newcomers were placed in the same groups as their assigned buddy. Grouping was not adjusted for the intermediate level students because they could communicate well enough to be successful in groupwork. In addition to checking for social support in group membership, Ms. Carroll assigned roles to each student for center activities, which were quite structured and would require students to work independently while she met with the study groups.

Ms. Carroll did not assign roles for the plant-use study groups. However, with her guidance, the groups devised their own division of labor when she met with them during the first week of the unit. In so doing, Ms. Carroll utilized her third strategy, which was to make sure that within each task there was a variety of ways for students to participate and contribute. By meeting with the study groups one at a time, she was able to make sure that each student had an appropriate way to contribute to both knowledge building and knowledge sharing.

Thematic Unit Summary

Developing study into thematic units provided students with several levels of learning. All students were provided numerous opportunities to use oral language, reading, and writing for learning. The variety of whole-class and small-group tasks in conjunction with concrete materials and experimentation provided constant opportunities for concept development as well as language learning. Involvement in the scientific method offered opportunities to use such terms as "hypothesize," "classify," "predict," and "conclude." Moreover, in using such terms, students were involved in higher-level thinking processes. In addition to the rich learning

These boys have worked hard in their cooperative group preparing their oral and visual presentation on "Aquaculture" as part of the class theme cycle on plants.

opportunities through oral language use, the students made use of written language for a variety of functions. For example, all students kept careful observations of plant changes in their science learning logs for the four different experiments they conducted, including drawing and labeling plant parts and functions. They also read the directions and information sheets for carrying out the activities provided at the science centers. They wrote letters requesting pamphlets on the rain forests and thank-you notes to the nursery following their visit. In addition, they used textbooks, encyclopedias, and magazines to locate information on their plant-use topics.

In order to summarize the strengths provided by the thematic unit, let's take a look at how Yen, an advanced beginner/early intermediate ESL student, participated in the plants unit, but first we will present a little background information about her. Yen arrived three years ago at the age of seven and was placed in a first-grade class. Now ten years old, she is in the fourth grade. Yen speaks Cantonese at home, as her family is ethnic Chinese from Vietnam. Though fluent in spoken Cantonese, Yen has had little opportunity to learn to write in her native language. However, her written English is fairly good, and she takes great pride in the appearance of her work. Given the choice, Yen likes to illustrate her writing with line drawings. Yen's oral English is adequate for most purposes. She understands Ms. Carroll's instruction and is aided by the sheltering techniques

Ms. Carroll uses to make herself understood. At times, Yen herself is hard to understand, however, and she is often asked to repeat herself for clarification.

Ms. Carroll has taken a few special measures with Yen in mind. First of all, she has made Yen the buddy to a new Cantonese-speaking girl, Li Fen, and she has grouped them with two supportive advanced English speakers, Jerome and Linda, for the plant unit activities. Ms. Carroll has noticed that Yen's oral English gets better as she uses it on behalf of her newcomer friend, and, of course, Li Fen benefits from Yen's Cantonese explanations. At the same time, Ms. Carroll has made sure to place them with two advanced English speakers who will be receptive to their communication efforts.

Yen is readily able to do the majority of the activities required for the plant experiments and the science center activities. She draws, labels, records notes in her science log, and negotiates tasks with her group members. For her contribution to the poster display, she researched the topic of herbal remedies in Chinese medicine. She and Li Fen developed this topic together, at the suggestion of Ms. Carroll. They began by interviewing family members and looking for information in the encyclopedia. By providing a number of sheltering techniques combined with social support, Ms. Carroll has created an environment in which Yen can learn with others in the class. Because Yen has the opportunity to assist another child, she gains in self-esteem and advances in her own content thinking.

ASSESSMENT

Assessment of reading and writing for academic learning is similar to assessment in writing and literature. Therefore, we will reiterate some basic informal ways you can assess students such as using portfolios and informal observation and child self-assessment. However, the most important point we want to make here is that all children, and especially non-native English speakers, should be assessed in a great variety of ways, through work in groups and with partners, through participation in projects, through drawings, experiments, and oral talk, as well as through reading and writing. If what you want to know is whether a student has learned about plants, you may find that some students can show you with drawings better than with essays while others can perform science experiments meticulously showing a clear understanding of the content. Always try to evaluate students' knowledge through their own strengths.

Portfolio Assessment

Whether you use a thematic unit approach or some other approach, there are many things you can evaluate beyond just whether students have understood basic concepts or know the vocabulary of a content area. Using portfolio assessment throughout a unit, for instance, you can ask students to keep their work and evaluate it with you so that they know where they are and what they need to do. In their portfolios they keep their learning logs or other journals; they keep a record of an experiment they have performed; they keep notes they took from oral interviews, or tapes or pictures they may have collected for a group publication. All of these materials can then be evaluated with the students to determine their level of participation in your class. In addition to the portfolio assessment, your daily observations of students will help you evaluate their work in your class.

Using Multiple Measures for Assessment

With all students, but particularly with second language students, we recommend that you assess their participation in many different ways. The oral abilities of many second language learners will surpass both their ability to read or write. Therefore, if you assess them only through written exams, you will surely underestimate their capabilities and knowledge of your content. We have a friend who understands and speaks Italian fairly well and has participated in classes where the language was used, but, if her knowledge of what happened in these classes were assessed in writing only, she would probably fail miserably. If assessed orally or in reading, however, she would perform better. If given a chance to show her abilities with concrete materials, she might receive an "A" for exhibiting her knowledge. Students who may not be able to perform well on a written test may be able to show you through a scientific experiment, for example, that they understood the information at a very high level. If you do not assess students in many different kinds of ways, you will not find out what they really know.

SUMMARY

In the upper elementary grades and beyond, students must read and write longer, more complex texts. They move from short, familiar stories and fables to longer chapter books containing a variety of characters involved in multiple problems, settings, and solutions. Students need strategies that will assist them with these longer narrative texts. Similarly, in curriculum areas such as history or science, students face texts that are longer, filled with new information, and structured differently from the short narrative texts with which they may be familiar from their earlier years of schooling. Therefore, students need special help in negotiating meaning in this new territory. In this chapter, we presented theory, research, and strategies to assist students in their journey.

Reading for academic learning involves reading to understand and reading to remember. We presented strategies pertaining to three phases of the reading process: prereading, during-reading, and postreading. To be successful, students must learn to set a purpose for reading, use their background knowledge, monitor their reading based on their purpose, and organize and remember what is important. Strategies for all of these processes were presented within the context of real classrooms. We also described a variety of ways to use writing for learning purposes across the curriculum, including journals, learning logs, reports, as well as integrating writing into oral and written research projects.

Next we presented an example of a thematic unit that incorporates many of the strategies discussed in the reading and writing sections of this chapter.

In this way, we illustrated how to select and integrate strategies into the larger learning process in which students are actively engaged in acquiring information and insights to be shared with their peers in written research reports, oral presentations, and creative audiovisual works. In our example, we focused on the use of sheltering techniques, peer support, and oral and written language use aimed at student learning.

Finally, we described assessment procedures emphasizing multiple modes of assessment, including portfolios, informal observation, and student self-assessment. Multiple modes of assessment help you to gain a complete picture of a child's progress and to determine adjustments in your teaching approach. Most important of all, we reiterated that the best way to become an informed teacher is to watch and listen to the children in your classroom.

SUGGESTIONS FOR FURTHER READING

Cantoni-Harvey, G. (1987). *Content-area language instruction: Approaches and strategies.* Menlo Park, CA: Addison-Wesley.
  This well-written book is one of the few that discuss second language reading and writing adequately within the context of content instruction. Chapters include topics such as science, social science, and mathematics, and the book contains many specific examples of second language reading and writing in these content areas.

Chamot, A. U., & O'Malley, J. M. (1986). *A cognitive academic language learning approach: An ESL content-based curriculum.* Rosslyn, VA: National Clearinghouse for Bilingual Education.
  The authors present their own approach to ESL content-based instruction, one that has made the handbook a classic. Their model is presented for content-based instruction along with a discussion of the characteristics of learning from different types of content texts. The emphasis throughout is on English language development, and the book contains numerous specific examples of how development can be embedded within content instruction.

Crandall, J. (Ed.). (1987). *ESL through content-area instruction: Mathematics, science, social studies.* Englewood Cliffs, NJ: Prentice Hall Regents.
  A thorough discussion along with many specific examples of teaching content to ESL students. The book contains perhaps the best collection of specific examples in each of the content areas mentioned. The emphasis is on classrooms and teachers.

ACTIVITIES

1. Observe how different teachers use writing in the content areas. What are the varieties of ways children write? What kind of prewriting activities do teachers use to make sure students will succeed in their assignments? Does the teacher respond to the children's writing? Do children respond to one another? Are the content area writing activities authentic and meaningful?

2. Many children who have been "good" readers in the first few grades where mainly stories and narratives are used begin to have difficulty with their content texts. Why do you think this is so? What are some possible differences between narrative and

expository texts in terms of structure and content? What kinds of procedures or strategies can a teacher use in order to assist children with content reading?

3. How do teachers seem to use prereading, during-reading, and postreading activities to assist children with content reading? Do all teachers follow a prereading, during-reading, and postreading model? Do teachers you have observed assist children with text structure and with using headings and subheadings to create questions and a purpose for reading?

4. Develop a lesson in one content area: English, social science, science, or mathematics and discuss how you will use the prereading, during-reading, and postreading model to teach the lesson. For example, what are the best prereading strategies for mathematics lessons or history lessons? What kinds of postreading activities can assist children in remembering what they learned? Why would you use one strategy over another in a particular content area?

5. Visit a class that uses thematic units to integrate content areas, and ask the teacher how a thematic approach might assist children in reading and remembering content materials. Observe for yourself the strengths and weaknesses of a thematic approach to instruction.

CHAPTER **6**

Summary and Conclusion

Teaching reading and writing to students who are limited in English language proficiency presents a challenge to an increasing number of teachers each day. In our effort to help with this task, we have summarized theory and research on second language acquisition and described specific teaching strategies consistent with current research and practice. Two goals underlie our approach: (1) the creation of a classroom environment that welcomes all students and promotes mutual respect and acceptance; and (2) the organization of instruction so as to maximize learning for students whose English language proficiency is limited. With these goals in mind, we present a view of learning that emphasizes social interaction and student initiative with the guidance of the teacher, who is also a learner. Fundamental to such learning are positive interpersonal relationships and communication among the students and the teacher. As the teacher, you set the tone and model the ways of listening, speaking, and relating that form the social matrix from which each child's learning may emerge.

Among the various possible classroom contexts of learning, we emphasize ample opportunity for small-group collaboration. When children express their opinions and feelings about a piece of literature, when they suggest reasons for the outcome of a science experiment, when they decide how to divide a task to share the work, then they all have the chance to exercise and develop their cognitive abilities and knowledge. Moreover, when students bring a variety of experiences and cultural perspectives to the classroom, their divergent viewpoints provide a potentially rich source of learning, provided the ground rules have been firmly laid for listening, considering, and accepting different opinions and views.

Of course, there is more to be gained from collaborative groupwork than just intellectual development. Learning to work together to accomplish a task requires students to develop socially in cooperation, patience, consideration, and helpfulness. At the same time, they build confidence in their ability to contribute and grow from the experience of persisting through chaos to consensus. Home groups, or groups that remain stable for long periods of time, pay special dividends for newcomers by creating a safe and receptive social unit ready to embrace them. In addition, the cognitive, social, and linguistic processes that interweave during groupwork offer optimal second language learning opportunities, another big payoff for students new to English.

Merely placing students in groups, however, guarantees neither cooperation nor learning. As the teacher, you must guide the direction of social interaction and curriculum content. With this in mind, we have outlined strategies for teaching students how to participate effectively during groupwork for different kinds of reading and writing tasks. Furthermore, we have shown ways that such participation might vary, depending upon the nature and purpose of the task. If ground rules for collaboration are made explicit, all students come to the task equally prepared for cooperation, the ultimate goal being independence, through which students accomplish their own goals, solve their own problems, and work through their own differences. As they do so, oral and written language uses proliferate, and opportunities for language development abound.

Given the multiple benefits of groupwork, we have described strategies throughout this book that involve pairs and small groups of students working together—writing response groups, literature response groups, research interest groups, informal groups, and others. Whole-group activities are important also, both for practical purposes and to maintain a cohesive whole-class identity. Within a variety of individual, small-group, and whole-class formats, we have provided numerous activities to involve students in writing and reading for various purposes, from self-discovery and disclosure to learning about the world around them. At each step, we have underscored our overarching goal: to make all classroom learning activities accessible to students who are still learning English, firmly based on a welcoming social-emotional environment. To this end, we have suggested scaffolding strategies to help beginning and intermediate ESL students read and write. In addition, we have incorporated sheltering techniques to make sure that students can understand the language of instruction and thereby benefit both in content learning and English language development.

At the heart of optimal instruction for all students is effective communication. For learners new to English, special care is required to make instruction "meaningful." The use of visuals, concrete objects, and direct experiences provides access to instructional meaning and the language that conveys it. At the same time, opportunities for broader conceptual understanding are increased when instruction is organized around semantic networks based on a theme or topic. Therefore, we have described in some detail ways to involve students in thematic units, theme cycles, and group research projects. Within thematic instruction, students often work in small groups to process, review, and extend information through the negotiation of meaning with their peers. Finally, conceptually organized thematic learning becomes even more meaningful when it is based on students' own experiences and when they have chosen their own interests to pursue. Throughout this book, we have suggested ways to incorporate student experience and choice within learning tasks. Thus, through the use of sheltering techniques, through conceptually focused thematic instruction, and through student collaboration and choice, instruction is constantly made meaningful and relevant for LEP students.

Finally, when learning goals are focused on social interactions and knowledge building that is meaningful, relevant, and interesting, multiple uses of oral and written language follow naturally to accomplish those goals. With student attention to function, the forms of language emerge gradually and naturally. At the same time, you, as the teacher, are on hand to facilitate students' awareness of the many forms and functions of oral and written language, while encouraging them toward the most appropriate and effective usage of which they are capable. For example, process writing offers a powerful source of language and literacy development for LEP students, with its emphasis on student choice, writing for a real audience and purpose, peer response, and polishing a piece for publication. Similarly, literature response groups create a forum for clarifying and negotiating meanings, benefitting students new to English. We discuss writing and literature response groups at length in this book because they tend to deepen interpersonal sensitivity and understanding of the human condition, as young writers share themselves on paper and as young readers explore the lives of literary characters. At their best, response groups provide exceptional social units for mutual acceptance and respect, while geared to the task of making meaning from written English. As a result, they serve the needs of LEP students exceptionally well.

For assessing second language learners, we have urged the use of a variety of measures, emphasizing day-to-day observation and the development of portfolios to document growth over time in oral language, reading, and writing. We have emphasized the need to look beyond English language limitations to find ways for students to express their knowledge and strengths, noting that all students bring a wealth of experiences to classroom learning.

Thus, the essence of our message calls for creating a welcoming classroom climate, one that provides each student with a variety of ways to be an active participant and successful contributor. We do not downplay the challenge of creating classroom unity out of student diversity, but we believe strongly that it can be done. Teaching linguistically and culturally diverse students presents an exciting learning opportunity for all of us! Is it easy? Certainly not! The opportunity for any learning and growth, our own and that of our students, is accompanied by great challenge and risk. Successful teaching with culturally diverse students calls for a willingness to go the extra mile, to observe ourselves critically, to question our assumptions and perhaps to try doing things a little differently: continual teacher learning with open eyes and open minds!

References

Aardema, V. (1975). *Why mosquitoes buzz in people's ears.* New York: Dial Press.

Aaronson, E. (1978). *The jigsaw classroom.* Beverly Hills: Sage.

Ada, A. F. (1988). The Pajaro Valley experience. In J. Cummins (Ed.), *Empowering language minority students* (pp. 223–238). Sacramento: California Association for Bilingual Education.

Ahlberg, J., & Ahlberg, A. (1981). *Peek-a-boo!* London: Puffin Books.

Allen, R. V. (1976). *Language experience in communication.* Boston: Houghton Mifflin.

Altwerger, B., & Flores, B. (1991). The theme cycle: An overview. In K. Goodman, L. B. Bird, & Y. Goodman (Eds.), *The whole language catalogue* (p. 95). Santa Rosa, CA: American School Publishers.

Ammon, P. (1985). Helping children learn to write in ESL: Some observations and hypotheses. In S. W. Freedman (Ed.), *The acquisition of written language: Response and revision* (pp. 65–84). Norwood, NJ: Ablex.

Ashton-Warner, S. (1963). *Teacher.* New York: Simon and Schuster.

Atwell, N. (1984). Writing and reading literature from the inside out. *Language Arts, 61,* 240–252.

Au, K. H., & Jordan, C. (1981). Teaching reading to Hawaiian children: Finding a culturally appropriate solution. In H. Trueba, G. P. Guthrie, & K. H.-P. Au (Eds.), *Culture and the bilingual classroom: Studies in classroom ethnography* (pp. 139–152). Rowley, MA: Newbury House Publishers.

Ausubel, D. P. (1968). *Educational psychology: A cognitive view.* New York: Holt, Rinehart and Winston.

Baker, L., & Brown, A. L. (1984). Metacognition skills and reading. In P. D. Pearson (Ed.), *Handbook of reading research.* New York: Longman.

Banks, J. A. (1991). *Teaching strategies for ethnic studies* (5th ed.). Boston: Allyn & Bacon.

Bartlett, B. J. (1978). *Top-level structure as an organizational strategy for recall of classroom text.* Unpublished doctoral dissertation, Arizona State University, Tempe.

Bauman, R., & Scherzer, J. (1974). *Explorations in the ethnography of speaking.* New York: Cambridge University Press.

Beck, I., McKeown, M., Omanson, R., & Pople, M. (1984). Improving the comprehensibility of stories: The effects of revisions that improve coherence. *Reading Research Quarterly, 19,* 263–277.

Boggs, S. (1972). The meaning of questions and narratives to Hawaiian children. In C. B. Cazden, V. P. Johns, & D. Hymes (Eds.), *The functions of language in the classroom.* New York: Teachers College Press.

Boyle, O. (1982). Writing: Process vs. product. In O. Boyle (Ed.), *Writing lessons II: Lessons in writing by teachers* (pp. 39–44). Berkeley: University of California/Bay Area Writing Project.

Boyle, O. (1990). *The magician's apprentice.* Unpublished manuscript: San Jose State University, San Jose, CA.

Boyle, O., & Peregoy, S. (1990). Literacy scaffolds: Strategies for first- and second-language readers and writers. *The Reading Teacher, 44*(3), 194–200.

Boyle, O. F., & Peregoy, S. F. (1991). The effects of cognitive mapping on students' learning from college texts. *Journal of College Reading and Learning, XXIII*(2), 14–22.

Bromley, K. (1989). Buddy journals make the reading–writing connection. *The Reading Teacher, 43*(2), 122–129.

Bruner, J. (1960). *The process of education.* New York: Vintage Books.

Bruner, J. (1978). The role of dialogue in language acquisition. In A. Sinclair, R. J. Jarvella, & W. J. M. Levelt (Eds.), *The child's conception of language* (pp. 44–62). New York: Springer-Verlag.

Buckley, M. H., & Boyle, O. F. (1981). *Mapping the writing journey.* Berkeley: University of California/Bay Area Writing Project.

Burt, M., Dulay, H., & Hernandez-Chavez, E. (1975). *Bilingual syntax measure.* Orlando: Harcourt Brace Jovanovich.

Busching, B. (1981). Reader's theater: An education for language and life. *Language Arts, 58,* 330–338.

Buswell, G. T. (1922). Fundamental reading habits: A study of their development. *Supplementary Educational Monographs, 21.* Chicago: University of Chicago Press.

Caldwell, K. (1984, February). *Teaching using the writing process.* Speech presented at the Bay Area Writing Project Workshop. Fairfield, CA.

Calkins, L. M. (1986). *The art of teaching writing.* Portsmouth, NH: Heinemann Educational Books.

Canale, M., & Swain, M. (1980). Theoretical bases of communicative approaches to second language teaching and testing. *Applied Linguistics, 1*(1), 1–47.

Cantoni-Harvey, G. (1987). *Content-area language instruction: Approaches and strategies.* Reading, MA: Addison-Wesley.

Carrell, P. (1984). Schema theory and ESL reading: Classroom implications and applications. *Modern Language Journal, 68*(4), 332–343.

Carrell, P., Devine, J., & Eskey, D. (1988). *Interactive approaches to second language reading.* Cambridge: Cambridge University Press.

Cazden, C. (1983). Adult assistance to language development: Scaffolds, models and direct instruction. In R. Parker & F. Davis (Eds.), *Developing literacy: Young children's use of language* (pp. 3–18). Newark, DE: International Reading Association.

Cazden, C. (1986). Classroom discourse. In M. C. Wittrock (Ed.), *Handbook of research on teaching* (pp. 432–463). New York: Macmillan.

Chamot, A. U., & O'Malley, J. M. (1986). *A cognitive academic language learning approach: An ESL content-based curriculum.* Rosslyn, VA: National Clearinghouse for Bilingual Education.

Chang, H. N.-L. (1990). *Newcomer programs*. San Francisco: California Tomorrow Immigrant Students Project.

Charlip, R. (1987). *Fortunately*. New York: Macmillan.

Chittenden, L. (1982, July). *Teaching writing to elementary children*. Speech presented at the Bay Area Writing Project Workshop, University of California, Berkeley.

Cohen, E. G. (1986). *Designing groupwork: Strategies for the heterogeneous classroom*. New York: Teachers College Press.

Collier, V. P. (1987). Age and rate of acquisition of second language for academic purposes. *TESOL Quarterly, 21,* 617–641.

Collier, V. P. (1987/1988). *The effect of age on acquisition of a second language for school* (Occasional Papers in Bilingual Education No. 2). Rosslyn, VA: National Clearinghouse for Bilingual Education.

Connor, U., & Kaplan, R. B. (Ed.). (1987). *Writing across languages: Analysis of L2 text*. Reading, MA: Addison-Wesley.

Cooper, C. (1981, June). *Ten elements of a good writing program*. Speech presented at the Bay Area Writing Project Institute. University of California, Berkeley.

Crandall, J. (Ed.). (1987). *ESL through content-area instruction: Mathematics, science, social studies*. Englewood Cliffs, NJ: Prentice Hall.

Cummins, J. (1979). Cognitive-academic language proficiency, linguistic interdependence, optimal age and some other matters. *Working Papers in Bilingualism, 19,* 197–205.

Cummins, J. (1980). The construct of language proficiency in bilingual education. In J. E. Alatis (Ed.), *Georgetown University Roundtable on Languages and Linguistics* (pp. 76–93). Washington, DC: Georgetown University Press.

Cummins, J. (1981). The role of primary language development in promoting educational success for language minority students. In California State Department of Education (Ed.), *Schooling and language minority students: A theoretical framework* (pp. 3–49). Los Angeles: Evaluation, Dissemination and Assessment Center, California State University.

Cunningham, J., Cunningham, P., & Arthur, S. (1981). *Middle and secondary school reading*. New York: Longman.

Dishon, D., & O'Leary, P. W. (1984). *A guidebook for cooperative learning: A technique for creating more effective schools*. Holmes Beach, FL: Learning Publications, Inc.

Dixon, C. N., & Nessel, D. (1983). *Language experience approach to reading and writing: LEA for ESL*. Hayward, CA: Alemany Press.

Dulay, H., Burt, M., & Krashen, S. (1982). *Language two*. Oxford: Oxford University Press.

Duncan, S. E., & De Avila, E. (1977). *Language assessment scales*. Larkspur, CA: De Avila, Duncan and Associates.

Dyson, A. (1982). The emergence of visible language: Interrelationships between drawing and early writing. *Visible Language, 16,* 360–381.

Edelsky, C. (1981a). *Development of writing in a bilingual program*. Final Report, Grant No. NIE-G-81-0051. Washington, DC: National Institute of Education.

Edelsky, C. (1981b). From "JIMOSALCO" to "7 naranjas se calleron e el arbol-est-triste en lagrymas": Writing development in a bilingual program. In B. Cronnel (Ed.), *The writing needs of linguistically different students* (pp. 63–98). Los Alamitos, CA: Southwest Regional Laboratory.

Edwards, P. A. (1989). Supporting lower SES mothers' attempts to provide scaffolding for book reading. In J. B. Allen & J. M. Mason (Eds.), *Risk makers, risk takers, risk breakers: Reducing the risks for young literacy learners*. Portsmouth, NH: Heinemann Educational Books.

Elbow, P. (1973). *Writing without teachers*. New York: Oxford University Press.

Emig, J. (1981). Non-magical thinking: Presenting writing developmentally in schools. In C. H. Frederickson & J. F. Dominic (Eds.), *Writing: Process, development and communication.* (pp. 21–30). Hillsdale, NJ: Lawrence Erlbaum Associates.

Enright, D. S., & McCloskey, M. L. (1988). *Integrating English: Developing English language and literacy in the multilingual classroom.* Reading, MA: Addison-Wesley.

Ferguson, C. A., & Heath, S. B. (1981). *Language in the U.S.A.* New York: Cambridge University Press.

Fillmore, C., & Kay, P. (1981). *Text semantic analysis of reading comprehension tests* (Progress Report No. 79-0511). Washington, DC: National Institute of Education.

Fishman, J. (1981). Language policy: Past, present, and future. In C. A. Ferguson and S. Heath (Eds.), *Language in the U.S.A.* (pp. 516–526). New York: Cambridge University Press.

Frank, M. (1979). *If you're trying to teach kids how to write, you've gotta have this book.* Nashville, TN: Incentive Publications.

Freire, P. (1970). *Pedagogy of the oppressed.* New York: Seabury Press.

Freire, P., & Macedo, D. (1987). *Literacy: Reading the word and reading the world.* South Hadley, MA: Bergin and Garvey.

Gardner, J. (1983). *The art of fiction: Notes on craft for young writers.* New York: Vintage Books.

Gass, S., & Madden, C. (Eds.). (1985). *Input in second language acquisition.* Rowley, MA: Newbury House.

Goodenough, W. H. (1981). *Language, culture and society.* New York: Cambridge University Press.

Goodman, K. (1967, May). Reading: A psycholinguistic guessing game. *Journal of the Reading Specialist, 126–135.*

Goodman, K., & Goodman, Y. (1978). *Reading of American children whose language is a stable rural dialect of English or a language other than English* (Final Report No. C-003-0087). Washington, DC: National Institute of Education.

Goodman, K., Goodman, Y., & Flores, B. (1979). *Reading in a bilingual classroom.* Rosslyn, VA: National Clearinghouse for Bilingual Education.

Goodman, K. S. (1973). *Miscue analysis: Application to reading instruction.* Urbana, IL: National Council of Teachers of English.

Goodman, K. S., Goodman, Y. M., & Hood, W. J. (Eds.). (1989). *The whole language evaluation book.* Portsmouth, NH: Heinemann Educational Books.

Goodman, Y. (1978). Kid watching: An alternative to testing. *Journal of National Elementary Principals, 57* (4), 41–45.

Goodman, Y. M., & Burke, C. L. (1972). *Reading miscue inventory manual: Procedure for diagnosis and evaluation.* New York: Macmillan.

Grabe, W. (1991). Current developments in second language reading research. *TESOL Quarterly, 25* (3), 375–406.

Graves, D. (1983). *Writing: Children and teachers at work.* Portsmouth, NH: Heinemann Educational Books.

Graves, D., & Hansen, J. (1983, February). The author's chair. *Language Arts, 60,* 176–183.

Grosjean, F. (1982). *Life with two languages: An introduction to bilingualism.* Cambridge: Harvard University Press.

Hakuta, K. (1986). *Mirror of language: The debate on bilingualism.* New York: Basic Books.

Halliday, M. A. K. (1975). *Learning how to mean: Exploration in the development of language.* London: Arnold.

Hanf, M. B. (1971). Mapping: A technique for translating reading into thinking. *Journal of Reading, 14,* 225–230.

Harley, B. (1986). *Age in second language acquisition.* London: Multilingual Matters.

Harste, J. (1988). *Creating classrooms for authors: The reading-writing connection.* Portsmouth, NH: Heinemann Educational Books.

Hawkes, K. S., & Schell, L. M. (1987). Teacher-set prereading purposes and comprehension. *Reading Horizons, 27,* 164–169.

Heald-Taylor, G. (1987). Predictable literature selections and activities for language arts instruction. *The Reading Teacher, 41,* 6–12.

Healy, M. K. (1980). *Using student writing response groups in the classroom.* Berkeley: University of California/Bay Area Writing Project.

Heath, S. B. (1983). *Ways with words: Language, life and work in communities and classrooms.* New York: Cambridge University Press.

Heath, S. B. (1986). Sociocultural contexts of language development. In California State Department of Education (Ed.), *Beyond language: Social and cultural factors in schooling language minority students* (pp. 143–186). Los Angeles: Evaluation, Dissemination and Assessment Center, California State University.

Heath, S. B., & Mangiola, L. (1991). *Children of promise: Literate activity in linguistically and culturally diverse classrooms.* Washington, DC: National Education Association.

Herber, H. L. (1978). *Teaching reading in content areas* (2nd ed.). Englewood Cliffs, NJ: Prentice-Hall.

Herbert, C. H. (1977). *Basic inventory of natural language.* San Bernardino, CA: CHECpoint Systems.

Hinds, J. (1983a). *Contrastive rhetoric: Japanese and English.* Edmonton, Calgary, Canada: Linguistic Research.

Hinds, J. (1983b). Linguistics and written discourse in particular languages. Contrastive studies: English and Japanese. In R. B. Kaplan, (Ed.), *Annual review of applied linguistics, III* (pp. 75–84). Rowley, MA: Newbury House.

Hoban, R. (1960). *Bedtime for Frances.* New York: Harper & Row.

Holdaway, D. (1979). *The foundations of literacy.* Portsmouth, NH: Heinemann Educational Books.

Holmes, B. C., & Roser, N. (1987). Five ways to assist readers' prior knowledge. *The Reading Teacher, 40,* 646–649.

Howard, K. (1990). Making the writing portfolio real. *The Quarterly of the National Writing Project and the Center for the Study of Writing, 12*(2), 4–6.

Hudelson, S. (Ed.). (1981). *Learning to read in different languages.* Washington, DC: Center for Applied Linguistics.

Hudelson, S. (1984). "Kan yu ret an rayt en ingles": Children become literate in English as a second language. *TESOL Quarterly, 18,* 221–238.

Hudelson, S. (1986). ESL children's writing: What we've learned, what we're learning. In P. Rigg & D. S. Enright (Eds.), *Children and ESL: Integrating perspectives* (pp. 23–54). Washington, DC: Teachers of English to Speakers of Other Languages.

Hudelson, S. (1987). The role of native language literacy in the education of language minority children. *Language Arts, 64,* 827–841.

Jackson, S. L. (1980). Analysis of procedures and summary statistics of the language data. In B. J. Mace-Matluck (Ed.), *A longitudinal study of the oral language development of Texas bilingual children (Spanish-English): Findings from the first year.* Austin, TX: Southwest Educational Development Laboratory.

Johnson, C. (1955). *Harold and the purple crayon.* New York: Harper & Row.

Johnson, D. M., & Roen, D. H. (1989). *Richness in writing: Empowering ESL students.* White Plains, NY: Longman.

Johnson, D. W., Johnson, R. T., & Holubec, E. J. (1986). *Circles of learning: Cooperation in the classroom*. Edina, MN: Interaction Book Company.

Kagan, S. (1986). Cooperative learning and sociocultural factors in schooling. In California State Department of Education (Ed.), *Beyond language: Social and cultural factors in schooling language minority students* (pp. 231–298). Los Angeles: Evaluation, Dissemination and Assessment Center, California State University.

Karlsen, B., Madden, R., & Gardner, E. (1976). *Stanford Diagnostic Reading Test*. New York: Harcourt Brace Jovanovich.

Kids of Room 14. (1979). *Our friends in the water*. Berkeley, CA: West Coast Print Center.

Kloss, H. (1977). *The American bilingual tradition*. Rowley, MA: Newbury House.

Koch, K. (1970). *Wishes, lies and dreams: Teaching children to write poetry*. New York: Perennial Library.

Krapels, A. R. (1990). An overview of second language writing process research. In B. Kroll (Ed.), *Second language writing: Research insights for the classroom* (pp. 37–56). Cambridge: Cambridge University Press.

Krashen, S. (1981). Bilingual education and second language acquisition theory. In California State Department of Education (Ed.), *Schooling and language minority students: A theoretical framework*. Los Angeles: Evaluation, Dissemination and Assessment Center, California State University.

Krashen, S. (1982). *Principles and practices in second language acquisition*. Oxford: Pergamon Press.

Krashen, S. D., & Terrell, D. (1983). *The natural approach: Language acquisition in the classroom*. Hayward, CA: Alemany Press.

Kreeft, J. (1984). Dialogue writing—Bridge from talk to essay writing. *Language Arts, 61*, 141–150.

Kroll, B. (Ed.). (1990). *Second language writing: Research insights for the classroom*. New York: Cambridge University Press.

LaBerge, D., & Samuels, S. J. (1976). Toward a theory of automatic information processing in reading. In H. Singer & R. B. Ruddell (Eds.), *Theoretical models and processes of reading*. Newark, DE: International Reading Association.

Lambert, W. (1987). The effects of bilingual and bicultural experiences on children's attitudes and social perspectives. In P. Homel, M. Paliz, & D. Aaronson (Eds.), *Childhood bilingualism: Aspects of linguistic, cognitive and social development* (pp. 197–222). Hillsdale, NJ: Lawrence Erlbaum Associates.

Langer, J., Bartolome, L., Vasquez, O., & Lucas, T. (1990). Meaning construction in school literacy tasks: A study of bilingual students. *American Educational Research Journal, 27* (3), 427–471.

Leal, L., Crays, N., & Moetz, B. (1985). Training children to use a self-monitoring study strategy in preparation for recall: Maintenance and generalization effects. *Child Development, 56*, 643–653.

Lessow-Hurley, J. (1990). *The foundations of dual language instruction*. White Plains, NY: Longman.

Loban, W. (1968). *Stages, velocity, and prediction of language development: Kindergarten through grade twelve*. Urbana, IL: National Council of Teachers of English.

Los Angeles County Office of Education (n.d.). *Sheltered English checklist*. Los Angeles: Los Angeles County Office of Education.

MacDonald, J. (1986). Self-generated questions and reading recall: Does training help? *Contemporary Educational Psychology, 11*, 290–304.

Mace-Matluck, B. J. (1980). General characteristics of the children's language use in three environments. In B. J. Mace-Matluck (Ed.), *A longitudinal study of the oral language development of Texas bilingual children (Spanish-English): Findings from the first year.* Austin, TX: Southwest Educational Development Laboratory.

Mace-Matluck, B. J. (1981). General characteristics of the children's language use in three environments. In B. J. Mace-Matluck (Ed.), *A longitudinal study of the oral language development of Texas bilingual children (Spanish-English): Findings from the second year.* Austin, TX: Southwest Educational Development Laboratory.

Martin, B. (1967). *Brown bear, brown bear, what do you see?* New York: Holt, Rinehart and Winston.

Maslow, A. H. (1968). *Toward a psychology of being.* New York: Van Nostrand Reinhold.

McKissack, P. (1988). *Mirandy and brother wind.* New York: Knopf.

McLaughlin, B. (1985). *Second language acquisition in childhood* (Vol. 2). Hillsdale, NJ: Lawrence Erlbaum Associates, Inc.

Mehan, H. (1979). *Learning lessons.* Cambridge, MA: Harvard University Press.

Meyer, B. J. F., Brandt, K. M., & Bluth, G. J. (1980). Use of top-level structure in text: Key for reading comprehension of ninth grade students. *Reading Research Quarterly, 16,* 72–103.

Michaels, S. (1979). A study of sharing time with first grade students: Discourse narratives in the classroom. *Proceedings of the Fifth Annual Meeting of the Berkeley Linguistics Society,* Berkeley, CA.

Mullen, N., & Olsen, L. (1990). You and I are the same. In J. A. Cabello (Ed.), *California perspectives* (pp. 23–29). San Francisco: California Tomorrow.

Murphy, S., & Smith, M. A. (1990). Talking about portfolios. *The Quarterly of the National Writing Project and the Center for the Study of Writing, 12*(2), 1–3.

Myers, M. (1980). *A procedure for writing assessment and holistic scoring.* Urbana, IL: National Council of Teachers of English.

Ninio, A. (1980). Picture-book reading in mother-infant dyads belonging to two subgroups in Israel. *Child Development, 51,* 587–590.

Ninio, A., & Bruner, J. (1978). The achievement and antecedents of labeling. *Child Language, 5,* 1–15.

Nolte, R., & Singer, H. (1985). Active comprehension: Teaching a process of reading comprehension and its effects on reading achievement. *The Reading Teacher, 39,* 24–31.

Northcutt, M., & Watson, D. (1986). *Sheltered English teaching handbook.* San Marcos, CA: AM Graphics & Printing.

Norton, D. (1989). *Effective teaching of language arts.* Columbus, OH: Merrill.

Ochs, E., & Schieffelin, B. (1984). Language acquisition and socialization: Three developmental stories. In R. A. Shweder & R. A. LeVine (Eds.), *Culture theory: Essays on mind, self and emotion* (pp. 276–322). New York: Cambridge University Press.

Odlin, T. (1989). *Language transfer: Cross-linguistic influence in language learning.* Cambridge: Cambridge University Press.

O'Hare, F. (1973). *Sentence combining: Improving student writing without formal grammar instruction* (Report No. 15). Urbana, IL: National Council of Teachers of English.

Olsen, L., & Mullen, N. (1990). *Embracing diversity: Teachers' voices from California's classrooms.* San Francisco: California Tomorrow.

O'Malley, J. M., & Chamot, A. U. (1990). *Learning strategies in second language acquisition.* Cambridge: Cambridge University Press.

Ovando, C. J., & Collier, V. P. (1985). *Bilingual and ESL classrooms: Teaching in multicultural contexts.* New York: McGraw-Hill.

Palinscar, A., & Brown, A. (1984). Reciprocal teaching of comprehension-fostering and comprehension-monitoring activities. *Cognition and Instruction, 1,* 117–175.

Pappas, C., Kiefer, B., & Levstik, L. (1990). *An integrated language perspective in the elementary school: Theory into action.* New York: Longman.

Paterson, K. (1978). *The Great Gilly Hopkins.* New York: Avon/Camelot.

Peregoy, S. (1989, Spring). Relationships between second language oral proficiency and reading comprehension of bilingual fifth grade students. *Journal of the National Association for Bilingual Education, 13*(3), 217–234.

Peregoy, S., & Boyle, O. (1990a). Kindergartners write! Emergent literacy of Mexican American children in a two-way Spanish immersion program. *Journal of the Association of Mexican American Educators, 6*–18.

Peregoy, S., & Boyle, O. (1990b). Reading and writing scaffolds: Supporting literacy for second language learners. *Educational Issues of Language Minority Students: The Journal, 6,* 55–67.

Peregoy, S., & Boyle, O. (1991). Second language oral proficiency characteristics of low, intermediate, and high second language readers. *Hispanic Journal of Behavioral Sciences, 13*(1), 35–47.

Peterson, A. (1981, June). *Working with the sentence.* Speech presented at the Bay Area Writing Project Workshop. Fairfield, CA.

Peterson, R., & Eeds, M. (1990). *Grand conversations: Literature groups in action.* New York: Scholastic.

Philips, S. U. (1983). *The invisible culture: Communication in classroom and community on the Warm Springs Indian Reservation.* White Plains: Longman.

Pollard, J. (1985). *Building toothpick bridges.* Palo Alto, CA: Dale Seymour Publications.

Raimes, A. (1983). *Techniques in teaching writing.* Oxford: Oxford University Press.

Readence, J., Bean, T., & Baldwin, S. (1981). *Content area reading: An integrated approach.* Dubuque, IA: Kendall/Hunt.

Richard-Amato, P. (1989). *Making it happen: Interaction in the second language classroom.* White Plains, NY: Longman.

Rico, G. L., & Claggett, F. (1980). *Balancing the hemispheres: Brain research and the teaching of writing.* Berkeley: University of California/Bay Area Writing Project.

Right to Read Conference (1972). Out of print passage used in workshop. Anaheim, CA.

Roche Rico, B., & Mano, S. (1991). *American mosaic: Multicultural readings in context.* Boston: Houghton Mifflin.

Rosenblatt, L. M. (1978). *The reader, the text, the poem.* Carbondale: Southern Illinois University.

Rosenblatt, L. M. (1983). The reading transaction: What for? In R. P. Parker & F. A. Davis (Eds.), *Developing literacy: Young children's use of language* (pp. 118–135). Newark, DE: International Reading Association.

Rosenblatt, L. M. (1984). *Literature as exploration* (3rd ed.). New York: Modern Language Association.

Rowe, M. B. (1974). Wait time—Is anybody listening? *Journal of Psycholinguistic Research, 3,* 203–224.

Ruddell, R., & Boyle, O. F. (1989). A study of cognitive mapping as a means to improve summarization and comprehension of expository text. *Reading Research and Instruction, 29,* 12–22.

Rupert, P. R., & Brueggeman, M. A. (1986). Reading journals: Making the language connection in college. *Journal of Reading, 30,* 26–33.

Rylant, C. (1989). *When I was young in the mountains.* New York: Bantam Books.

Saville-Troike, M. (1978). *A guide to culture in the classroom.* Rosslyn, VA: National Clearinghouse for Bilingual Education.

Schieffelin, B. B., & Eisenberg, A. (1984). Cultural variation in children's conversations. In R. L. Schiefelbusch & J. Pickar (Eds.), *The acquisition of communicative competence* (pp. 377–420). Baltimore: University Park Press.

Schifini, A. (1985). *Sheltered English.* Los Angeles: Los Angeles County Office of Education.

Schmidt, B. (n.d.). Story mapping. In unpublished manuscript, California State University, Sacramento, CA.

Scieszka, J. (1989). *The true story of the three little pigs by A. Wolf.* New York: Viking Penguin.

Shepherd, J. (1971). *Wanda Hicky's night of golden memories and other disasters.* New York: Doubleday.

Shultz, J., Erickson, F., & Florio, S. (1982). "Where's the floor?": Aspects of social relationships in communication at home and at school. In P. Gilmore & A. Glatthorn (Eds.), *Children in and out of school: Ethnography and education* (pp. 88–123). Washington, DC: Center for Applied Linguistics.

Silva, T. (1990). Second language composition instruction: Developments, issues, and directions in ESL. In B. Kroll (Ed.), *Second language writing: Research insights for the classroom* (pp. 11–23). New York: Cambridge University Press.

Sinatra, R., Beaudry, J., Stahl-Gemake, J., & Guastello, E. (1990). Combining visual literacy, text understanding, and writing for culturally diverse students. *Journal of Reading, 8,* 612–617.

Singer, H. (1978). Active comprehension: From answering to asking questions. *The Reading Teacher, 31,* 901–908.

Singer, H., & Donlan, D. (1989). *Reading and learning from text* (3rd ed.). Hillsdale, NJ: Lawrence Erlbaum Associates.

Sloyer, S. (1982). *Reader's theater: Story dramatization in the classroom.* Urbana, IL: National Council of Teachers of English.

Snow, C. (1977). The development of conversation between mothers and babies. *Journal of Child Language, 4,* 47–56.

Spradley, J. P. (1980). *Participant observation.* New York: Holt, Rinehart and Winston.

Stauffer, R. G. (1970). *The language–experience approach to the teaching of reading.* New York: Harper & Row.

Stauffer, R. G. (1975). *Directing the reading–thinking process.* New York: Harper & Row.

Takaki, R. (Ed.). (1987). *From different shores: Perspectives on race and ethnicity in America.* New York: Oxford University Press.

Taylor, M. D. (1976). *Roll of thunder, hear my cry.* New York: Dial Press.

Terkel, S. (1974). *Working.* New York: Pantheon.

Terrell, T. D. (1981). The natural approach in bilingual education. In D. Dolson (Ed.), *Schooling and language minority students: A theoretical framework.* Sacramento: California State Department of Education.

Tharp, R., & Gallimore, R. (1988). *Rousing minds to life: Teaching, learning and schooling in social context.* New York: Cambridge University Press.

Thonis, E. (1981). Reading instruction for language minority students. In California State Department of Education (Ed.), *Schooling and language minority students: A theoretical framework* (pp. 147–181). Los Angeles: Evaluation, Dissemination and Assessment Center, California State University.

Tiedt, P. L., & Tiedt, I. M. (1990). Multicultural teaching: A handbook of activities, information, and resources (3rd ed.). Boston: Allyn & Bacon.

Tierney, R., Readence, J., & Dishner, E. (Eds.). (1990). *Reading strategies and practices: A compendium* (3rd ed.). Boston: Allyn & Bacon.

Tinajero, J. V., & Calderon, M. E. (1988). Language experience approach plus. *Educational Issues of Language Minority Students: The Journal, 2,* 31–45.

Vacca, R., & Vacca, J. (1989). *Content area reading.* Glenview, IL: Scott, Foresman.

Varonis, E. M., & Gass, S. M. (1985). Non-native/non-native conversations: A model for negotiation of meaning. *Applied Linguistics, 6*(1), 71–90.

Vygotsky, L. S. (1962). *Thought and language.* Cambridge, MA: MIT Press.

Waddell, M., Esch, R., & Walker, R. (1972). *The art of styling sentences: 20 patterns to success.* New York: Barron's Educational Series.

Wallat, C. (1984). An overview of communicative competence. In C. Rivera (Ed.), *Communicative competence approaches to language proficiency assessment* (pp. 2–33). London: Multilingual Matters.

Wells, G. (1986). *The meaning makers: Children learning language and using language to learn.* Portsmouth, NH: Heinemann Educational Books.

White, E. B. (1952). *Charlotte's web.* New York: Harper & Row.

White, E. M. (1985). *Teaching and assessing writing: Recent advances in understanding, evaluating, and improving student performance.* San Francisco: Jossey-Bass.

Wong Fillmore, L. (1980). Learning a second language: Chinese children in the American classroom. In J. E. Alatis (Ed.), *Current issues in bilingual education: Georgetown University Roundtable on Languages and Linguistics* (pp. 309–325). Washington, DC: Georgetown University Press.

Wong Fillmore, L. (1982). Instructional language as linguistic input: Second-language learning in classrooms. In L. C. Wilkinson (Ed.), *Communicating in the classroom* (pp. 283–296). Madison: University of Wisconsin Press.

Wong Fillmore, L. (1983, February). *Levels of language proficiency: The view from second language acquisition.* TESOL Forum Lecture presented at Teachers of English to Speakers of Other Languages, Austin, TX.

Wong Fillmore, L. (1985). When does teacher talk work as input? In S. Gass & C. Madden (Eds.), *Input in second language acquisition* (pp. 17–50). Rowley, MA: Newbury House.

Wong Fillmore, L. (1990). Latino families and the schools. In J. Cabello (Ed.), *California perspectives: An anthology from the immigrant students project.* San Francisco: California Tomorrow.

Wong Fillmore, L., Ammon, P., Ammon, M. S., DeLucchi, K., Jensen, J. A., McLaughlin, B., & Strong, M. (1983). *Language learning through bilingual instruction* (Second Year Report No. 400-80-0030). Washington, DC: National Institute of Education.

Yochum, N., & Miller, S. (1990). Classroom reading assessment: Using students' perceptions. *Reading Psychology: An International Quarterly, 11,* 159–165.

Yopp, R. (1987). *Active comprehension: Declarative knowledge for generating questions and procedural knowledge for answering them.* Unpublished doctoral dissertation, University of California, Riverside.

Index